Losing Pravda

What happens when journalism is made superfluous? Combining ethnography, media analysis, and moral and political theory, this book examines the unravelling of professional journalism in Russia during the 1990s and 2000s and its effects on society. It argues that contrary to widespread assumptions, late Soviet-era journalists shared a cultural contract with their audiences that ensured that their work was guided by a truth-telling ethic. Postcommunist economic and political upheaval led not so much to greater press freedom as to the deprofessionalization of journalism because journalists found themselves having to monetize their truth-seeking skills. This has culminated in a perception of journalists as political prostitutes, or members of the "second oldest profession", as they are commonly termed in Russia. Roudakova argues that this cultural shift has fundamentally eroded the value of truth-seeking and truth-telling in Russian society. Beyond Russia, this book illustrates what could happen to a country's public life when collective truths are regularly displaced by systematic falsehoods and fabrications.

NATALIA ROUDAKOVA is Assistant Professor of Communication at the University of California, San Diego. Educated in both the Soviet Union and the United States, she draws on her linguistic, political and social knowledge of the region. Her work combines cultural anthropology, political communication, political theory, moral philosophy, and the study of Russian history and contemporary society and culture.

Losing Pravda

Ethics and the Press in Post-Truth Russia

NATALIA ROUDAKOVA
University of California, San Diego

CAMBRIDGE
UNIVERSITY PRESS

CAMBRIDGE
UNIVERSITY PRESS

University Printing House, Cambridge CB2 8BS, United Kingdom

One Liberty Plaza, 20th Floor, New York, NY 10006, USA

477 Williamstown Road, Port Melbourne, VIC 3207, Australia

314-321, 3rd Floor, Plot 3, Splendor Forum, Jasola District Centre, New Delhi - 110025, India

79 Anson Road, #06-04/06, Singapore 079906

Cambridge University Press is part of the University of Cambridge.

It furthers the University's mission by disseminating knowledge in the pursuit of education, learning and research at the highest international levels of excellence.

www.cambridge.org
Information on this title: www.cambridge.org/9781316629772
DOI: 10.1017/9781316817117

© Natalia Roudakova 2017

First published 2017

A catalogue record for this publication is available from the British Library

ISBN 978-1-107-17112-1 Hardback
ISBN 978-1-316-62977-2 Paperback

For my parents, Anna Rudakova and Vladimir Rudakov

Contents

Acknowledgments

I have been very fortunate to have had the support of many people and institutions in the process of writing this book. First and most important, thanks go to the journalists in the city of Nizhny Novgorod in Russia, whose trust in me and in my project made fieldwork for this book possible. I am especially grateful to Vladimir Lapyrin, Irina Panchenko, Galina Shcherbo, Olga Morozova, Yulia Sukhonina, Natalia Rezontova, Larisa Solovyova, and Valentina Buzmakova for guiding me through fieldwork. I also thank numerous other journalists who appear pseudonymously in this text and many others who do not. Marina Metneva, Natalia Chistyakova, Xenia Zadorozhnaya, and Daria Miloslavskaya offered genuine friendship in Nizhny Novgorod and Moscow, making my time in those cities productive and enjoyable.

This book began as a doctoral dissertation at the Department of Cultural and Social Anthropology at Stanford University. There my deepest gratitude goes to my dissertation committee. Sylvia Yanagisako, my admirable advisor, patiently guided me through the process of becoming a scholar. Jim Ferguson joined the committee relatively late but became instrumental in helping me see my project's broader relevance, both in anthropology and beyond. His engagement with my work and his faith in me were a real privilege. I thank Ted Glasser for his open-mindedness and numerous discussions and for consistently being there for me. Thank you to Alexei Yurchak for giving me a unique perspective on the Soviet period early on in the project and for pushing me to think critically and creatively.

My colleagues at the Department of Communication at the University of California San Diego (UCSD) provided me with an outstanding intellectual environment that nurtured this project further. I am especially grateful to Dan Hallin, Val Hartouni, Robert Horwitz, Elana Zilberg, Kelly Gates, and David Serlin for their mentorship, inspiration, friendship, and sound advice. Beyond the department, I am grateful to have had the intellectual home within the Program for Russian, East European and Eurasian Studies at UCSD. There the academic fellowship and friendship of Amelia Glaser, Martha Lampland, and Bob Edelman have been invaluable.

Beyond my home institutions, I thank many colleagues in the fields of anthropology and communication for their stimulating engagement with my work over the years. In anthropology, I am particularly indebted to Naomi Schiller, Robert Samet, Tomas Matza, Dominic Boyer, Nancy Ries, Michele Rivkin-Fish, and Thomas Wolfe; in communication and media studies, my debt goes to John Peters, James Curran, Michael Schudson, Karin Wahl-Jorgensen, Isabel Awad, Olessia Koltsova, and Yuezhi Zhao. All of them have been very generous with their time and intellectual energy, and many of them have read and have helped to improve parts of the manuscript at critical stages.

My sincere thanks also go to Harry Humphries and Deborah Ballard-Reisch, the first US academics I came to know while I was an undergraduate student in Kazan, Russia. They inspired me to pursue graduate education in the United States, for which I am forever grateful.

The bulk of the fieldwork for this project was funded by a generous grant from the Wenner-Gren Foundation for Anthropological Research. Follow-up trips to Russia were supported by the American Councils for International Education and the International Research and Exchange Board. Another generous fellowship – from the Institute for International Studies at Stanford – funded my graduate studies and helped me complete the dissertation, and grants from the Soros Foundation, the Social Science Research Council, and the Havighurst Center for Russian and Post-Soviet Studies at Miami University, Ohio, offered valuable opportunities to present and discuss my work with wider audiences. I am grateful to all of those organizations.

The majority of the book was written while I was a Fellow at the Center for Advanced Study in the Behavioral Sciences at Stanford University in 2013–14, with additional funding from the University of California's President's Faculty Research Fellowship and the Hellman Research Fellowship. I wholeheartedly thank those institutions for their support. The intellectual atmosphere at the Center for Advanced Study at Stanford was truly unique, and this book owes much to the daily conversations that took place there.

Among colleagues and mentors at the center that year, my debt is greatest to Sam Fleischacker and Ethan Pollock.

I also take this opportunity to thank Lew Bateman, John Haslam, Claudia Bona-Cohen, Stephanie Taylor, Chloe Harries, and the rest of the editorial team at Cambridge University Press for their guidance, kindness, and patience. I also thank the three anonymous reviewers of the manuscript for their enthusiasm and their thorough and detailed engagement with the text. I also gratefully acknowledge the work of Jonathan Walton, who did a phenomenal job creating the book's index.

I dedicate this book to my wise and loving mother, Anna Rudakova, and to the memory of my father, Vladimir Rudakov. They came from very humble backgrounds, and they taught me how to focus and to work hard. To a large extent, I think, the spirit behind this book comes from my father, who believed in state socialism, who was not a party member, but who did not hesitate to speak unpleasant truths into the faces of his superiors, many times putting his engineering job on the line. The only reason he never lost his position was because he continued to do the most challenging work that others relied on and could not perform themselves. He was tolerated for his frankness but respected for his talent and skill. In many ways, the Soviet Union lasted as long as it did because of people like him.

Finally, this manuscript owes most to my partner of many years, Roger Levy. His unending love and support gave me strength and confidence to continue, and his editorial brilliance helped me to sharpen my arguments at many critical junctures. This book very simply would not exist without him. I thank him from the bottom of my heart.

Introduction

This is a book about the momentous transformation in Russia's political and public culture that took place after the fall of the Soviet Union. I take political culture to be what people know, understand, believe, and feel about politics – how it is conducted, by whom, to what ends, and with what consequences for people's individual and collective lives. Political culture thus has an epistemic and an ethical dimension. It has an institutional dimension as well: politics is practiced more visibly in particular locales and contexts and by people in particular occupations.

The sudden dissolution of the Soviet Union – and the vertiginous political transformation that ensued – offered social scientists a rare opportunity to closely observe social and political change in the making. A key concern among post-Soviet reformers and lay and academic observers was whether the intended rebuilding of political institutions away from authoritarianism would be accompanied by a corresponding shift toward liberal political beliefs among citizens. The worry was that the change in beliefs might lag behind, because beliefs are presumably harder to transform than institutional practices (or so we are told).

This book speaks to this set of concerns. However, instead of treating culture as a desired aftereffect of institutional change, I see it as a constitutive component of that change. Political regimes and people's knowledge about the world – the common and collective world people inhabit together – are closely intertwined (Glaeser 2011). Political regimes do not exist without particular epistemologies and ethics built into them; regimes and knowledge about politics stand together and change together.

This book, then, is about the ethical and epistemic dimensions of post-Soviet political change. Put differently, it is a study of political change as a cultural process. Methodologically, it was imperative for a study like this to proceed at two levels of analysis – going back and forth between the institutional level and the level of meanings. Given these goals, several political institutions slated for a democratic

1

transition in Russia could have served as good research locales for a study such as this. If we understand democratic politics to be about the righting of wrongs and the pursuit of justice (Ranciere 2004), then I believe that the legislative branch, the courts, and the press would all have made particularly fitting research sites.

I chose to focus on the press because access to journalists and newsrooms was far easier to secure for a single ethnographer without political connections than gaining unmitigated entry to courtrooms and legislative chambers. Another reason in favor of studying the press was the fact that I shared the educational background of many Russian journalists. Lastly, and crucially, journalism remains one of the quintessential *political* professions in modernity, alongside diplomacy and law, as Max Weber remarked a century ago. Political advocacy – taking a stance, fighting for a cause, and bearing responsibility for it – is "the politician's element" (Weber 1946: 95). "To an outstanding degree, politics today is in fact conducted in public by means of the spoken or written word," and "the journalist is nowadays the most important representative of the demagogic species" (Weber 1946: 96). Studying journalism's transformation after the fall of the Soviet Union, then, offered a particularly good vantage point for studying how people's knowledge and sentiment about politics might have transformed in that process as well.

Studying Russia's political culture *as a process* means giving up on a predetermined set of stereotypes about how Russians *are* or what they *wanted* from the transition. Studying political culture through the vantage point of journalism in particular means going against the grain of the dominant narrative about the curtailment of press freedom in Russia over the past twenty years. More generally, it means challenging the conceptual binary between journalism and propaganda where the two are seen as mutually exclusive.[1] The dominant narrative goes like this: press freedom was granted to the (then) Soviet press by Mikhail

Dominant narrative

[1] Several admirable attempts have recently been made to unsettle that binary – whether by exposing its Cold War roots (Nerone 1995, 2013; Sparks 2000; Szpunar 2012) or by attempting to theoretically decouple journalism from democracy (Josephi 2013; Zelizer 2013; Gronvall 2015), but doing so remains difficult. This is so because it goes against the grain of centuries of liberal political thought, where journalism is conceptually tied to freedom of the press as a historical coconspirator and constitutive element of liberal democracy. And liberal democracy, in turn, remains the primary source of modern political legitimacy. Recent suggestions to think beyond democracy as the privileged site of political legitimacy in the contemporary West (Crouch 2004) inevitably push

Gorbachev and carried forward by Russia's first president, Boris Yeltsin. Powerful media moguls and oligarchs who emerged in the 1990s began to put various kinds of pressure on media outlets, which began to derail press freedom's movement from its tracks. With the arrival of President Putin in 2000, press freedom was further and unequivocally curtailed as private media began to be harassed, censorship was reintroduced, and independent journalists began to be threatened and even murdered.[2]

While acknowledging the significance of these stark and tragic developments, I wish to point out that this particular narrative has many unexamined and often contradictory assumptions built into it. The shift from government propaganda to a free press, for instance, is imagined – conceptually – as a clean, 180-degree turn. Journalism in the authoritarian period is imagined as having been either a vehicle of indoctrination or an outlet for resistance, with little room in between or outside that binary. Soviet media audiences are imagined to have been fully indoctrinated or, alternatively, to have been yearning for freedom and capable of seeing through propaganda's mystifications. Soviet journalists, in their turn, are variously imagined as cynical careerists, spineless yes-men, or closeted dissidents. With the lifting of censorship by Mikhail Gorbachev, Soviet journalists are understood to have tapped into their freedom-loving nature, quickly transforming themselves into fearless watchdogs shining the light of publicity on the abuses of power. In Yeltsin's Russia, independent journalists fought for equality and justice, educating citizens on matters of public concern and providing an open forum for multiple political voices. Where they failed to do that, they were marred by their backward cultural "legacies" or by pressure from oligarchs and media moguls. With the reemergence of censorship under Putin, the freedom switch is understood to have been turned back off, and things more or less went back to where they were before the fall of the Soviet Union.

I find these assumptions and the entire metaphor of press freedom's progressive movement derailed from its tracks not very helpful because they force us to see Russia's media-political transformation as driven primarily by powerful actors (presidents, oligarchs, media moguls)

against a strong conviction that democracy is one thing that Western liberals cannot afford to give up (Brown 2010).

[2] Russia's Center for Journalism in Extreme Situations (CJES) and Glasnost Defense Foundation (GDF) documented over 200 murders and countless beatings and intimidations of journalists in Russia between 1991 and 2006.

while overlooking the sociocultural dimensions of that transformation. Those broader social and cultural dynamics and their unintended consequences can tell us much more about what has been going on in Russian media and politics over the past three decades.

Instead of perpetuating these common assumptions yet again, this book offers a new vocabulary for discussing journalism and its political and cultural significance in nondemocratic and postauthoritarian settings. It is an ethics-based vocabulary, where ethics is a continuously evolving set of practices and criteria of judgment rather than a set of normative rules. I use the trope of truth-seeking and truth-telling as the central category of my analysis. The relationship between journalism and truth-telling is at least as old as between journalism and press freedom but is not identical with it. This is because the vocabulary of truth-telling is broader than the vocabulary of political liberalism, to which the concept of press freedom belongs.

Again, the classic narrative about journalism and truth in the Soviet Union is well known. It is captured by an old Soviet dissident joke: "There is no *izvestia* in *Pravda*, and there is no *pravda* in *Izvestia*," where *Izvestia* and *Pravda* are the names of Soviet newspapers and *izvestia* means "news" and *pravda* means "truth." Cold War communication scholar Wilbur Schramm (1956) offers a classic elaboration of this view in his influential essay, "The Soviet Communist Theory of the Press."[3] The difference between the Soviets' and "our own" approach to truth, says Schramm, is that the Soviets believe that there is only one truth out there – that of Marxism-Leninism. "The teachings of Marx are immovable because they are true," Schramm quotes Lenin as saying. The job of the Soviet mass communicator, then, was to interpret daily events from the standpoint of class struggle, to penetrate behind appearances, to abstract away from specifics, in order to uncover the underlying Marxist reality behind events. Truth is thus *revealed* to Soviet audiences through the mass media, whereas in the liberal tradition, Schramm (1956) says, truth is always *contested* through rigorous argument, confrontation of evidence, and exchange of ideas. At its most fundamental, Schramm (1956: 145) sums up, "the differences between the Soviet tradition and ours are the differences between Marx and Mill ... on the one side, man as a mass, malleable, unimportant in himself, in need of Promethean leadership; on the other side, man as

---

[3]   On the institutional overlap between the emerging fields of mass communication and Soviet studies during the Cold War, compare Simpson (1994) and Engerman (2009).

intelligent, discriminating, perfectly able to purchase by himself in a 'free market place of ideas.'"

Leaving Schramm's self-congratulatory rhetoric aside for the moment, let me point out how he is in fact drawing on an approach to knowledge and truth that has long been prevalent in Western epistemology. This is the view that knowledge – whether in science or in politics – is properly formed only when truth claims are subjected to doubt, skepticism, and rigorous questioning from all sides. As influential as this approach has been historically, it is not the only way to understand knowledge formation. There is a lesser-known tradition in Western epistemology that views knowledge production as dependent as much on *trust* as on skepticism and doubt. Knowledge in this tradition is understood to be a social institution and a collective good, and cognitive and moral orders here are seen as closely intertwined. In *A Social History of Truth*, historian of science Steven Shapin (1994) reminds us, for instance, that for most of our history, the credibility of someone's truth and knowledge claims was assessed through face-to-face interactions. "Premodern society looked truth in the face. Veracity was understood to be underwritten by virtue … Truth flowed along the same personal channels as civil conversation" (Shapin 1994: 410). The same was the case, Shapin demonstrates, in early-modern Europe, where modern scientific practices first took hold. Only those who were known as virtuous persons could successfully participate in the creation of scientific truths; knowledge production was a collective effort, and practitioners relied on one another's honesty, integrity, civility, and a sense of proportion to succeed. Today, elaborate systems of institutional expertise, with checks and balances and rigorous internal monitoring, are said to guarantee scientific truthfulness instead of "the personal qualities of scientists" (Shapin 1994: 413). Yet, Shapin points out, when it comes down to it, any particular subfield of science today is still made up of interdependent actors who are pushing the limits of knowledge together. And like their early-modern predecessors, they make judgments about one another's personal integrity that are simultaneously judgments about the scientific merits of one another's work.

Shapin's approach to truth as a social product underscores how skepticism and doubt live on the margins of trust. Our ability to doubt someone's words or actions depends on our "ability to trust *almost everything else* about the scene in which [we] do skepticism" (Shapin 1994: 417, original emphasis). Doubting is still a social and communicative engagement; it is an attempt to calibrate "one dubiously trustworthy source by others assumed to be trustworthy" (Shapin 1994: 21). When trust is fully severed, a community of discourse and knowledge falls apart: it is not only that people cannot agree with one another; rather, the *possibility of disagreement* itself is withdrawn (Shapin 1994: 36, original emphasis).[4]

That trust is the solution to the problem of moral order, Shapin sums up, is not news: it intuitively makes sense and has been commented on countless times. But the argument that knowledge depends on trust *is* counterintuitive because we tend to think that knowledge (cognitive order) and belief (moral order) are antithetical: "modern epistemology has systematically argued that legitimate knowledge is defined precisely by its rejection of trust" (Shapin 1994: 16).

So, if even the hardest of scientific facts are formed through ethical practices such as the granting or withdrawal of trust, then the "softer" varieties of political knowledge – such as the knowledge about what constitutes justice and fairness, what it means to be a citizen, to have a voice, to have rights, to mount grievances, to fight for a cause, to be represented – *must* also depend on the moral judgments people make about those in their midst who "do" politics. Government officials, party activists, people's deputies, judges, political advocates, and of course journalists have always been recognized as people who engage in politics. These groups of people existed, acted, and were judged for their actions both before and after the fall of the Soviet Union. Other groups of actors – election consultants, private media owners, campaign strategists, and other varieties of political operatives – joined them after 1991.

To play the devil's advocate, we may ask: Do politicians, activists, journalists, and other public figures even *care* whether and how they are judged by their mass publics? Some of them probably do not, and others certainly do. Does it matter? It most certainly does. As media scholar Daniel Hallin (1994) observed with respect to journalists (and as most ideological workers understand very well), there are actually limits beyond which even the most instrumental or strategic use of communication cannot be pushed. "Every process of communication involves a social relationship, in fact, a network of relationships, among active human subjects," Hallin (1994: 32) writes. "The maintenance of

---

[4] Jumping ahead of the story, this is precisely what happened to a substantial portion of public discourse in Russia throughout the 2000s.

these relationships imposes demands on institutions like the media ... [in that they] have to attend to their own legitimacy. [The media] must maintain the integrity of their relationship with their audience and also the integrity of their own self-image and of the social relationships that make up the profession of journalism. Maintaining these relationships requires a certain minimum of honesty." If the media fail to attend to their own integrity in this way, Hallin (1994: 33) sums up, they face the risk that they "may become ineffective ideological institutions."

Paradoxically, this aspect of the Soviet media system and its satellites has received very little attention from scholars. Aside from important work by Ellen Mickiewicz (1981, 1988), who, from the early 1980s, was demonstrating through Soviet opinion polls that Soviet mass audiences trusted their media on some topics but wanted more honesty on others, few attempts have been made to systematically examine the mechanisms through which the credibility of Soviet-style media offerings was challenged and maintained.[5] This book offers such an examination. It is centrally concerned with those relations between journalists and their publics that Hallin (1994) talks about, and especially with journalists' efforts to maintain the integrity of those relations during and after Russia's encounter with press freedom in the 1990s.

This book argues that contrary to conventional narratives, Soviet-era journalists did share a truth- and justice-seeking[6] ethic for which they were recognized by their audiences. Soviet journalism carried on elements of social and intellectual critique from the nineteenth century, modeling itself on the writings of prominent justice-seekers who inspired the Russian Revolution such as Alexander Herzen and Vissarion Belinsky.[7] Bona fide journalism thus coexisted with official propaganda in the Soviet Union, at times standing more clearly apart and at other

---

[5] But see Boyer (2003); Meyen and Schwer (2007); Muller (2013); Wolfe (2006). Earlier examples of scholarship that paid some attention to the social and moral aspects of relations between Soviet mass communicators and their audiences include Dzirkals et al. (1982), Hopkins (1970), and Inkeles (1950).

[6] In Russian, *iskat' pravdu* – "to seek truth" – simultaneously means to seek justice as well. See the entry for *pravda* in Cassin (2014).

[7] Alexander Herzen (1812–1870) was one of Russia's most prominent political writers and philosophers of the nineteenth century. Influenced by Proudhon, Rousseau, and Hegel, he is credited with creating the political climate that led to the emancipation of the serfs in 1861. Vissarion Belinsky (1811–1848) was Russia's most preeminent literary critic and magazine editor of liberal persuasion, advocating for a socially conscious approach to literature.

times blending more easily together. The majority of Soviet journalists, though, worked hard to maintain the trust of their audiences and
were recognized by readers for their efforts. After the fall of the Soviet
Union, those social and moral relations began to strain and were
eventually severed. Media privatization at a time of economic collapse in the early 1990s led to the fragmentation of journalism as
a profession, alienating journalists from one another and from their
audiences, undercutting their moral authority, and bringing about
a public discourse in which journalism began to be framed as political
prostitution ("the second oldest profession") that had been absent in
the USSR.

The broader and more ambitious argument that this book makes is
that this spectacular institutional unraveling brought about a society-
wide erosion of the *value* of seeking truth and of speaking it to power.
Because journalism is linked to the most cherished of Enlightenment
ideals – the idea of freedom of speech and of speaking truth to power –
when journalism devolves, those values, I argue, devolve with it.
The ability (and the need) to seek truth and justice and to do so publicly
is fundamental to the maintenance of most social and political orders.
Citizens' ability to seek justice, and the society-wide appreciation of
those efforts, was just as central for the workings of socialism as it is
for the maintenance of liberalism. To suggest that post-Soviet society
lost its taste for truth- and justice-seeking is thus to suggest that the
collapse of the Soviet Union wreaked moral havoc in the lives of many
Russians. This profound moral disorientation is what much of this
book is about.

Last but not least, this book examines how this devolution in journalism has articulated with forms of state-sponsored cynicism that
President Putin has actively pursued during his tenure. Putin bolstered
his authority in part by trying to discredit Western ideals and practices,
particularly those of democracy promotion and civil society building.
My study shows why his efforts succeeded – because they had been
prepared by the crisis of journalism as an institution of truth-seeking
that had set in before Putin came to power. By the time Putin began to
consolidate his influence, manipulation of public opinion was simply
expected; indignation about it was absent; it was no longer news. This
untied Putin's hands and those of his allies to the point that by the end
of the 2000s, Russian officials and other power brokers (including
some journalists) began to get away not only with displays of cynicism

directed at liberal institutions but also with periodic open admissions of manipulation and deceit.

With this erosion of the value of truth-seeking, neither journalism nor press freedom make much sense. This crucial development paved the way for the emergence, and the society-wide acceptance, of rabid ultranationalist propaganda in Russia since 2014 (leading up to and following the annexation of the Crimean Peninsula from neighboring Ukraine) that would not have occurred without the tacit acquiescence of the majority of Russia's journalists who had only recently thought of themselves as representatives of an independent Fourth Estate.

Before moving on any further, any book claiming to say something new on the subject of truth-telling in Russia must first deal with an older, familiar claim that Soviet public life was full of falsehoods and lies and that those lies were perpetuated out of collective timidity or convenience, or both. The appeals by Alexander Solzhenitsyn (1974) and Vaclav Havel (1989) to their fellow citizens to "Live Not by Lies" and to "Live in Truth" are well-known examples of this position. So a discussion of truth-telling in Russia is necessarily linked to the discussion of the morality of the Soviet political project as a whole. It is to this discussion that we must first turn.

Truth in the USSR: An Ethical Turn

A moral condemnation of all things Soviet is a perspective with substantial intellectual pedigree, beginning with what was loosely known as the totalitarian school of Sovietology – a body of scholarship about the Soviet Union produced at the height of the Cold War. These works considered Soviet political rule fundamentally illegitimate and therefore immoral, based on coercion and indoctrination rather than consent (Conquest 1968; Friedrich and Brzezinski 1956; Kennan 1954; Schlesinger 1949).[8] The early works of the totalitarian school saw "the new Soviet man" to be a victim of propaganda and terror, atomized from

[8] Consider also Arendt (1951), Hayek (1944), Koestler (1941), and Orwell (1949). In addition to Sovietology, speculations about the degree of legitimacy of Soviet political order were a major current in other academic fields that similarly came of age at the height of the Cold War and were nurtured by it, including modernization and development studies, social psychology, comparative political science, and mass communication scholarship (Pletsch 1981; Simpson 1994; Engerman 2009).

fellow human beings, "dissolved in communist 'patterns of thought,' and unable to sustain a critical distance between himself and society" (Krylova 2000: 9). Historian Anna Krylova (2000: 8) argues that this image of the new Soviet man – easily suggestible, fearful, unable to relate to others, unwilling to think critically – was none other than "an immoral opposite of the liberal self," Western modernity's alter ego. Krylova (2000: 4) suggests that this kind of knowledge production took place in the particular, post–World War II environment when Western intellectuals felt "an uneasy sense of connectedness" to their totalitarian alter ego and were searching for "the roots of totalitarian deviation" so as to protect Western modernity from a potential internal enemy.[9]

In the 1940s, Western social scientists had to rely primarily on official Soviet documents for their knowledge about the Soviet Union. In the 1950s, new sources of data became available: interviews with émigrés who did not return to the Soviet Union after the end of World War II (the large-scale Harvard Émigré Interview Project) and the so-called Smolensk Archive – a large trove of archival documents from the Smolensk Oblast Committee of the Communist party that was captured intact by Nazi Germany in 1941, retained by West Germany, and subsequently made available to Western scholars.[10] Those new data helped to substantially refine the views of Cold War Sovietologists on "how Russia [was] ruled."[11] On the one hand, there was now clear evidence that many Soviet citizens genuinely endorsed state socialism as a legitimate form of government and that many recognized the gap between political ideals and attempts at their implementation. On the other hand, Cold War scholars discovered that the Soviet Union also had plenty of "non-believers" who had learned to manipulate the system to their personal advantage. The presence of these calculating, self-interested individuals supported Sovietologists' earlier suspicion that even in the midst of a social totality, there must have been "islands

---

[9] Krylova (2000: 8) points out the irony involved in some of the juxtapositions from that period. Some accounts (e.g., Erikson 1954) distinguish "the balanced, organic wholeness" of the liberal self from the "one-sided, mechanical totality" of the new Soviet man. The contrast thus drawn is between "'wholeness' as good and 'totality' as bad" (Krylova 2000: 8).

[10] Many of the classic texts of Cold War Sovietology were based on those two sources of data, including Inkeles (1950), Fainsod (1953), Bauer, Inkeles, and Kluckhohn (1956), Inkeles and Bauer (1959), and others.

[11] The title of Fainsod's (1953) classic text.

of separateness" where "non-indoctrinated individuality survives" (Krylova 2000: 10). While calculated self-interest was hardly an illustration of high moral probity presumably expected of "non-indoctrinated individuality," finding it in the Soviet Union partially answered the question of "why did they not resist?" that haunted American postwar Sovietology (Krylova 2000: 10).

The 1960s witnessed the birth of the dissident movement in the former Soviet bloc, and this brought about another dramatic shift in how the field of Soviet studies understood the basic morality of the Soviet political project. The emergence of underground periodicals (*samizdat*), the steady stream of manuscripts smuggled out of the Soviet bloc to be published in the West, the growing number of forced émigrés and political prisoners among the dissidents – all of this gave the dissident voice the authority to tell Western audiences the truth about what was "really" going on in the Soviet bloc. The question of "why did they not resist?" was no longer posed; "they" were obviously resisting, even if they were the brave few. With that, the basic morality of the Soviet order had shifted once again, and the possibility for maintaining individual dignity and moral integrity in the midst of a social totality was reinstated in the subject-position of the dissident. Moreover, the nondissident majority of Soviet citizens began to be viewed primarily as calculating conformists rather than as true believers. The story told by the Soviet dissidents and retold by Sovietologists featured the manipulative rather than the manipulated Soviet majority: people from all walks of life using the system for their advantage, avoiding public confrontation with it, "while mocking it in the private realm, at the kitchen table" (Krylova 2000: 15). In this narrative, the nondissidents appeared as persons of compromised morality – at best, as individuals who made arrangements "between one's conscience and convenience" and, at worst, as "moral invalid[s] who both lacked inner integrity and laughed about it" (Krylova 2000: 15–16).

In the 1970s and 1980s, against the grain of the totalitarian school, and under the influence of détente in US-Soviet relations, there began to emerge scholarship that came to be loosely known as the *revisionist school* in Soviet area studies. The revisionists challenged the totalitarian school's views on many counts, including the negative portrayal of Soviet society as under siege and crippled from an all-powerful dictatorship established as a result of the Bolshevik conspiracy plot in 1917.[12] Drawing attention to the existence in the USSR of upward mobility, of professional groups and ideologies, and of interbureaucratic and center-periphery conflicts, revisionist historians were arguing that Soviet socialism-building was a form of state-sponsored modernization and, as such, enjoyed some degree of legitimacy from the population at large (Viola 2002; Fitzpatrick 2007, 2008).[13]

Interesting

Not surprisingly, such perspectives were bound to be interpreted as whitewashing Bolshevism and Stalinism. Revisionists' work on the Great Purges – especially Arch Getty's (1985) study arguing that the Purges might have been an unintended outcome of power struggles, disorganization, and considerable autonomy at lower levels of government and not necessarily a top-down relay of Stalin's bloodthirstiness – was equated to Holocaust denial. "If the Nazis had won, we would have had revisionist scholarship pointing out Hitler's good sides," wrote one proponent of the totalitarian school in a *New York Times* editorial (quoted in Fitzpatrick 2008: 687). At every opportunity, revisionists were thus expected to offer public acknowledgment that "the purges were a bad thing and that Stalin and the Soviet system were responsible for them" (Fitzpatrick 2008: 692). As Fitzpatrick (2008: 694) sums it up, until the mid-1980s, revisionism was seen as an "unpardonable exercise in *'tout comprendre, c'est tout pardonner'*."[14]

With the end of the Cold War, the intellectual climate in the West once again shifted, the range of intellectual perspectives on Soviet history widened dramatically, and research into the human and moral dimensions of state socialism no longer carried the high political stakes it did before. Ironically, in the 1990s, the revisionists began to focus on resistance to, rather than support for, the Soviet rule, since there was now plenty of evidence of resistance from the newly opened

[12] As Sheila Fitzpatrick (2008), a leading figure among the revisionists, points out, challenging the grand narrative of Cold War Sovietology on moral grounds was only one of the tasks of the revisionists. The other, stronger impulse, according to Fitzpatrick, was the push toward greater empiricism through a more detailed use of archives (following the data wherever they led) and away from abstract model building and ideological partisanship that had dominated the totalitarian school.

[13] See also Fitzpatrick (1979); Getty (1985); Suny (1983); Viola (1987).

[14] "To understand all is to forgive all," a phrase said to originate in Tolstoy's *War and Peace*. For a contemporary iteration of this attitude to revisionist scholarship, see Etkind (2005).

archives (Fitzpatrick 2007). It was now a new cohort of scholars, sometimes called the *postrevisionists,* who continued to be interested in the legitimation mechanisms of Soviet rule. The works that have come out in this tradition in the 1990s and 2000s have been interdisciplinary and have been as much an exercise in cultural theory as in Soviet historiography. *Love Foucault!*

A substantial body of postrevisionist scholarship to date has been produced in direct engagement with Michel Foucault's ideas about modern disciplinary power and governmentality (Collier 2011; Engelstein and Sandler 2000; Halfin 2000, 2003, 2009; Hellbeck 2006; Kharkhordin 1999; Kotkin 1995; Wolfe 2006). There continues to be disagreement among Russia specialists as to the appropriateness of wholesale (or even piecemeal) appropriation of Foucault's frameworks to Russian historical realities (Boym 2002; Engelstein 1993; Etkind 2005; Kharkhordin 2001; Plamper 2002). Yet this Foucauldian turn has served a very important purpose in Russian studies: it has allowed the conversation about the moral valence of Soviet rule to continue *without* scholars having to commit themselves, explicitly or implicitly, to either denouncing or exculpating the Soviet political project, as had been the case in the past. The moral ambivalence of many of Foucault's philosophical positions[15] – including his unwillingness to reproduce the dichotomies of truth and falsehood, of conformity and resistance – struck a welcome cord with the new cohort of Russia scholars who similarly did not want to have to choose sides. Foucault's ambiguity around the moral valence of truth and power allowed these scholars to move beyond the polarities of good and evil to speak instead of Soviet "governmentality" and "subjectivity" from a position of seeming moral neutrality.[16] *Foucault → for essay*

One of the most nuanced accounts of the ethical dimension of Soviet life has been offered by anthropologist Alexei Yurchak (2006). While not drawing directly on Foucault (the theoretical debt is instead to Derrida, Deleuze and Guattari, Bakhtin, and others), Yurchak's (2006) historical ethnography is similarly committed to not reproducing any of the dichotomies of modernity, including truth

---

[15] On some possible explanations for this ambivalence, see Rorty (1992).

[16] Oleg Kharkhordin's (1999) work is clearly an exception here. For a thorough review of Western historians' approaches to Soviet subjectivity and personhood, see Chatterjee and Petrone (2008).

and falsehood, liberation and oppression, and so on. Yurchak's (2006: 10) aim was to "rehumanize Soviet life," to understand how that life could be simultaneously experienced as dull, stagnating, and coercive, on the one hand, and meaningful, creative, and ethical, on the other. Drawing on J. L. Austin's theory of performatives, Yurchak argues that, especially in late socialism (after Stalin's death in 1953), most elements of Soviet public discourse – official speeches and reports, newspaper editorials, ritualized acts such as party meetings, political information sessions, public demonstrations, parades, and so on – lost much of their *literal* meaning for Soviet citizens (but not all meaning). People participated in those acts not because they supported a particular candidate or endorsed this or that party position on an issue – most of the time, those positions were seen as irrelevant. The reason people delivered official-sounding speeches at meetings, took part in public events, voted in favor of resolutions, paid membership dues, and so on was in the *performative value* that such participation carried. Such acts "did things" beyond their literal meaning: they signaled to others that one was a particular kind of person – one who was bored by the dullness of public ritual but who nevertheless espoused the values of sociality, inquisitiveness, altruism, equality, creativity, and self-fulfillment that were at the heart of the socialist project. Soviet ideology in the late socialist period thus claimed a certain "hegemony of form," as Yurchak (2006) puts it, but left much of ideological content indeterminate and open-ended.

This was the key paradox of late socialism: the more humane, creative, and meaningful aspects of socialism could be experienced only if, and sometimes even *in the process of,* taking part in ideological formalities. In moments of such collective togetherness (even if those occasions were explicitly ideological), a particular community of like-minded people was produced – a community of *svoi*, or "our own kinds of persons," as Yurchak calls it.[17] These communities of *svoi* would pop up whenever and wherever people recognized themselves as belonging to *svoi* – often in the spaces of official public events and *through the act of* reproducing official Soviet discourse. An open refusal to participate in those events would have meant risking exclusion from these communities.

[17] *Svoi* is a reflexive possessive pronoun in Russian meaning "one's own." It is similar to Latin *sui*, Spanish *suyo*, German *sein*, and so on.

"ordinary Soviet morality"

Such a refusal could get the communities of *svoi* "into trouble" with the authorities, so there was a certain "moral responsibility not to cause problems to one of *svoi*" (Yurchak 2006: 109).

This account of ordinary Soviet morality, as I am calling it here, and its relations with official discourse significantly improves our understanding of the moral worlds Soviet citizens inhabited in late socialism (from the 1960s onward). It shows that one might partake in official events and discourses for a host of reasons, including not only the cynical pretense or the full identification with Soviet power, as had been suggested before, but also a complex ethical mechanism theorized through the concept of *svoi*. Yurchak (2006) here makes a very important contribution to our understanding of how Soviet ideology was coproduced by speakers and listeners in everyday practice: the *act* of saying or doing something in public – including officially sanctioned words and actions – could transform the mean- ✗ ing of that act for those involved, sometimes in unexpected or unpredictable directions. The performative dimension of an ideolo- gically marked utterance would routinely get unhinged, as it were, from its literal meaning and would begin to drift in some other direction (commonly, toward reaffirming the sociality of *svoi*). The meaning of a public act would therefore undergo an internal displacement, unnoticeable on the level of form but nevertheless recognized by all involved.

This influential account of how Soviet citizens related to official dis- course does, however, gloss over some important aspects of ordinary ethics in late socialism that are crucial for understanding the social and moral relations Soviet journalists maintained with their audiences, so it is to these overlooked aspects of ordinary morality that we must now turn. One issue that needs to be addressed in greater detail is Soviet attitudes toward political dissidents and the phenomenon of nonconformity more broadly. Yurchak (2006) controversially places dissidents and party activists on the same plane – as people who took the official Soviet discourse too literally and too seriously.[18] The committed party activists defended the official positions, the dissidents denounced them as lies, while the most sensible position, according to the self-described "normal people" Yurchak interviewed, would have been to treat official Soviet

---

[18] See also Oushakine (2001).

ambivalence?

language simply as irrelevant or uninteresting.[19] As historians Kevin
Platt and Benjamin Nathans (2011: 316) have pointed out, Yurchak's
account leaves us with a view of the dissidents that borders on caricature.
Taking official ideological pronouncements too seriously, the dissidents
come across as people of compromised morality who were willing to
jeopardize the sociality of *svoi* – the human bonds that would have
emerged *if* one were willing to perform ideological formalities together
with others.[20]

More recent studies of nonconformist practices and attitudes in the
Soviet Union (e.g., Boobbyer 2005; Nathans 2007; Firsov 2008; Suslov
2011) show that there was actually substantial ambivalence toward
both dissidence *and* conformity in Soviet Russia. Even if dismissive
attitudes toward nonconformists were as widespread as some of
Yurchak's interlocutors claim, such dismissal might have been due to
 psychological repression rather than indifference[21] (Platt and Nathans
2011: 314). It is likely that the dissidents' open nonconformity was
"uncomfortable and stressful" (Platt and Nathans 2011: 309) for many
educated people in the Soviet Union because it reminded them of their
own conformism, which was in conflict with the value of frank and
honest speech they also espoused (Boym 1994: 95–102). Behaving
contrary to one's value orientations can generate strong cognitive dissonance, so Yurchak's interlocutors might have been trying to reduce
such dissonance, coming up with ways to rationalize their conformist
behavior. One way would have been to talk oneself into devaluing
nonconformity, choosing to see the dissidents as fighting political

---

[19] In discussing common perceptions of the dissidents as "abnormal," as "having
a screw loose," and, borrowing from poet Joseph Brodsky, as "the sick" who
were "written off" by "the healthy majority," Yurchak (2006: 106) is oddly
silent about the links begging to be made between these characterizations and
the normalizing practices of European insane asylums examined by Foucault.
This seems like a most fitting application of a Foucauldian frame to Soviet
realities, given the notorious Soviet practice of actually incarcerating some
dissidents in mental hospitals.

[20] Negative attitudes toward individuals willing to jeopardize the well-being of the
group are an instantiation of the larger social phenomenon of *krugovaya poruka*
(variously translated as "forced trust," "imposed cooperation," "the circle of
collective responsibility," or "coverup") that, for historical reasons, has
a particularly rich genealogy in Russia (see Ledeneva 2006).

[21] In his earlier work, Yurchak (1997) did invoke Freud's metaphor of repression
to explain the proliferation of political jokes in the Soviet Union, but he seems to
have moved away from Freud's vocabulary in his later work.

windmills, as it were, and deciding that such fighting was pointless and therefore irrelevant and uninteresting.[22]

Continuing with the idea of cognitive discomfort, sociologist Alena Ledeneva (2011) explores the other side of the same phenomenon – the uneasiness many people felt when faced with evidence of their own and others' *conformist* rather than dissident behavior.[23] Ledeneva (2011) zooms in on the phenomenon of the "knowing smile" – a signal people can send to one another in situations of moral squeeze – when they recognize that they are complicit in some morally ambiguous behavior, feel awkward about it, but do not want to openly acknowledge it. People in the Soviet Union experienced moral squeeze, Ledeneva (2011: 730) argues, when they found themselves in situations that were governed by contradictory values or logics – such as wanting to help a friend in need but feeling ashamed about using public resources to do so or wanting to speak bluntly and directly but sensing the group's "ambivalence about the idea of being honest [and] upright." Ledeneva (2006, 2011) argues that in such situations, most Soviets gravitated toward decisions that privileged silence over speech and people's personal well-being, or the well-being of a small group (*svoi*), over the public interest or the common good.

Yet the notions of the common good and of speaking out did have their place in a Soviet system of moral, if not always political, coordinates – which is precisely why acting as if those ideals did not matter created uncomfortable situations of moral squeeze. Sharing an awkward "knowing smile" was one way to handle this moral discomfort: it allowed participants to mutually recognize that what they were doing

---

[22] Poet Joseph Brodsky seems to have been thinking along the same lines when he invoked "the healthy majority" for whom the dissidents were "a convenient example of the wrong deportment" and "a source of considerable moral comfort" (quoted in Yurchak 2006: 101).

[23] Alena Ledeneva's (2011) work is among the first to bring the concepts from social and cognitive psychology "back in" to discussions of Soviet ideology and subjectivity in Russian area studies. Psychologists, particularly Raymond A. Bauer (1952, 1956), were active participants in the initial production of knowledge about the Soviet Union, but psychology and Sovietology rather quickly parted ways. There are, I believe, more discoveries to be made if we incorporate concepts that have since been developed in social and cognitive psychology (e.g., rationalization, self-deception, cognitive dissonance, motivated reasoning, wishful thinking, learned helplessness, rational and willful ignorance, and so on) into our theories of the working of social and power relations both in the Soviet Union and beyond.

was not quite right, but it took away the pressure to openly acknowledge the transgression. In this way, a knowing smile worked as a safety valve in the repression mechanism theorized by Freud – similar to winks, political jokes, or a genre of talking that literary scholar Svetlana Boym (1994: 1) called "communication with half-words." Speaking with half-words protected communities of Soviet intellectuals "from outsiders and, in a way, from its own members," Boym (1994: 1) noted. "If all at once those other halves of words were to be spoken, intimate gatherings of friends might end – in fistfights" (Boym 1994: 2). This, Boym explained, was because the values of honest and sincere speech were also prevalent in that milieu. Official de-Stalinization reinforced those values in the late 1950s and 1960s, encouraging a new round of soul-searching among the intellectuals and a renewed desire to share the results of such introspection with others.

Historian Marci Shore (1998) documents similar developments for Czechoslovakia in the late 1950s and 1960s. There, as in all countries of the former Soviet bloc, the state needed the cultural and moral support of intellectuals for socialism's continued political survival. During the high-mobilization Stalinist period, the tasks of developing class consciousness, becoming attuned with the proletariat in order to lead them forward, building faith in the socialist project while practicing comradely criticism and self-criticism – these tasks were central to Marxist intellectuals' understanding of their moral and cultural roles. But after the Twentieth Party Congress in Moscow in 1956 with which official de-Stalinization began, the language of intellectual Marxism across the former Soviet bloc became more existentialist, "a language made up more of questions than of answers" (Shore 1998: 439).[24] What is the relationship of individual to society? What does it mean for the intellectuals to be "the conscience of the nation"? What is individual conscience and responsibility? These were the new concerns of educated people across Eastern Europe, Marxists or not, from the late 1950s forward (Shore 1998, 2013; see also Boobbyer 2000, 2005). This new focus on conscience and individual responsibility brought about a renewed concern with frank speech. Speaking frankly and honestly might be one of humankind's earliest virtues, and it acquires special – political – significance if it is done in front of many others (Arendt 2005) and delivers a message the majority does not necessarily

[24] See also Sartre 1974.

want to hear (Foucault 2010, 2011). Frank speech demands courage; it is thus antithetical to conformity and is a key element of the truth/power nexus that is often overlooked in discussions of truth, power, and subjectivity. In his final two years of lectures at the *Collège de France*, Michel Foucault (2010, 2011) concentrated on the ancient Greek concept of parrhesia – the practice of frank and courageous speech delivered at the risk of angering a majority or a more powerful interlocutor.[25] As a practice of truth-telling, parrhesia for Foucault has several distinct characteristics. It is speech that is clear and direct, with nothing left to interpretation. It is an ethical act because it is based in conviction (which distinguishes it from rhetoric, where public speakers need not be personally invested in what they argue). It is ethical in another sense: it is experienced as a moral duty. Parrhesia is also a political act: it is criticism from a position of less power. Classic examples of parrhesia Foucault gives are of a philosopher criticizing a tyrant, a citizen criticizing a majority, or a student criticizing a teacher.

This focus on the courage of truth-telling is an important shift, or perhaps an important refinement, in Foucault's broader thinking about the relationship between subject, truth, and power. In interviews given in his final years, Foucault admitted that his earlier work might have been misunderstood as claiming that truth, like freedom, is merely an effect of power and does not exist outside of it (Foucault 1997a; Laidlaw 2002). Foucault clarifies that he draws a distinction between power and domination. The latter is an abuse of power, when the governing of others becomes fixed, "blocked, frozen," whereas power itself is "mobile, reversible, unstable" and is thus permeable to ethics (Foucault 1997b: 283, 292). The practice of parrhesia therefore becomes the bridge that connects ethics and politics as the exercise of power. When people speak openly and courageously in front of others, they try to bring ethics back into politics, aiming to realign the political with the ethical that they perceive had gotten out of sync. The practice

[25] "Calling things by their real names," "telling it like it is," "not mincing words," and "speaking out" are some of the ways people acknowledge courageous speech in English. The Russian equivalents include *govorit' pravdu v glaza* (*v litso*), *govorit' priamo, rubit'(rezat') pravdu-matku*. I thus disagree with Svetlana Boym (1994: 1), who noted that "the American metaphors" for open and frank speech such as *saying what you mean* and *being straightforward* "do not translate properly into the Soviet and Russian contexts."

of parrhesia, Foucault suggests, is the thread through which the genealogy of the critical tradition in Western political thought and practice can be traced.[26]

Important
↓
for
essay

This somewhat modified and clarified perspective on truth and power, where truth is seen as close and connected but not subsumed by power, is particularly useful for approaching the nexus of conformity and dissidence in the Soviet Union because it helps us to move beyond the common view that it was either the party or the dissidents who held a monopoly on truth-telling in the former Soviet bloc. This book argues that courageous speech was a rare but highly valued occurrence across many different strata in Soviet society and was not limited to the dissident milieus; it occurred in both private and public settings, and it was particularly important and meaningful for journalists. Understandably, the safest place to practice courageous speech was among the like-minded communities of *svoi* (Boym 1994: 94–102; Pudovkina 2000; Yurchak 2006: 131–157). But recall that those communities often existed in official Soviet spaces, such as public "Palaces of Culture," youth organizations, after-school clubs and programs, and, as Chapter 1 will show, in newspaper offices that were open to the public.[27] In one such after-school club in Leningrad, for instance, appropriately termed *Derzanie* ("Daring"), participants gathered regularly to discuss literature, films, and current events. The club was open to young people from all walks of life and was led by a team of older teachers; local authors, poets, and other dignitaries were often present at discussions. According to one member of the club, participants "argued about everything, harshly and freely," with "teachers and students ... disputing on an equal basis" (Pudovkina 2000, quoted in Yurchak 2006: 136). When the work of a local author was being discussed, few attendees felt "any special 'reverence' for the author." "We were the impudent young fellows [*yunye nakhaly*], allowing ourselves to aim critical arrows at our older colleagues. I don't particularly recall them objecting to it" (Pudovkina 2000). Those gatherings are often remembered as giving people an opportunity to pursue their

[26] Foucault's death in 1984 prevented him from undertaking a historical investigation into the role such nonconfessional varieties of truth-telling played in the formation of modern subjectivity (Kotkin 1995: 392, n90).

[27] For the genesis of these youth initiative clubs that proliferated throughout the Soviet Union after Stalin's death and for the rationality behind the official endorsement of them, see Tsipursky (2012).

own *pravda* (truth), but perhaps because of the official devaluation of the word itself, participants refer to those experiences as having been about a pursuit of "truer truths" (Boym 1994: 96), "deep truths" (Yurchak 2006: 130), or even "horse doses of truth" (Pudovkina 2000).

Courageous speech also belonged in Soviet workplaces, where, again, it was a rare but valued occurrence, marking someone as a person of integrity. Whenever one publicly expressed one's frustrations, drew attention to an injustice, confronted superiors, urged a colleague to "think with his or her own head," reminded others of their responsibility for their actions, or acted in a myriad other ways that drew on one's faculty of thinking and demanded some amount of courage – one was "luring what [would] otherwise [be] passed over in silence into the area of discourse" (Arendt 1968: 78). As historian Stephen Kotkin (1995) argued in his influential study of social and power relations in a Soviet industrial town in the 1930s, even at the height of Stalinism, workers spoke out about their frustrations and grievances during production meetings. Those "occasional public moments of catharsis," especially when "brief but blunt words" were coming from "the most authoritative 'core' proletarians, hard-working ... men who had sufficient clout to say what others could not and just had had enough," were, Kotkin (1995: 229) argues, part and parcel of "speaking Bolshevik."[28] Such public instances of frank

[28] Historian Jochen Hellbeck (2000: 81; 2006) has both derived inspiration from Kotkin's work and criticized it for endowing Soviet subjectivity with a certain "extrahistorial kernel" from which Soviet power could be resisted. For Hellbeck, Kotkin (1995) reads too much resistance into the acts of speaking out he describes. Hellbeck (2000: 81) suggests that Soviet subjects not only "spoke Bolshevik" but "thought Soviet" – that is, sought to align their intimate selves with the revolutionary project. They could and did speak out and often experienced the need to do so as a duty, but they owed the authority to do so "to their self-alignment with the revolutionary master-narrative" (Hellbeck 2000: 95). I am generally sympathetic with Hellbeck's arguments, especially his insistence that we do not treat "only negative, resisting statements as indices of a true speaking out" (2000: 85). But I also believe that Hellbeck leaves too little space between power and ethics, doing what Foucault's critics accused him of doing – that is, suggesting that freedom and truth are an effect of power and do not exist outside of it. Perhaps it is the need to theorize the space from which power can be spoken to, and not only inhabited, that led Foucault to his interest in parrhesia in his late work. For this reason, I think Kotkin's (1995) take on "speaking Bolshevik" – with an important inclusion of parrhesia in it – still stands.

speech were a key component in the "subtle, if unequal negotiation" of the terms of political and moral engagement between the workers and the state that was supposed to represent them.[29] Such negotiation was possible to the degree that Soviet power itself was "pliable" – that is, productive of new moral frameworks but also amenable to moral exhortation (Kotkin 1995: 22).[30] It would be a mistake, Kotkin says, to privilege such moments of catharsis as "moments of truth" that revealed the basic falseness of the rest of life under Stalin. Rather, such behaviors coexisted with people's belief in the basic rightness of socialism, the sense of purpose people derived from being part of the socialist project *and* with their ambivalence, or perhaps even a "willing suspension of disbelief," about the mismatch between revolutionary ideals and their everyday implementation (Kotkin 1995: 230).[31]

As mentioned earlier, it would be incorrect to see these instances of frank speech, delivered in public, as necessarily examples of dissidence, just as it would be wrong to see them as manifestations of conformity. Rather, they are better thought of as instances of people risking to take an ethical stance in public – effectively saying, "This I *can't* do" (Arendt 2003: 78) in front of others – and *not* quite knowing what will follow. I purposefully invoke Arendt's ideas on individual responsibility here because they take us back full circle to the question of the moral valence

29 See also Lynn Viola's (2000: 57) discussion of peasant *vystuplenia* – acts of public defiance, of "stepping out of line" – as the most frequently used word in police reports about peasant disturbances during the Stalinist 1930s. Importantly, *vystuplenie* can also be translated as "speaking out," which sets it apart from other acts of peasant resistance under Stalinism, including peasant insurrections and riots. *Vystuplenie* thus can be seen as an act of speaking *to* power in the hope of being heard.

30 Kotkin (1995: 392, n90) mentions that Foucault's lectures and seminars on parrhesia, or the courage of truth-telling, delivered at Berkeley in 1983 were a crucial inspiration for Kotkin's analytical framework.

31 Following official de-Stalinization, portrayals of workplace parrhesia – of speaking bluntly in front of others while "meaning well" – began to make it into official Soviet popular culture. One good example is from *Moscow Does Not Believe in Tears*, an Oscar winner for Best Foreign Film in 1980. There is a scene in the film where the protagonist, a worker-turned-factory-director named Katia, is preparing to give a shop-floor interview on television, to be filmed by a man who was once her lover. As Kristin Roth-Ey (2011: 283) describes it, "An imperious and distinctly foreign-looking [television] producer shoves a script into [Katia's] hands to memorize, but once the camera begins to roll, Katia is flustered and blurts out her own, contrarian opinions instead. The contrast between honest Katia and the slick and manipulative world of broadcasting could not be clearer."

of state socialism as a political project with which this section began. In Arendt's (1951) estimation of Stalinism, it differed little from Nazism in that both regimes aimed to eliminate diversity of thinking and independence of judgment and employed mass terror to achieve those goals. There is indeed much historical evidence today that at the height of Stalinist "dark times" (Arendt 1968), it was conformity and withdrawal from politics, rather than speaking out, that allowed many people to physically survive in the Soviet Union (Fitzpatrick 1999; Geyer and Fitzpatrick 2009). There are also many indications that following de-Stalinization, Soviet society continued to be susceptible to conformism and privatism, albeit of a somewhat different variety, perhaps owing to the growing postwar emphasis across the Soviet bloc on consumption and mass entertainment.[32]

This does not mean, however, that the value of speaking honestly and openly disappeared in late socialism. As I just argued, and will do so again throughout this book, taking courageous stances in public continued to be valued precisely because they were rare, unpleasant, inconvenient, risky, but no longer potentially deadly as they often were under Stalinism.[33] In fact, it was Soviet journalists, cultural producers, educators, and other intellectuals who, in late socialism, continued to remind their fellow citizens of the significance of frank and honest speech – both for personal integrity and for society's well-being. For journalists in the late Soviet period, courageous action, among other things, came to mean speaking on behalf of readers who were unjustly wronged by Soviet bureaucracies. As Chapter 1 argues, most readers knew that in cases of conflict between citizens and bureaucracies, journalists were on their readers' side, even though they were often limited in what they could openly publish. Readers' knowledge that journalists and readers were

[32] On conformity within bureaucratic circles in late Stalinism, see Hooper (2006). On the increased importance of consumption and entertainment in post-Stalin's Russia, see Crowley and Read (2010), Koenker and Gorsuch (2006), Lovell (2003), Roth-Ey (2011), Siegelbaum (2008), and Tsipursky (2012).

[33] See Hooper (2008); Kozlov (2013); Schattenberg (2006). See also the rapidly expanding body of scholarship on everyday life and social relations during Khrushchev's thaw, including Bittner (2008), Jones (2006), and Kozlov and Gilburd (2013). On political protest, dissent, and diversity of thinking during the Khrushchev and Brezhnev periods, see Boobbyer (2005), Firsov (2008), Hornsby (2013), Kozlov et al (2011), Nathans (2007, 2011), and Suslov (2011).

"in it together" was very important for maintaining the integrity of journalist-reader relations that broke down after the fall of the Soviet Union. It was also important for the credibility of Soviet journalism as a profession and even for the legitimacy of the Soviet political project as a whole. It is to these topics that we must now turn.

Soviet Journalism, Professionalism, and Political Legitimacy

Just as we needed to identify whether courage and individual responsibility (1) existed and (2) were valued in Soviet society so that we could make better judgments about the moral valence of state socialism as a political and moral project, we now need to perform a similar kind of excavation for Soviet journalism – to see if we can speak of it as a legitimate social and political institution. If, as many Western scholars have argued, press freedom and liberal democracy were crucial to the emergence of journalism as a phenomenon, were people working in Soviet media organizations under conditions of censorship journalists in name only? Or can we still call what they did journalism? To answer these questions, we need to take an institutional look at the Soviet press, examining its role in the social and political structure of Soviet society, including its role as a legitimating mechanism of the political order of which it was part.

When discussing the conjoined histories of journalism and liberal democracy, Western scholars usually focus on several developments. Initially, the press played an important role in creating the liberal bourgeoisie as a distinct social class by connecting disparate economic actors and providing them with relevant information about prices, major events, and technological innovations that could affect their business interests (Hallin and Mancini 2004: 26). From the Reformation onward, the press was also centrally involved in political mobilization of large groups of people for revolutionary causes (the political advocacy role that Weber flagged as paramount). And in the eighteenth and nineteenth centuries, the press was crucial to the emergence of the new phenomenon of public opinion that became an important counterweight to the political authority of the bourgeois state (Habermas 1989).

How did the press aide in the creation of public opinion? Most important, it did so by monitoring government actions and by shining the light of publicity on abuses of power and by providing a platform

providing a platform for discussion

for a public discussion on these topics. This is precisely what philosophers ranging from Immanuel Kant to Thomas Carlyle to James Mill meant by the notion of the press as the Fourth Estate (Habermas 1989; Peters 1995). Over time, this monitorial or watchdog role for the press became the key normative feature of liberal-democratic media systems.[34] ✦

Christians et al. (2009) provide a good overview of this monitorial role for journalists in liberal democracies. Journalists are needed, Christians et al. (2009) argue, to continuously survey what goes on in the life of a democratic society for signs of anything that might pose a threat to the survival of that society. Christians et al. (2009) ground this normative view of journalism in what Harold Lasswell (1948) identified, in structural-functionalist terms, as the surveillance function of communication in social life. Journalists, according to Lasswell, are akin to the sentinels in the animal kingdom who "stand apart from the herd or flock and creat[e] a disturbance whenever an alarming change occurs in the surroundings" (Lasswell 1948: 39). Similarly, sociologist Robert Park (1967) has argued that journalists are the modern equivalents of town-criers whose job was to relay information of vital importance to the community (fires, births, deaths, major disturbances) so that townspeople could "keep track of their neighbors and to offer help or initiate criticism as appropriate" (Tuchman 1978: 3).

The journalistic monitoring of what goes on in the life of a society is clearly not the same as the intelligence gathering that we have come to associate with the modern concept of surveillance. Journalists conduct their investigations to make them public so that citizens, in the preferred phrase of media theorists, have the information they need to govern themselves effectively. The data gathered through spying and other covert operations, however, is not for public consumption; it is often done to manage or manipulate the behavior of those under surveillance and likely benefits those who initiate such data gathering rather than the public at large (although officials working for security agencies around the world would probably beg to differ). Nevertheless, the continuous monitoring of people's actions has been an inescapable element of actual governing practices – whether this monitoring is done openly by journalists in the name of transparency of government or by

---

[34] See Baker (2002); Christians et al. (2009); Curran (2011); Muhlmann (2010); Overholser and Jamieson (2005); Schudson (2008).

various covert agents in the name of security and order.[35] This is so because governing and self-governing are more difficult when polities are comprised of large numbers of people who have little or no face-to-face contact with one another (cf. Tocqueville 1954). Face-to-face contacts make it easier to (self) govern – both when it comes to policing and to deliberations on matters of common concern. Surveillance is thus central to governing and self-governing in *modernity*, which is why another name Christians et al. (2009: 142) give to journalism's monitorial role is that of "good" surveillance.[36]

What, then, makes the mechanism of "good" surveillance tick, we may ask? What precisely is good about it? How exactly does it work as a key component of governing – that is, of generating and sustaining authority, solidarity, and value? Of central importance here is the notion of publicity or publicness, which has both a participatory and a spectator dimension (Peters 1995). The public is both what matters or belongs to the whole society and what the whole society sees or witnesses. It is thus about openness and exposure but also about people "being in this together." Publicity in these interlocking senses is a powerful mechanism both for the enforcement of values and norms and for the rearticulation of those norms. Paul Lazarsfeld and Robert Merton (1948) recall anthropologist Bronislaw Malinowski's (1922) observation that among the Trobriand islanders, deviations from social norms were tolerated unless or until a public announcement of those deviations was made. Publicity – as the public exposure of deviation – is a mechanism that forces members of a group to recommit, as it were, to

---

[35] Investigative journalists' unease about some of the methods they (or their colleagues) might use to get to the story, such as going undercover, points to the porousness of boundaries between "good" and "bad" surveillance. Our language also offers evidence of such porousness: *investigation* belongs both to journalism and to police work, *survey* shares the same root with surveillance, and the meanings of *informant* and *informer* can be uncomfortably close. On concerns about doing journalism in the era of mass (digital) surveillance, see Andrejevic (2008) and Allen (2008).

[36] Historian Peter Holquist (1997) makes a related point in his influential article on Bolshevik surveillance practices and their modern European counterparts. Following early-twentieth-century usage, Holquist (1997) suggests that we distinguish between *policing* (activities designed to prevent delinquency and maintain order within a territory) and *surveillance* (gathering information on large numbers of people to make effective interventions into their behavior). Surveillance, for Holquist (1997), is a modern governmental practice that transcends the socialism-capitalism divide.

the social norm that has been violated. Publicity, in Lazarsfeld and Merton's (1948: 103) terms, "closes the gap between 'private attitudes' and 'public morality.' [It] exerts pressure for a single rather than a dual morality by preventing continued evasion of the issue."[37] That is, when many people are paying attention, a particular kind of moral certainty is produced – certainty that comes from committing to, or watching others commit to, a set of moral coordinates. Publicity's moral pull on us is so strong, anthropologist Roy Rappaport (1979: 198) explained, because "failure to abide by the terms of an obligation that one has accepted [in front of others] is generally, perhaps even universally, categorized as immoral, unethical, or wrong." *paradox of publicity*

So people govern and self-govern through publicity because it is a powerful way to get individuals to realign their behavior and even their beliefs with the prevailing social norms. One could thus conclude that publicity encourages conformism, and in many ways it certainly does. But, paradoxically, publicity also makes room for the opposite: it creates openings for rearticulating society's commitments and values – and that is publicity's *political* (rather than its social) role. The public realm, as Hannah Arendt (1958) famously argued, is the space where human plurality and distinctness manifest through people's speech and action. When people speak in public, they not only recommit to existing social norms but also create opportunities for new beginnings, including new relations, norms, and values. This is possible because risk, courage, novelty, and unpredictability are also built into human action. When we address a public, in that moment we do so as peers (Arendt 1958). Acting in public puts us in a position that is both vulnerable and powerful: it forces us to confront our private reservations, to pass judgment, to make choices, and to stand by them. *publicity and accountability*

This combination of freedom and obligation makes publicity a particularly important mechanism through which political leaders can be made accountable for their actions. Publicity – in the sense of transparency of government – became the rallying cry of Enlightenment reformers against the arbitrary rule of monarchs and their lack of accountability and disclosure (Lucas 1996; Peters 1995). The idea of the press as the Fourth Estate, mentioned earlier, is built on the same idea of democratic government through openness, transparency, and "good" surveillance.

[37] See also Katz (1982).

Now, when one thinks about surveillance under state socialism, one likely thinks of the interception of letters and phone calls, secret police informers, and other ignoble aspects of covert surveillance. But can one speak of any good surveillance – in the senses described earlier – under state socialism? Is it even possible to conceptually separate the "good" from the "bad" surveillance in communist political systems? These are high-stakes questions because answers to them crucially weigh in on whether there were any elements of popular rule in state socialism – which, in turn, taps into the issue of basic legitimacy of Soviet-style political projects as such.

In line with Marx's vision of human emancipation, and driven by the need to retain power, the Bolsheviks made a number of key governing decisions early on: away from multiparty elections, legal proceduralism, and freedom of the press and in favor of what they saw as more informal and more flexible mechanisms for adjusting policy and delivering justice and accountability.[38] Major emphasis was placed on soliciting citizens' appeals, grievances, complaints, suggestions, criticisms, and other kinds of input as forms of popular control from below, as it was officially known. Citizens were encouraged to bring their complaints against local and regional authorities to other levels and branches of government, including the press, and many people appealed to different governing agencies at once. Those appeals were not unlike petitions in imperial Russia when peasants complained to the tsar of abuse at the hands of local administrations or police (V. Kozlov 1996; Verner 1995). The key difference after the Revolution was that citizens could now *expect* that their grievances would be examined and investigated – because citizens were now invited to be the "eyes and ears of Soviet power," assessing the performance of their coworkers, including managers and officials, at building socialism.[39]

---

[38] For how and why some of those decisions were made in the first few years after the Revolution, see Berman (1948), Boim (1974), Burbank (1995), Huskey (1992), Kenez (1985a, 1985b), and Solomon (1985).

[39] Historians David Hoffmann (2011) and Peter Holquist (1997) have argued that these attempts to monitor the performance of lower-level bureaucrats, carried out both overtly and covertly, can be placed on a broader continuum of forms of modern European surveillance that were not unique to revolutionary Russia. Hoffmann (2011) suggests that such initiatives were in fact rather "progressive" compared to governing practices during the monarchy, when popular moods and input were largely disregarded because people were simply expected to obey. Now Soviet authorities *wanted* to involve the masses into politics, and to

For most of the Soviet period, but especially under Stalinism, popular denunciations – voluntary reports of wrongdoing by some citizens against others, brought before any level of authority, including the press – became a constant feature of Soviet governmental landscape.[40] Some denunciations, particularly during the Stalinist 1930s, were accusations of fellow citizens' lack of loyalty to the regime and reports of marital infidelity or of concealing one's class background. More serious accusations, widespread throughout the entire Soviet period, were so-called abuse-of-power denunciations (*zloupotreblenie vlast'yu*). They arrived both from people in subaltern positions and from people working within Soviet administrative or managerial bureaucracies. English speakers would recognize such practices as instances of whistle-blowing. In Soviet Russia, whistle-blowing quickly became a key feedback channel in the new communicative relationship, however poor and imperfect by democratic standards, between average citizens, local and midlevel officials, and central authorities (V. Kozlov 1996). In the absence of many legal avenues for the resolution of conflicts between citizens and bureaucracies, Russian historian Vladimir Kozlov (1996) argues, whistle-blowing became a singularly important means of popular oversight of lower and midlevel managers and administrators, who thus could be held at least somewhat accountable for their actions. Whistle-blowing

More than any other institution, whistle-blowing, given its public nature, "belonged" to the Soviet press. Newspapers actively encouraged signals from below and received the lion's share of letters containing abuse-of-power denunciations (Fitzpatrick 1996: 834). With readers' and correspondents' input, newspapers published relatively frequent exposés of misappropriation of funds, negligence, malfeasance, and other misdeeds at different levels of industrial and administrative bureaucracies.[41] So, while Soviet journalists did not enjoy freedom of the press in the liberal sense of the marketplace of ideas, they did have the mandate from the political system at large, in fact, an

---

do so effectively, they needed to both understand them and to be seen as responding to their needs and concerns – hence the prevalence of both overt and covert surveillance over lower-level bureaucracies.

[40] See Fitzpatrick (1996); Goldman (2007, 2011); Heinzen (2007); Hoffmann (2011); Hooper (2006); Kozlov (1996); Tsipursky (2010).

[41] On worker-peasant correspondents in the 1920s and early 1930s and on their struggles for authority within their communities, including through "abuse of power" denunciations, see Coe (1996) and Gorham (1996).

obligation, to partake in governing by providing administrative and managerial oversight with the help of overt surveillance from below. This is not to say that every case of whistle-blowing that came to journalists' attention turned into an abuse-of-power exposé or that interested officials did not try to actively prevent the publication of damaging information about them. It is also not to diminish the historical role of high-pitched diatribes that were especially prevalent during the Stalinist period – when, under the appearance of an exposé, the state would come down harshly on its critics, nonconformists, and other inconvenient individuals falsely accused of acts they did not commit.[42]

Another paradox

The press thus occupied an important but ambiguous position in the Soviet system of governance. Being an organ of the Communist party, the press was clearly subordinate to it; however, the party was dependent on the publicity the press generated – because publicity has the power to both enforce social conformity and challenge prevailing values and norms, as discussed earlier. In any political system, this capacity of public criticism to both maintain and challenge moral orders is what allows political communication scholars to speak of the legitimating function of the press vis-à-vis the political order of which it is part (Alexander 1981; Habermas 1975; Paletz and Entman 1981; Tuchman 1978). In liberal democracies, when the press, in its watchdog role, enters into fierce conflicts with other major institutions (the parliament, political parties, or the presidency, such as what arguably happened in the United States during the Watergate era or toward the end of the Vietnam War), this standoff between the press and other institutions does not mean that the legitimacy of the entire political order is about to collapse (Paletz and Entman 1981). Rather, journalists in their "good surveillance" role understand themselves and are likely to be seen by audiences as upholders of democracy who "present the correction of abuse as the ultimate proof of its soundness"

---

[42] See especially Brooks (2000) and Lenoe (2004). Denunciations in Soviet Russia have often (and sometimes primarily) been discussed in conjunction with Stalin's Great Terror – as something that actually oiled the terror machine (Arendt 1951; Fainsod 1953; see also Goldman 2011). Russian historian Vladimir Kozlov (1996: 871) argues that while, indeed, denunciations became "dry kindling" for the most notorious wave of massive political repressions during the late 1930s, by themselves, denunciations did not cause the repressions because, as a phenomenon, they stretched over a much longer period in Russian history both prior to and after the Purges.

(Hallin 1994: 33). We could make a similar argument for the role of whistle-blowing, and its manifestations through journalism, under state socialism. Soviet authorities could not afford to be *seen* as ignoring signals from below without jeopardizing socialism's legitimacy.[43] A public acknowledgment of (at least some) official wrongdoings, as unpleasant and risky as it was, was governmentally important because it performed a measure of justice both to those affected by the wrongdoing and to those watching the act of public judgment.[44] *A Interesting...*

This is not to say that denunciations were not used instrumentally. Because of its public and political character, denunciation is a highly charged act both for the whistle-blower and for those he or she denounces. As already mentioned, in Stalinist Russia, denounced officials commonly became targets of direct political repression. Denunciations, especially by bureaucrats against one another, could be made out of spite, as a way to settle personal disputes, to seek revenge, or to deflect blame (V. Kozlov 1996; Tsipursky 2010).[45] To protect themselves against denunciations, bureaucrats tried to discredit the character of the denouncer, questioning his or her integrity and motives. For this reason, some of the whistle-blowers sought anonymity (in effect, asking to speak "off the record"), which newspapers and other authorities handling denunciations did not guarantee. Another way a denunciation could backfire on its author was when the denunciation letter would be sent back to the offending bureaucracy with a request to investigate into the matter and to take action as appropriate. Needless to say, in such cases, the action taken would often involve punishing the denouncer for his or her betrayal. This, in turn, might prompt the denouncer to launch another complaint against the offending bureaucracy, this time directed at higher-level authorities, and adding "suppression of criticism" to the original list of grievances (Fitzpatrick 1996; V. Kozlov 1996).

---

[43] The same ambiguity has been built into China's mass communication system, starting from the Maoist period and continuing to some extent today (Zhao 2011, 2012). For the role of public criticism in the maintenance of party-state legitimacy in socialist Czechoslovakia, see Larson (2013: chap. 3).

[44] On public judgment as a nonlegal act of justice and on the liberal fear of judging and the problems it poses for democratic politics, see Arendt (2003: 18–22).

[45] Silvio Waisbord (2000: 103–118) describes a similar practice in Latin America known as *denuncismo*, in which political insiders use journalists to fight intraelite battles through media denunciations.

It is interesting that even in liberal democracies, whistle-blowing can be seen as a morally ambiguous activity, and journalists have an ambivalent relationship to it (Carr 2013; Wahl-Jorgensen and Hunt 2012). This is despite the fact that the majority of investigative reporters crucially depend on whistle-blowers for their stories (Waisbord 2000). Journalists' (and everyone else's) ambiguity toward whistle-blowing, Fitzpatrick and Gellately (1996) explain, owes to competing notions of loyalty and citizenship and to remaining uncertainty about the legitimacy of governments. Who do we, modern citizens, primarily owe our allegiance – to our families, to our friends, or to political entities such as our community, our nation, our country? The morality of denunciation seems to depend on whether one approves or disapproves of the political project at hand, say Fitzpatrick and Gellately (1996). "If we disapprove of a regime, church, or party and regard its interests as distinctly separate from and opposed to the interests of its citizens, we are likely to condemn the citizen who voluntarily offers information on another citizen to the authorities and will characterize his or her action disparagingly as collaboration or betrayal. Conversely, if we approve of the regime, we will tend to minimize the distinction between state and citizen interests, perhaps even regarding 'the state' as synonymous with 'the community of citizens,' and will see the citizen-denouncer as performing a necessary civic duty" (Fitzpatrick and Gellately 1996: 766). These distinctions – between state and citizen interests – become increasingly difficult to make in times of revolutions and major political upheavals, when moral foundations of states are changing and people's loyalties and senses of citizenship are in formation.[46]

To sum up thus far, Soviet journalists did not enjoy freedom of the press as the power of the better argument or as a platform for the

---

[46] This was precisely the dilemma with the attitudes toward denunciations during the French Revolution, according to historian Colin Lucas (1996). Proponents of the Revolution made an effort to distinguish between *délation* (informing and spying, a much-hated practice of the Old Regime) and *dénonciation*, which the revolutionaries struggled to define as a critical act of citizenship, as vigilant concern for public virtue and common good. The press (with such titles as *Sentinelle, Observateur, Véridique, Censeur,* and *Dénonciateur*) became a natural ally of the Revolution. "The debate on press freedom turned precisely on these issues of denunciation," Lucas (1996: 776) notes. To defenders of press freedom, journalists and publishers were "a vigilant eye of the People," and their denunciations were "rays of light shining into the darkness of evil" (Lucas 1996: 776). To defenders of the Old Regime, "journalists were in effect *délateurs*, purveyors of calumny, and thus generators of fatal discord" (Lucas 1996: 777).

workings of "the public sphere" where private citizens come together to discuss matters of common concern. They were unmistakably representatives of the state; and in that role, they were entrusted with two very different governmental tasks. One was symbolically representing the state to citizens – in Jürgen Habermas's (1989) sense of representation as outward display, performance, or pomp (Brooks 2000).[47] The other task, however imperfectly accomplished, was monitoring the very governing bureaucracies of which the press was part, helping to "strengthen the hand of the upright elements in the government … and weaken the hand of the corrupt" (Lazarsfeld and Merton 1948: 104). In this monitorial capacity, the Soviet press could perhaps be compared with the Scandinavian institution of an ombudsman (Boim 1974) or with the office of Inspector General in the United States (Schudson 2010).

Another way to speak about Soviet journalism in institutional terms would be through the concept of professionalization. After all, citizens in liberal democracies tend to trust journalists in part because of journalism's relatively successful efforts at professionalization over the past century (Schudson 1999; Schudson and Anderson 2009). As contemporary sociologists understand it, professionalization is an occupational project where occupational groups struggle for jurisdiction over a particular domain of knowledge and practice (Abbott 1988; Waisbord 2013). In that process, members of an occupation develop a sense of common interests and commitments. As a group, they negotiate relations with other social institutions, including the state. The aim of such negotiations is to settle on a social contract where the state guarantees professional groups a degree of autonomy in exchange for those groups' expertise and commitment to public service. As part of the same process, members of professionalizing groups strive to also be recognized by their clients – the public at large – as legitimate bearers of particular forms of knowledge and expertise.

Can one speak of journalism in communist media systems in these terms – as a professional institution, recognized as such by society and by the state? For decades, in US media scholarship, the notion of journalistic professionalism was equated with the idea of commercial independence of media outlets from political parties and the state

---

[47] See also the growing literature on the anthropology of the state, where representations of the state are a crucial component of what the state is and does (Geertz 1980, 1995, 2005, 2012; Navaro-Yashin 2002; Sharma and Gupta 2006; Steinmetz 1999).

(Hallin 2000). Any kind of party-affiliated press, communist or not, was understood to lack professionalism precisely because of its dependent, partisan character. This has begun to change, as evidence of professional practices and logics in communist media systems began to grow.[48] As Jane Curry (1990) in particular has demonstrated, professional and political logics in communist media systems do not cancel each other out.[49] Polish journalists whom Curry (1990) studied in the late 1970s understood themselves as "experts first and communists second," as "loyal opposition in the English sense," as they themselves put it. Many of them moved back and forth between the political and professional worlds to advocate for fellow journalists, to weigh in on government policies, to put pressure on politicians, and to expand their professional options – much like lawyers do in the United States (Curry 1990: 161–204).

What *were* the professional logics and goals of Soviet-era journalists, then? For a variety of reasons (prepublication censorship, unavailability of official data, citizens' fear of going on the record), a focus on *news* – as fast-paced, event-driven reporting of current events, as it is known in Western journalism – was almost absent in communist media systems.[50] This was further augmented by a more general orientation of Soviet-style societies and their media systems not to current events but to the future – to the building of socialism and communism – and to "life as it was becoming rather than as it was" (Fitzpatrick 1999: 9).[51] For Soviet journalists, this meant that at any given time and in any given locale, "socialism was both present and absent" (Wolfe 2006: 29). In this context, being a good journalist came to mean devoting effort to exploring this tension between socialism's reality and potentiality in the genre of long-form nonfiction essays (*ocherk*).

There was, however, an occupational feature that journalists in liberal democracies and their colleagues in socialist Eastern Europe

---

[48] See Boyer (2003, 2005, 2006); Curry (1990); French (2014); Huxtable (2012, 2013, 2016); Mueller (1992); Wolfe (2006).

[49] Neither do they cancel each other out in continental Europe, where party-affiliated press has had a long history (Hallin and Mancini 2004).

[50] It was also, as Jean Chalaby (1996) has argued, absent in continental Europe until the early twentieth century.

[51] Anthropologist Katherine Verdery (1996) has identified a related phenomenon she called "etatization of time" in socialist Romania. See also Mihelj and Huxtable (2016) on the flow of time on socialist television in the Soviet Union and former Yugoslavia.

did share – it was the belief in the desirability of social progress as such.[52] This belief went hand-in-hand with the confidence journalists, as public intellectuals, felt that they were better equipped – better than political elites or the public at large – to judge whether a behavior, a position, or a policy was in line with progressive ideals or was falling short of them. While in the United States journalists embraced social progressivism without the state's involvement or encouragement (Schudson 1978, 2001, 2007), both in capitalist and in socialist Europe, the state played a more direct role in tacitly acknowledging journalists' (and other cultural producers') claims to cultural and social leadership (Boyer 2003, 2005; Hoffmann 2011). In Western Europe, the development of journalistic professionalism was aided by the growth of the rule-bound authority of the civil service,[53] with the all-important exception that journalism always remained a political profession, straddling bureaucracy and politics. In Soviet Russia and other state socialist countries for which there is evidence, journalism similarly exhibited many of the classic features of a political profession, as theorized by Weber (1946) in *Politics as a Vocation*. Soviet journalists were trained in professional programs, not in special schools for party cadres (Mueller 1992; Remington 1988); they had a professional union since 1959 (French 2014); they understood themselves as social progressives who could push back against political decisions that contradicted those principles; they maintained strong group solidarity, recruited colleagues based on merit, engaged in peer review, and defined their own criteria of excellence. And, as recent archival data show,[54] there was at least some understanding among the Soviet officialdom that to remain an effective channel of communication with the citizenry, journalism needed to maintain some identity of its own.[55]

---

[52] On the Progressive roots of US journalism, see Daly (2012), Gans (1979), Nord (2001), Peters (1989), and Schudson (1978, 2001, 2007).

[53] Karl Bücher, a late-nineteenth-century German economist and public figure, "argued that journalists were similar to civil servants in their social functions and that systematic journalism education should for that reason be supported by the state" (Hardt 1979, quoted in Hallin and Mancini 2004: 195).

[54] See French (2014); Huxtable (2012, 2013, 2016); Wolfe (2006).

[55] It is likely, though, that in the first few years after the Revolution, there was some confusion around precisely that issue. In a letter published in *Rabochaya Gazeta* [*Workers' Gazette*] in 1924, for instance, a party official instructs his audience of worker-peasant correspondents: "You are not informers ... you are organizers of the workers' affairs ... you are public opinion ... workers' opinion" (Brooks 1989: 23).

As a result, Soviet journalism ended up having negotiated two kinds of social contracts – one with the Soviet state and another with the public at large. The state both distrusted journalists and relied on them for the production of social values. As Chapter 1 will show, this relationship between journalists and the state was conflictual and tense but relatively stable, and only *glasnost* and *perestroika* broke open that social contract for renegotiation. On the other end, journalists worked hard to establish their *own* relationship with audiences, and they were largely successful at it. Audiences across the Soviet bloc understood that journalists were limited in what they could air and publish (Curry 1990: 95; Meyen and Schwer 2007). Nevertheless, the press maintained credibility with audiences as "the most humane (*chelovekoobraznyi*) department of Soviet power," as Pavel Gutiontov (2005), a well-known Soviet journalist, put it – a department to which the average citizen, wronged by Soviet bureaucracies, could reliably turn for help. Similarly, in socialist Poland, for instance, journalists "tended to lend an aura of credibility" to party and state bodies when they publicly participated in policy discussions, giving those "usually faceless [bodies] a clear, publicly recognizable face" (Curry 1990: 7).

How were those moral ties between Soviet journalists and their audiences created and maintained? What led to their near-total breakdown in post-Soviet Russia? Finally, how does one begin to restore faith in the possibility of honest public communication after that belief had been severed? These are the questions at the heart of this book; in the remainder of this Introduction, I put forward some theoretical tools with which to approach them.

Truth-Telling as Virtue and Practice

German philosopher Jürgen Habermas (1984, 1990) usefully distinguishes between instrumental uses of communication (advertising, propaganda, public relations) and more genuine forms of discourse oriented toward reaching understanding. This distinction is a good entry point into this part of the discussion. For Habermas, speech and action are instrumental, or utility maximizing, when speakers treat their interlocutors as means to an end and turn to manipulation, deception, coercion, rewards, and punishments to reach their goal. Speech and action are oriented toward understanding, however, when communication is interactive, cooperative, and uncoerced.

Of central importance to this book is Habermas's insight that to avoid a legitimation crisis, modern societies and their media systems *must* make enough room for a kind of communication where people can genuinely connect with one another on a human level. Without that opportunity – when public discourse is dominated by the instrumental logic of money and power, as happens in advertising, propaganda, and public relations – media institutions (and political regimes of which they are part) eventually lose their credibility. To put it another way, the mass media and other institutions of cultural production risk becoming ideologically ineffective if what they offer has nothing to do with people's life-worlds or the intersubjective domain of lived experience.

It might be important to acknowledge at this point that I am making a conceptual distinction between propaganda and ideology. In line with Habermas's (1984) notion of strategic action, I understand propaganda as a variety of instrumental or purposive communication that is not bound by the need for communicatively achieved understanding or agreement. Classically, propaganda is a one-way rather than a feedback-driven mode of communication: it is singularly oriented to changing the beliefs and behaviors of others; it treats its audiences as opponents rather than as coparticipants; and it frequently involves deception. Ideology is a broader and more complex phenomenon than propaganda; it is a system of ideas linked to particular social, political, and economic institutions rather than a direct instrumental intervention aimed at changing people's behaviors and beliefs. This is not to say that ideological content (ideas, images, assertions about the world) cannot be advanced through propaganda – they certainly have been, in the Soviet Union and elsewhere. But it is to say that ideological production is fundamentally a cultural process that must respond to people's life-worlds and lived experiences, and as such, it cannot be reduced to (or replaced by) propaganda's means-ends calculus.

One of the objections raised against Habermas's (1984) division of communication into instrumental and genuine or uncoerced is that it sets up too neat a dichotomy, presupposing on one end a communicative domain that is free of power, whereas in the real world power can never be excised from social and communicative relations. This is a valid objection, and one response to it might be to treat instrumental and uncoerced communication as Weberian ideal types of speech and action that do not exist in pure form but may in fact be copresent in any particular communicative situation. Another way to respond to this objection would be to recall the distinction Michel Foucault (1997a) made between power and domination, mentioned earlier. Foucault operates from the assumption that power permeates human relations, but he sees it as distinct from domination that he defines as abuse of power. When power – as domination – resorts to coercion, thereby becoming "blocked" or "frozen," as Foucault puts it, it seems to map onto the concept of strategic action advanced by Habermas. But when power is "mobile, reversible, and unstable" (Foucault 1997b: 292), when it responds to ethical challenges, such as those of parrhesia (open and frank speech directed at more powerful interlocutors) – we seem to go back to Habermas's domain of life-worlds, intersubjectivity, and reaching understanding.

And yet, beyond Habermas's core insight that uncoerced public communication is central to the legitimacy of a political order, the utility of his theory is limited if we want to explain the actual mechanisms through which the integrity of Soviet journalist-audience relations was maintained. This is so because Habermas's theory remains explicitly normative and relies on participants approximating what Habermas calls an "ideal speech situation" in order for those communicative experiences to count as genuine, real, and true. A fundamental requirement of the ideal speech situation is that it is modeled on rational face-to-face interactions where everyone can speak, express their desires and needs, introduce assertions, and question the assertions of others. Some of the rules of the ideal speech situation require that speakers assert only what they really believe, that they not contradict themselves, avoid ambiguity, use words consistently, and so on (Habermas 1990, 2001). There is no question that rational, rule-bound interactions between public speakers and their audiences (where audiences, ideally, also speak and respond, ask questions and give answers) would be crucially important for building audiences' trust in the speakers. But trust is built not only through rational interactions of this sort (even assuming that such interactions do sometimes occur) but also through the entire range of social relations public speakers maintain with their audiences in particular historical and cultural settings. As early as in *Rhetoric*, Aristotle states that in addition to argumentation (*logos*) and emotional appeal (*pathos*), a key determiner of whether or not the words of a speaker will resonate with the audience is the speaker's *ethos*, or moral character. Listeners' judgment of the speaker's moral character is necessarily social, contextual, and historical, extending beyond the immediate speech act taking place in a particular place and time. This judgment is also processual and cumulative, in that it is reinforced or transformed over a span of multiple communicative encounters.

To understand what allowed Soviet audiences to trust journalists and how that trust was severed in the 1990s and 2000s, we need a theoretical tool kit that would ground the ethics of public discourse *not* in following the rules of the ideal speech situation, as Habermas suggests, but in the actual practices of public speaking to mass audiences – practices that would be judged as well executed, believable, appropriate, meaningful, and worthwhile. This requires making a shift from rule-based to practice- and virtue-based approaches to ethics – a move that has been made by many moral philosophers over the past few decades (Cavell 1979; MacIntyre 1981; Williams 1985, 2002). Following this *neo-Aristotelian turn in ethics*, as it has come to be known, contemporary media scholars are just beginning to theorize what a virtue-based approach to speaking in public, in and through the media, might look like in different historical and cultural settings (Asen 2013; Couldry et al. 2013; Scannell 2014; Silverstone 2007). This book contributes to those growing efforts.

A key advantage of introducing virtue-based vocabulary into discussions of ideology, as I am doing, is that it gives us new tools to theorize the *uncertainty* that accompanies the practices of ideological production and reception. Over three decades ago, Stuart Hall (1986) reminded us of the fundamental *problem* of ideology. As a dominant system of ideas and beliefs, ideology in any society is tied to the social, political, and economic institutions at hand, but those links are never permanent or secure. The problem with Marxist theories of ideology, Hall (1986: 29) argued, is that they cannot guarantee how at any particular time "ideas of different kinds [would] grip the minds of the masses." Scholars of ideology, Marxist or otherwise, "have to acknowledge the real indeterminacy of the political" (Hall 1986: 43). A virtue-based approach, I believe, does offer some new tools for how to account for this fundamental indeterminacy of ideology – that is, for whether and how people in various historical settings will accept certain ideas, and political institutions behind them, as legitimate. One of the reasons they will do so, this study argues, is when the bearers of those ideas – in our case journalists – come across as people of moral integrity, as people who argue soundly, judge fairly, blame justifiably, warn rightly, advise well, and so on.

Ethics and morality constitute a dimension of human life that is fundamentally about dealing with the uncertainty of social experience and with the need to act in the face of that uncertainty. Ethics entails continuously making judgments about the actions of others and of oneself; it also entails confronting the limits of those judgments (Lambek 2010). For this reason, ethics – as an ongoing practice – is open-ended, and it is grounded in previously established but continuously revised criteria of judgment. Such criteria are usually tacit and are outside people's conscious awareness, but they rise to the surface and become "available for conscious discernment and deliberation" (Lambek 2010: 43) when people are unsure of, or disagree about, how to interpret the actions of others.

What, then, might be some of those criteria according to which people tacitly judge the truthfulness of public speakers, particularly those endowed with institutional power, such as journalists? Drawing on the work of moral philosophers and anthropologists of ethics, I believe we can identify several such criteria, including a concern with accuracy, willingness to stand by one's words, sincerity, seriousness, reflexivity, and courage. We could, following moral philosopher Bernard Williams (2002: 7), also understand these as the virtues of truth-telling – that is, "qualities of people that are displayed in wanting to know the truth, in finding it out, and in telling it to other people." This list of criteria (or virtues) of truthful speech I am suggesting is by no means exhaustive. But it is, I believe, important not to extend it to all known virtues simply so that we can keep our focus on the actions and practices most centrally associated with public truth-seeking and telling – such as wanting to get to the bottom of things, wanting to avoid comfortable falsehoods, and calling on power to correct abuse, bias, or error.[56]

A concern with *accuracy* is the first criterion of truthful speech Williams (2002) identifies. The way accuracy is usually discussed in relation to journalism is along the lines of what philosophers call the *correspondence theory of truth*: as fidelity to reality or correspondence

---

[56] For this reason I am not including in this list the virtue of *hospitality*, for instance, that media theorist Roger Silverstone (2007: 136) identified as "the first virtue of the mediapolis" and that Nick Couldry (2012: 197) has extended into a broader virtue of *care* – as in the care for the consequences of what media producers do on the airwaves, in print and online. See also Scannell (2014) for another admirable attempt, drawing on Heidegger, to make "care" a central category of media analysis.

between our knowledge about the world and the world itself. This is indeed the answer one will get from most professional journalists: accuracy to them is reporting the world as it is, without fabricating characters or events, with proper attribution of words and deeds, and so on. But journalists also know that with this commitment to facts, they are rarely on firm ground: more often than not, "correspondence to the facts is necessary but neither simple nor sufficient" to the truthfulness of a news story (Ettema 2009: 116). Moreover, as journalism scholars Ettema and Glasser (1998) have masterfully shown, the harder the facts that need to be established in a news story, the more they seem to involve the hard *moral* work of corroboration and justification.

A different way to think about accuracy, Williams (2002) suggests, is to see it as the care one takes in trying to find out what is going on. Unlike with sincerity, seriousness, or courage, a concern with accuracy is more centrally a concern with truth-*seeking* rather than truth-telling. Williams (2002: 87) suggests we think of accuracy in terms of an "investigative investment" – what it might cost somebody "in time, energy, opportunities lost, perhaps dangers run" to try "to get to the bottom of things" or "to get it right." Despite the cost-benefit language, a commitment to accuracy for Williams is not (only) an instrumental value but a matter of dignity and conscience. When one is committed to finding out what is going on, one is likely to encounter obstacles, both external (people withholding information) and internal (laziness, wishful thinking, bias, and so on). Overcoming those obstacles might be a source of both public recognition and self-respect.

As a virtue, a concern with accuracy manifests itself primarily through practice, through speech and action. As such, it becomes amenable to ethnographic investigation. We can pay attention to the persistence, the effort, even the obstinacy with which one might (or might not) try to get to the bottom of things. We can study whether, how, and in what situations accuracy is "prized, praised, cultivated" (Williams 2002: 127). All of this can yield an understanding of the qualities of people recognized as truth-seekers. In Chapter 1, we will see that when it comes to the virtues of accuracy, Soviet journalists' record was mixed. On the one hand, there was toleration of guesswork, use of direct quotes reconstructed from memory, journalists' subjective evaluations of events and persons, and other narrative embellishments that would be disapproved of in Western journalism. On the other hand, there is evidence that Soviet journalists did value perseverance in overcoming obstacles when

investigating abuses of power by Soviet officials, scrupulously following
up on readers' complaints. Many of those investigations never made it to
print, but this does not mean that they did not happen or that they were
not valued for what they were. Post-Soviet Russia saw the emergence of
Western professional norms of reportorial accuracy (properly sourcing
a story, not using composite characters, taking care in quotations and
paraphrasing, not taking statements out of context, and so on). At the
same time, there emerged a flaunting disregard of those norms by
many newcomers to the profession. As Chapter 2 will show, especially
during election campaigns, some journalists would display no qualms
and in fact show a certain amount of pride in producing what has
come to be known as *kompromat* ("black PR") – character assassination pieces of political opponents based on partly or fully fictitious
claims about the lives of those opponents.[57]

Another criterion, or virtue, of truthful speech I would like to flag is
simply *standing by one's words*. Following through on a commitment
one has publicly accepted is perhaps the most fundamental ethical act
(Lambek 2010; R. Rappaport 1999). Since, as mentioned earlier, ethics
is about acting in the face of uncertainty, making and keeping promises
and watching others commit to a course of action (or to a set of moral
coordinates) are crucial to reducing that uncertainty. Knowing, or at
least expecting, that others will follow through on their promises
allows us to take our bearings in the world (Arendt 1958). This is
what anthropologists of ethics call the *truth-producing* feature of
ritual: promises made in public help to lay the ground for people to
trust one another. It activates the link between publicity and truthfulness discussed earlier: publicity helps to keep people in check as they act
in front of many others, putting their honor on the line.[58]

---

[57] For more on the production and reception of *kompromat* and "black PR," see
Ledeneva (2006) and Shevchenko (2009).

[58] There have been several important works in communication scholarship
treating mass media as ritual, building on James Carey's (1989) pioneering call
for a cultural model of communication, away from a "transmission" model
(Couldry 2003; Dayan and Katz 1992; Ettema 1990; Liebes et al. 1998; Schill
2009). Most of these accounts have focused on analyses of mass-mediated
events as public ceremonies. There has not been (to my knowledge) an account
viewing ritual as a dimension of communication that deals with the truthfulness
of nonceremonial public utterances, the way I am doing it here. Eric
Rothenbuhler's (1998) account comes closest.

Unlike their Western colleagues, Soviet journalists were explicitly called on to govern, and they did so visibly, in open view.[59] To maintain legitimacy, the Soviet state needed to *be seen as* binding itself to its own declared principles of rationality, fairness, and justice. Soviet journalists thus were expected to perform that key task: to continuously demonstrate that the Soviet state was ready to stand by its own words, as it were. In many ways this was an impossible task to fulfill, given the suppression of the many politically sensitive topics in the media through censorship. Nevertheless, there *was* an aspect of journalist-reader relations in the Soviet Union that was akin to keeping a promise. Readers knew that if they brought a valid complaint to the attention of a newspaper, they were guaranteed a response (which was not the case with other branches of Soviet bureaucracy). It was also expected that if a problem had been written about in the newspaper, measures would be taken to correct it, and often quickly. Such *inevitability* of response (journalists bound to respond to readers, officials bound to respond to newspaper criticism) was a form of moral-political commitment that was upheld throughout the Soviet period, for which journalists took credit. As Chapter 2 will show, one of the first forms of "liberation" experienced by journalists with the arrival of press freedom in Russia in 1990–1 was liberation from this obligation to respond to readers' complaints. The "freedom" of officials to ignore criticisms leveled at them in the press soon followed.

The next criterion of speech that aims at truth, *sincerity*, has received substantial attention from moral philosophers, literary scholars, social scientists, and lay commentators. J. L. Austin (1962) identified sincerity as one of the key felicity criteria of successful utterances. Austin's theory of performative utterances – of "doing things with words" – is usually invoked as an illustration that speech acts can be felicitous or infelicitous (successful or not) rather than true or false. Austin's student, moral philosopher Stanley Cavell (1995, 2005), has argued that this view significantly underestimates the novelty of Austin's contributions. To the extent that a performative utterance is an invitation to participate in a moral order, its failure to secure uptake (to use Austin's term) is not only a pragmatic but also a moral and an epistemological

---

[59] For perspectives on US journalism as coparticipant in political governance, see Bennett (1990), Cook (1998), and Entman (2003).

problem as well.[60] Much of our knowledge about the world is acquired through what Austin called "implicit performatives," such as assertions about the state of affairs in the world and our relationship to it. We decide whether or not to trust the speaker in part by tacitly judging whether his or her assertions are backed up by conviction and belief. This is so because convictions take time and moral resources to develop and, once established, cannot be easily changed, so we inherently place some value on the process by which people come to hold a belief. It is precisely this expectation that one will not change their beliefs at will or under pressure that is at the core of our notion of integrity (Halfon 1989).

Sincerity, then, is how we signal through speech that our assertions correspond to our beliefs and internal states. The most important implication of this practice, for Williams (2002), is that in doing so, we establish bonds of solidarity, reciprocity, and trust and thereby signal our intention not to deceive our interlocutors.[61] Aiming for sincerity was important for Soviet journalists, for that is indeed where they drew the line between ideology and propaganda. Chapter 4 will examine the rise of a particularly disconcerting variety of cynicism in Russia in the 2000s, where people in positions of power (which sometimes includes journalists) periodically admit deceit rather openly.[62] After an

---

[60] Cavell (2005: 159) argues that with his theory of performatives, Austin wanted "to bring the philosophical concern with truth down to size" – that is, open an inquiry into how a sense of truthfulness is produced in ordinary speech. In Austin's own words, "It is essential to realize that 'true' and 'false' ... stand ... for a general dimension of being a right or proper thing to say as opposed to a wrong thing, in these circumstances, to this audience, for these purposes, and with these intentions" (Austin 1962: 145).

[61] There is a growing body of work in cultural anthropology on the practices of sincerity, probably because sincerity is closely tied to personhood, which has traditionally attracted anthropologists' attention. See, for instance, the work of Glaeser (2000), Keane (2007), Klumbyte (2011), Lambek (2007), and Yurchak (2008). These accounts underscore that sincerity manifests differently in various historical and cultural settings and that people display the perceived link between their words and interior states for many different purposes. Still, these anthropological accounts do not seem to dispute Williams' (2002) claim that the intention not to deceive is built into the concept of sincerity and connects it to trust.

[62] When Russian investigative journalist Anna Politkovskaya was assassinated in her apartment building in Moscow in October 2006, President Putin famously remarked that her murder "brought more damage to the Russian authorities than her publications ever did" (see Roudakova 2009). While not directly admitting deceit, Putin did indirectly admit with this statement that he saw no value in Politkovskaya's investigative work.

election campaign, for example, a journalist might admit in an interview that he or she did, indeed, try to manipulate public opinion to some desired effect. For all the shortcomings of the Communist party press, such public admissions of deceit would have been inconceivable in the Soviet Union. There is thus substantial moral erosion around the practice of sincerity in Russia in the 2000s. Some correspondence between people's words and their interior states presumably remains, but there is no longer the intention not to deceive associated with it. For many in the profession of journalism and outside of it, this has been a very disorienting development, signaling that people are dealing not only with a decline in trust but also with the erosion of the value of truthfulness itself.

Seriousness, I believe, is yet another helpful criterion for judging the truthfulness of one's public words and actions. It has obvious overlaps with sincerity and with standing by one's words, but it is not identical with them. Seriousness is distinctive because of its links to gravity, solemnity, suffering, and sacrifice – what the Greeks called *pathos*. In Russian, *pafos* is a native term and is very commonly used. Seriousness or pathos is thus a way of getting at what matters via a connection to the tragic dimension of life. There is a reason one can be "dead serious": at least in principle, it involves one's willingness to suffer for what one holds dear, even to risk one's life for one's convictions. For Durkheim (1961), the domain of the serious is where the sacred finds its shadow in secular societies. He coined the concept of *la vie sérieuse* ("life in earnest," "life for real") – a dimension of human affairs that is elevated above others, treated as "unquestionable, 'beyond interdiction' ... [dealing with] ideas, symbols, and activities ... so important that they deserve to be set aside and protected" (Rothenbuhler 1998: 24). For moderns, *la vie sérieuse* is about "the struggle for existence, the family, citizenship, duty, knowledge of the world" (Watts Miller 1996: 81). There is "grandiloquence" about these topics, Durkheim (1973: 172) noted, which would be "ridiculous" in discussions of other, more ordinary affairs.[63]

---

[63] A puritanical streak is evident in Durkheim's separation of *la vie sérieuse* from *la vie légère*, which for Durkheim covers everything "light-hearted" from game and recreation, to the frivolity of imagination, to the enjoyment of the arts (Watts Miller 1996: 81–82).

One important problem with seriousness is that it is easy to overuse it.[64] Signals of seriousness in speech, to use J. L. Austin's language again, can fail to secure uptake if they are performed incorrectly. It is worth recalling that Austin (1962) identified two kinds of infelicities or things that can go wrong with an utterance and prevent its successful uptake. One was misfires, or flaws in the execution of the procedure (inappropriate speaker or audience, saying the wrong words, saying them in the wrong order, and so on), that are more relevant for explicit performatives (e.g., marrying someone). The other kind of infelicity, abuses, is more relevant for implicit performatives such as assertions, interpretations, acts of warning, urging, challenging, doubting, taking sides, and so on. Austin pointed to insincerity as the main example of abuses, but I think that this is even more relevant for seriousness. If one overdoes it on pathos, one's public appeal might fall flat, being perceived as too pompous, fake, or simply false.

This, I believe, is what happened to much of the official language of Soviet propaganda – the familiar turns of phrases one would encounter on the front pages of Soviet newspapers and in official speeches delivered at various public events. Yet, as Chapter 1 will show, there were other modes of address in the Soviet press where pathos and conviction were not overused to the point of falling flat. Chapters 2 and 4 will then illustrate how during the 1990s and 2000s, many post-Soviet journalists once again began to "abuse" pathos, whether consciously or not. This, I will argue, is so because among the different criteria of truthful speech, pathos is the easiest to try to fake compared with, say, sincerity or courage. Finally, Chapter 5 will demonstrate how, since the early 2010s, one route to reestablishing the value of truth-telling has been a careful dance between reducing pathos in public speech, on the one hand, and simultaneously reaffirming its importance, on the other.

Presence or absence of signals of *reflexivity* is yet another criterion by which audiences may judge the truthfulness and trustworthiness of public speakers. At its broadest, reflexivity is about our capacity for self-awareness, self-distancing, and self-examination. It includes not presuming that one has the monopoly on truth, allowing that one might be mistaken, and simply being able to see things from another's point of

---

[64] This is where an Aristotelian approach to seriousness as a virtue is most helpful: for Aristotle, virtuous behavior entails maintaining the right balance between not displaying enough of something and displaying too much of it.

view. Reflexivity is about forming a relation with oneself, and as such, it is fundamental to thinking – that "soundless dialogue between me and myself" that is at the core of ethical life (Arendt 1971: 442; Foucault 1997a: 117; Keane 2014). Importantly, reflexivity is also about confronting the limits of one's knowledge. It thus involves a degree of epistemological and ontological risk: the risk of who I might become when I face the limits of what I can know (Butler 2001).

Reflexivity and mainstream Anglo-American journalism have not been especially good bedfellows (Ettema 2005; Niblock 2007; Mason 2014). "Journalism, supposing that it would lose itself in self-contemplation, is characteristically hostile to the mere mention of reflexivity" (Ettema 2005: 146). Journalism scholar James Ettema acknowledges that editorial pages in American newspapers do sometimes feature more contemplative styles of writing, especially when editorialists engage in what Ettema calls "acts of plural reflexivity" – moments when the editorialist encourages readers to consider "who we are" as a society (Ettema 2005: 143). But on news pages, Ettema (2005: 143) laments, the moral considerations of American journalists are hidden or "conveyed [only] surreptitiously through selection of stories and sequencing of facts."

As mentioned earlier, news reporting in the Soviet Union was almost absent as a genre, but long-form nonfiction essays and feature stories telling contemplative moral tales based on real events were very common. This genre of writing was known by a distinct name – *ocherk* – and was considered the most prestigious and most difficult genre for journalists to work in. Why was *ocherk* writing considered difficult? Because a good moral tale needs to *resonate* with readers instead of coming across as empty moralizing. Resonance is difficult for any writer to achieve. It requires (1) empirical credibility and (2) commensurability with our lived experience – with our fears, desires, longings, and visions of a good life and of the future (Schudson 1989; Ettema 2005). Anatoly Agranovsky, the Soviet Union's best known *ocherkist*, urged fellow journalists to open their own processes of thinking to readers to achieve greater resonance. "Thinking is the root of journalism. He who thinks well, writes well" – he apparently liked to repeat.[65] Leo Tolstoy, another inspiration for many Soviet *ocherkists*, advised

---

[65] For a detailed analysis of Agranovsky's essays and on reflexivity as a key feature of Agranovsky's style, see Wolfe (2006: 71–103).

writers to do the same: "In order to be influential, the author needs to be a genuine seeker. If he found everything and knows everything and begins to preach ... he does not act. Only when he is searching, the reader will join him in his search" (quoted in Agranovsky [1978] 1999).

Lastly, a discussion about the virtues of truth-seeking and truth-telling would be incomplete without considering the *courage* involved in speaking truth to power. Not every act of truth-telling involves speaking it to power; but to the extent that it does, it is important to understand what makes it distinctive and how it is recognized. "Speaking up," "not mincing words," "telling it like it is," "calling things by their real names," "without fear or favor" – these are some ways we acknowledge courageous words. As discussed earlier, this concern with truth-telling as a courageous activity (parrhesia), and its relationship to personal ethics and to politics, was central to Michel Foucault's later thought (2001, 2010, 2011). With his focus on parrhesia, Foucault could be seen as joining other social and political theorists who understand truth to be at arm's length from power – that is, close and connected but not subsumed by it (Lambek 2000; Laidlaw 2002). To the extent that there is any space between truth and power, ethics occupies that space, enabling power "to be reflected upon, to be addressed, to be harnessed or warded off, to be explicitly internalized" (Lambek 2000: 312).

This is a particularly useful perspective from which to approach the question of truth and power in Soviet journalism. Censorship eliminated parrhesia – the courage of truth – from the front pages of Soviet newspapers.[66] But in the back pages of newspapers, particularly in *ocherki*,[67] as well as in reviews of readers' letters, the courage of the writer pushing the limits of the sayable could come across. Moreover, as Chapter 1 will show, internal criticism was a common practice within Soviet editorial collectives and was regarded as a sign of personal and professional integrity. Editors valued their free-spoken

---

[66] There were a few institutionalized and carefully monitored avenues for critical speech in the Soviet press, including *feuilletons* (satirical pieces about select officials and their corrupt practices), as well as a rubric adopted by many newspapers titled, "If I were the director ...." The rubric began during Khrushchev's thaw and published letters to the editor containing constructive criticisms of the Soviet economy.

[67] *Ocherki* is the plural of *ocherk*.

colleagues (even if grudgingly) and at times engaged in acts of parrhesia themselves when confronting their party overseers.

As Chapters 2, 3, and 4 will argue, speaking truth to power lost much of its meaning and value in Russia in the decade and a half after the dissolution of the Soviet Union. The sudden destitution of privatized media outlets and the unending demands from new owners for political and electoral promotion created conditions for what Foucault (2010) called "bad parrhesia" – the practice of political speaking to audiences that is manipulative, pandering to crowds, done by many rather than a few, and motivated by personal gain rather than courage. Significantly, as my ethnographic material will show, a sense of solidarity and camaraderie, found in many Soviet editorial offices, was replaced in the 1990s and 2000s by cliquishness and an almost military variety of super- and subordination. Internal criticism was discouraged, disparaged, or dismissed; in that sense, paradoxically, many journalists in post-Soviet Russia ended up having an even narrower margin of freedom than their Soviet predecessors.

As the former Soviet journalist (now journalism educator) Nadezhda Azhgikhina, who is of the same generation as Anna Politkovskaya,[68] sums it up:

Between the official line of *Pravda* and the *samizdat* [Chronicle of Current Events] were the liberal *Literaturnaya gazeta, Yunost', Sovetskaya Rossiya* under Mikhail Nenashev, and *Komsomol'skaya pravda* under the editorship of Boris Pankin. These papers published the best minds of the era, and educated their readers in civic awareness, appealing for a better life and awakening a yearning for justice and truth that filtered through the Aesopian language to which the Soviet eye was accustomed. In fact, all the main tenets and ideology of perestroika were formulated latently in the Soviet liberal press. That press demanded that the truth be told about our tragic past, that its crimes be evaluated and that we cleanse ourselves of lies, definitively rehabilitate the victims of the repression, and call corruption and stupidity by their real names. It demanded respect for human rights, talent and independence. All of this completely corresponded with the high moral standards current among the journalistic community of the liberal press –

---

[68] As mentioned in an earlier footnote, Anna Politkovskaya was a human rights activist and an investigative journalist who worked for *Novaya Gazeta* in Moscow. She was very critical of President Putin's policies, especially resulting from the fallout of the two wars Russia fought in the Republic of Chechnya in the 1990s and early 2000s. Politkovskaya was assassinated in her apartment building in Moscow on October 7, 2006.

there was an unwritten ethical standard that journalists honoured as something sacred. Yea-saying propagandists seeking promotion and ready to curry favour were not respected by the community. (Azhgikhina 2007: 1250)

What made this state of affairs (or at least this perception of it) possible, how it unraveled, and where things go from there are the subject of this book.

1 | *Ethics and Politics in Soviet Journalism*

This chapter approaches Soviet journalists as simultaneously moral and political actors – as people who mediated between the Soviet state and the ethical ideals of that state. The chapter makes two related arguments. First, I argue that in the late Soviet period (during the 1970s and 1980s, for which I have data), journalists maintained two sets of relations – one with the Communist party and the other with readers and viewers – that helped to sustain journalism's legitimacy as "the most humane" institution of Soviet power, as described by Pavel Gutiontov in the Introduction. The party-state needed journalists (and not only propagandists) because at least once in a while the Soviet state needed to *be seen* as accountable to its citizens. For this reason, it was journalists (and not lawyers, union leaders, people's deputies, or other kinds of citizens' representatives) who were tasked by the party to handle citizens' grievances against Soviet bureaucracies. The party encouraged citizens to take their grievances to the press, journalists were obligated to investigate those grievances, and the party-state was, in turn, obligated to respond to those investigations by "taking measures" and punishing the culprits.

Despite its theoretical commitment to accountability, the party nevertheless preferred to keep the amount of negative publicity generated by the press to a minimum, opting to sweep as many issues as possible under the rug. This was thus the major tension journalists inhabited – between the party's encouragement of criticism and its simultaneous fear of it. In that space, Soviet journalists were able to push the limits of the "sayable" as long as they did one of two things: (1) abstained from criticizing the party itself[1] and (2) remained committed to the socialist project as a whole,

---

[1] Every Soviet newspaper was an official organ of a party or state organization at a particular level of governance (local, regional, national, or all-Union). Once in a while, newspapers that were higher up in the party hierarchy could criticize party officials at lower levels of that hierarchy, but never at higher levels. That is,

Just as they had to negotiate a particular set of relations with the party, Soviet journalists had to maintain another set of relations with their audiences to maintain *their own* legitimacy. Most Soviet readers understood that journalists were limited – by censorship and self-censorship – in what they could actually say in public. In the common turn of phrase, Soviet citizens knew that the authorities (and to some extent the journalists) "won't tell us the whole truth anyway" (*vse ravno vsei pravdy ne skazhut*) (Levada 2006). Nevertheless, readers trusted journalists in large part because they knew that journalists would be on their readers' side in cases of conflict with Soviet bureaucracies, effectively serving as readers' representatives and advocates. As this chapter will show, most journalists took this job as truth- and justice-seekers on behalf of citizens very seriously.

The second argument this chapter makes is that a certain understanding of truth was built into the Soviet governing project, of which journalism was a central part. As a philosophical movement, Marxism was grounded in what we may call *epistemological realism*: truth was a real thing, it was lofty and pure, it mattered, it was out there, and the value of seeking and finding it was high. Official propaganda no doubt laid its own claims to truth, but so did the dissidents and other Soviet intellectuals. So did Soviet scientists, and so did the journalists. What social and moral relations did Soviet journalists maintain with their audiences – relations from which journalists could aim at truth, as philosophers put it? How did journalists signal to their audiences that they were to be trusted, that they were on their readers' side, so to speak, when it came to the really important matters? What *were* the really important matters in that relationship between journalists and audiences?

This chapter draws on interviews, conducted between 2001 and 2012, with seventeen former Soviet journalists in the city of Nizhny Novgorod (former Gorky) who worked for the region's most popular daily newspaper, *Leninskaya Smena* (LS)[2]; on textual analysis of the

---

criticism could go down the party channels but not up. Additionally, the criticism always had to be leveled at a particular party official and not at the institution of the party as a whole.

[2] As a springboard for my ethnographic project, I chose to locate my study in the city of Nizhny Novgorod (known as Gorky during the Soviet period). I did it for several reasons. Nizhny Novgorod is a large industrial city of about a million and a half located 400 kilometers east of Moscow. During the Soviet period, Gorky and its satellite town, Sarov, were off-limits to foreigners. Most of the Western

back issues of *LS* from the 1970s and 1980s; on archival materials about *LS* from the GOPANO archive[3] in Nizhny Novgorod; on journalism textbooks published in the late Soviet period; and on over three dozen memoirs published by prominent Soviet journalists in the last

scholarship on Russia has focused on Moscow and St. Petersburg, and most of the scholarship in the field of journalism studies has focused on elite, urban, and national news organizations. My choice to ground the study at a regional and local level was thus meant to correct for those blind spots. Additionally, in most countries, local journalists are simply far more numerous than journalists working for the national outlets, and local outlets tend to be more trusted in their communities (Franklin 2006). The pressures on journalism – both technological and political – are also felt earlier and more fiercely at the local level and with more devastating consequences. There was another methodological advantage to locating my project in a smaller city: most journalists in Nizhny Novgorod knew and had worked with one another at some point. In the post-Soviet period, Nizhny Novgorod was representative of a dozen regional centers in Russia with similar media ownership structures and centers of power. Last but not least, there was an enormously popular youth daily (*Leninskaya Smena* [*LS*]), published in Gorky during the Soviet period, that played a crucial political role during *perestroika*. Before the fall of the Soviet Union, *LS* journalists led several citizen-driven campaigns to preserve the region's environment and Gorky's historical architecture. Many post-*perestroika* media owners and editors in Nizhny Novgorod had worked together at *LS* in the 1980s. *LS* thus served as an important bridge between the Soviet and the post-Soviet epochs. The late Boris Nemtsov, ex-Deputy Prime Minister of Russia and a prominent leader of the opposition in the 2000s, published his first interview with physicist and dissident Andrei Sakharov, exiled to Gorky, in *LS* in 1988.

3   The GOPANO Archive – the State Political Archive of Nizhny Novgorod Oblast – is the main source of archival material for this study. The GOPANO Archive is the main party archive in the region and one of the largest party archives in the country. It was founded in 1921 and contains all manner of documents generated by the Communist party and Komsomol organizations (the party's youth wing) in the Gorky region. It includes protocols of party and Komsomol meetings, correspondence with other party organizations, plans, reports, statistics on party and Komsomol membership, records of expulsions from the party and from Komsomol, and so on. The archive also contains the document flow for the main party newspapers of the region – *Gorkovskaya Pravda* and *Leninskaya Smena* (the organ of the Gorky Oblast Komsomol Committee), as well as a collection of letters to the editor for *Gorkovsky Rabochi* – the newspaper of the city council of the city of Gorky. The *LS* archival fund is unfortunately rather modest, because a substantial part of the *LS* archive had been kept by the newspaper itself and was lost in the process of privatization of the newspaper (see Chapter 2). Among the documents that had been preserved are the protocols of editorial meetings, orders issued by the chief editor, hiring records, records of awards and official reprimands issued to journalists, descriptions of editorial plans, and some readers' letters to the newspaper.

two and a half decades.[4] Many memoirs are written by people who worked at *Literaturnaya Gazeta* (*LG*), the official organ of the Soviet Writers' Union, the thickest (sixteen pages) and most prestigious of all Soviet newspapers. Another substantial portion of memoirs is written by journalists who worked at *Komsomolskaya Pravda* (*KP*), a very popular daily newspaper, the organ of the Soviet Union's Communist Youth Organization, Komsomol. While *LG*, known as the Soviet Union's "Hyde Park," was unique, *KP* in many ways was not, because many regional newspapers for youth were modeled on it.[5] *LS* was one such paper that was modeled on *KP*; another popular regional newspaper targeting youth and modeled on *KP* was *Smena*, published in Leningrad (now St. Petersburg).[6] Journalists in Gorky often compared their work to that of their colleagues at Leningrad's *Smena*, viewing them as their professional competition.

LG, KP, and regional newspapers modeled on *KP* were indeed flagship cases of what Russian journalist Nadezhda Azhgikhina, quoted in the Introduction, called the Soviet liberal press. It is important to be cautious in using the term *liberal* here so as not to reproduce the ahistorical liberal subject that continues to stalk Russian area studies (Krylova 2000). What Azhgikhina (2007) means by liberal is closer to what anthropologist George Faraday (2000) called a "secular humanist stance" in Soviet cultural production – a set of Enlightenment precepts about human dignity, talent, and self-realization but also

---

[4] Select memoirs include Loginova (1992), Nenashev (1995), Bogdanov and Zassoursky (1998), Matusevich (1999), Syrokomsky (2001), Tolkunova (2002), Gutiontov (2005, 2008), Shatunovsky and Rykovtseva (2003), Yakovlev and Nenashev (2003), Shinkarev (2005), Shchekochikhin ([1984]2003a, 2004), Rudenko (2005), Udaltsov (2005), Krasukhin (2005), Zakharko et al. (2006), Druzenko et al. (2007), Pankin (2002), Gamayunov (2009a, 2009b), A. Volkov (2010), and Vaksberg (2011).

[5] Newspapers such as *KP* targeting youth were read by audiences of all ages, as evidenced by those newspapers' mailbags. In the Soviet Union, newspapers for youth tended to be popular because they were afforded more room for experimentation and criticism than their adult counterparts such as *Pravda* and even *Izvestia*. The same was the case, and to a substantial degree still is, in China: consider, for instance, the continuing popularity of the *China Youth Daily* (Zhao 2008).

[6] Other popular regional newspapers modeled on *KP* include *Moskovsky Komsomolets* (published in Moscow), *Molodost' Sibiri* (published in Novosibirsk), *Komsomolets* (published in Rostov-on-Don), *Na Smenu* (published in Sverdlovsk), *Krasnoyarsky Komsomolets* (published in Krasnoyarsk), and many others.

about equality, fairness, and justice – precepts that liberalism and socialism to a large degree share. The Soviet "liberal" press indeed differed from publications such as *Pravda* ("*The Truth*"), *Voprosy Kommunizma* ("*Questions of Communism*"), *Partiinaya Zhizn'* ("*Party Life*"), and the like in that journalists' yearning "to call corruption and stupidity by their real names" that Azhgikhina talks about was stronger in the "liberal" press than anywhere else.[7] As this chapter will argue, this yearning was based on a parrhesiastic desire to bring ethics back into politics and was a rare but coveted practice in Soviet journalism. As such, this yearning could be seen as a structure of feeling that was shared across liberalism and socialism.

Focusing on what were arguably the best journalistic practices in the Soviet Union inevitably raises issues of method and data selection. One certainly could have chosen to focus on Soviet journalism's most reprehensible practices, such as attempts to manipulate public opinion through newspaper coverage of show trials of the dissidents, or on other instances of open vilification of nonconforming citizens in the press. Also, instead of the "liberal" newspapers, one could have chosen to focus on *Pravda* or *Voprosy Kommunizma*, whose language was much more formal, chiseled, and authorless and therefore more readily available for endless ideological reproduction in a variety of contexts. Finally, one could

---

[7] This pathos of secular humanism was also very salient at the flagship School of Journalism established at Moscow State University in 1952. Azhgikhina (2005: 58–59) recalls the prevailing spirit in the halls of the school in the 1970s and 1980s: "The beauty of our education was that we were surrounded by all manner of things. Literally. Fifteen minutes after the lecture on the wise policy of the party regarding the press, literature, and art (on the infamous resolution denouncing the writing of Akhmatova and Zoshchenko, for instance), there would be a lecture by Galina Andreyevna Belaya – precisely on the works of Akhmatova and Zoshchenko. And half of Moscow would gather to hear it. Of course, someone would snitch to the authorities afterwards. But the lectures continued, just like many other courses that were taught that did not fit into the hard ideological frames – and that was the paradox of the School. During the lectures on the theory of propaganda (the professor was a former party secretary and a bully who nowadays works in PR in America), the children of KGB officers would share forbidden books with their classmates – books for which you could get in trouble. And in all of this variety of experiences, one thing was very clear – the sense of the moral norm, the high moral bar. One learned to separate Mikhalkov [the author of the Soviet anthem] from Pasternak in the classrooms, just like one learned to separate courageous deeds [*postupok*] from propaganda in the newspaper ... Actually, this balancing act had existed in Russian literature and journalism ... even before the Revolution. The Soviet epoch fittingly continued this imperial tradition."

have focused on Soviet journalists who were journalists in name only and were primarily engaged in propaganda work that in most newspapers was explicitly delineated as such, confined to departments of propaganda that existed in almost every party and Komsomol newspaper. From the data I have collected, it appears that more often than not journalists working in propaganda departments were more cynical and opportunistic than their colleagues in other departments. Propaganda department workers were more likely to treat their positions instrumentally – as a step on the ladder toward a more promising party career. It was to them, I was told, that editors gave the tasks that journalists working in other departments did not want to do: praising the party and its policies, denouncing the party's enemies home and abroad, writing welcoming speeches for official events, and the like.[8]

Getting those people's take on what they thought they were doing is difficult: they refuse to grant interviews, and they do not write memoirs. This is an important methodological problem.[9] The data that are more readily available are the recollections of people who *want* to remember their experiences in the Soviet press as meaningful and valuable, and this skews this study in the direction of practices that were not fully representative of the entire picture of what was going on in the Soviet press. The problem is further compounded by the nostalgia factor: journalists willing to write and talk about their Soviet past are likely to recall their experiences more positively today than, say, in the early 1990s because of the profound degeneration of journalism as a profession that has occurred in Russia since then (the subject of Chapters 2–4).[10]

While acknowledging the weakness of the data collected here, I suggest that for the purposes of this study, such weakness can be treated as a strength in at least one important respect. For all their

---

[8] See the passage from Azhgikhina (2005) in the preceding footnote on the moral clarity of separating journalism from propaganda.

[9] It is also a disciplinary problem. The professional Code of Ethics of the American Anthropological Association states that the anthropologist's first and foremost obligation is to his or her informants: "anthropologists must do everything in their power to protect the physical, social, and psychological welfare and to honor the *dignity* and privacy of those studied" (AAA 1986, emphasis added). Protecting research subjects' dignity becomes a problem when the research involves studying behaviors that can be seen as morally reprehensible.

[10] See Bergman (1989), Kotkin (2002), and Hooper (2013) for discussions among historians of Soviet Russia on the inevitable partiality of memoir data.

shortcomings, interviews and memoirs are good at identifying what counted as professional and moral standards of excellence in Soviet journalism. Having such standards of excellence is what qualified Soviet journalism as a vocation, and not only as a job, in Weberian terms (cf. Boyer 2003).[11] As if writing about Soviet journalists, Weber (1946) remarked in *Politics as a Vocation*: "It is not astonishing that there are many journalists who have become human failures and worthless men. Rather, it is astonishing that, despite all this, this very stratum includes such a great number of valuable and quite genuine men, a fact that outsiders would not so easily guess" (Weber 1946: 99).

There is a reason the word *professional* continues to have positive moral overtones in many languages despite sociologists' efforts to see professionalism as a neutral analytical category (or even a morally suspect one, as in strands of Marxist sociology that approach professionalization as an elite class project). Standards of excellence, where the moral and the technical are fused together, are a key cultural component of a vocation: it is by reference to those standards that members of vocational guilds have long been educating newcomers and maintaining their distinct identities. This conflation between what *is* and what *should be* in how the professions understand themselves also translates into how they are studied academically. Journalism research in the United States and elsewhere, for instance, frequently draws on Pulitzer prize–winning stories and authors for evidence *both* of journalistic excellence *and* of journalistic norm (Ettema and Glasser 1998; Forde 2007; Wahl-Jorgensen 2013).

Unlike their Western colleagues, Soviet journalists saw themselves as coparticipants in the Soviet governmental project and took responsibility for it. That responsibility was unmistakably *personal* rather than corporate, which once again illustrates that Soviet journalism was a political vocation by Weber's (1946) standards. Soviet journalists often understood themselves as state agents whose responsibility was to bring morality back into politics when the two fell egregiously out of sync.[12] Often this meant standing up for what a journalist believed was

Bringing morality back into politics

[11] For a sociological argument about Soviet journalism as a profession, see Roudakova (n.d.).

[12] It is worth recalling the point made by anthropologist Talal Asad (2003: 255) that every modern state is "a complex arrangement of legal reasoning, moral practice, and political authority." As cultural formations, all modern states are inflected with the positive ethics of some normative categories, most commonly

right against pressures from the party, from one's own editor, or from an internal voice advocating for self-censorship. The memoirs and interviews I have collected are full of journalists' recollections of how they struggled with these moral choices. Certainly, for every story a journalist remembers where he or she ended up doing the right thing, there must have been plenty of cases where he or she gave in to party pressures, to editors' caution, or to the voice of the censor within (e.g., Gutiontov 2005).

Does this fact invalidate the memories of journalists who remember themselves as struggling and sometimes succeeding in upholding a value in which they believed? I do not think so. True, people's memories are selective and self-serving, but it is also true that people hold onto memories that were crucial to their self-formation and self-definition. Sociologist Philip Abrams (1982) argues for the importance of studying such moments of one's biography. Abrams (1982: 282) calls such moments "clarifying" because they simultaneously mark important milestones in a person's identity formation *and* call that person into being as a social and historical actor. The material I have collected is full of such moments. No matter how skewed those representations might be, they give us an insight into the social and political *ideals* Soviet journalists wished to uphold.

As legal scholar Kim Lane Scheppele (1996) reminds us, to gain proper insight into any political formation, one needs to take seriously its ideals and not only how those ideals failed to materialize in practice. Most of social science scholarship written across the Cold War divide, she argues, suffered from a fatal flaw: "comparing an empirical reality of one society with an ideal type of another" (Burawoy and Lukacs, quoted in Scheppele 1996: 636). This was the case with comparisons between socialism and capitalism in economics, legal theory, political science, mass communication research, and other fields. Under liberalism, would you rather have legally guaranteed rights, Scheppele asks, or racial profiling and police brutality? In a similar vein, "[W]ould you rather

of human rights, equality, justice, and the rule of law. In liberal democracies, Asad (2003) argues, the positive morality of the secular state tends to be stowed in the legal system that serves as the primary vehicle through which equality and justice are delivered to, and experienced by, citizens. State socialism as a political formation carried its own strong moral charge, but unlike the disguised morality of the liberal-democratic state Asad talks about, the moral dimension of the Soviet state was much more visible and palpable, in large part because of the weakness of its legal dimension.

have the solidarity and substantive equality of socialist legality or Party-dictated show trials? It is no contest within one system, and also no contest across systems. Ideals always win" (Scheppele 1996: 636).

Understanding how those ideals were sustained, eroded, or transformed would be crucial to understanding the inner workings of any political system. This is why attending to the admittedly skewed memories of people who lived with an acute awareness of those ideals is still a valuable practice in ethnographic and historical research. It does not protect us from the self-serving mistakes memory makes – in fact, I will offer an example of precisely that kind of mistake later on in this chapter. But it does offer us a glimpse into aspects of journalists' work that they found important, valuable, and meaningful. It does not give us an account of how the Soviet press objectively *was*, but it does tell us about the values that guided Soviet journalists and about the efforts they made to live up to those values. To the extent that *any* of those efforts were recognized as such by their audiences, they are important pieces of data with which to work.

The Story with Accuracy

As mentioned in the Introduction, adherence to factual accuracy is the most common way journalism distinguishes itself from other varieties of public speaking and writing. It is also where journalism draws its authority as a cultural form. Not making up characters or events, proper attribution of words and deeds, precision in quotations and paraphrasing – these are all understandings of accuracy shared by journalists in societies that value freedom of the press. Following Bernard Williams (2002), we can also shift our thinking about accuracy further into the moral plane and treat it as one of the virtues of truth-telling as a commitment to finding out what is going on, a perseverance in getting to the bottom of things despite possible obstacles, opportunities lost, and dangers run (Williams 2002: 87).

Soviet journalists' record on factual accuracy is clearly mixed. Given the official limitations on newsgathering, simply being a news reporter in the Western sense of the word was an impossible task. As is well known, every page of galley proofs in a Soviet newspaper had to be signed by a censor. Contrary to widespread belief, though, there was a fairly limited list of topics that the censors were guarding against. These included state secrets (primarily information about the Soviet

Union's military and industrial potential) as well as topics that would be deemed too sensitive to raise in the press, such as questioning the leading role of the party in society, the lives of Soviet leaders, the desirability of communism, and so on. Raising any of those topics was considered anti-Soviet propaganda, which was explicitly proscribed. Still, anything that was not on the censors' (admittedly very long) list of proscribed topics was, in principle, "fair game," especially in the late Soviet period (under Khrushchev's and Brezhnev's leadership).[13]

In practice, though, journalists faced additional restrictions on information-gathering. Accidents, natural disasters, and gruesome crimes were equally sensitive for the Soviet authorities, so reporting on them was very limited or simply out of bounds.[14] As a former *KP* correspondent in Gorky told me, for example, he would report to the *KP* Moscow office about a natural disaster or an accident that happened locally, including the number of human lives lost. The report would come out but would omit all mention of victims. Another category of information nearly impossible to obtain was government statistics. Once academic sociology began to take off in the 1960s and 1970s, some survey results began to be published in academic journals, and scholars and journalists started to draw on them (Grushin 2000; Kon 1999, 2000; Mickiewicz 1981).

As a result of these limitations, establishing facts and accurately reporting them were not priorities for Soviet journalists. Reportorial jobs were rare and frankly not very popular among journalists. In *Leninskaya Smena* (*LS*) in the 1970s and 1980s, for instance, there was a Department of News headed by a seasoned journalist, Valentina Buzmakova, who loved newsgathering and did not want to do anything else, but the rest of the workers in that department were interns who moved on to more desirable positions whenever they had a chance (to

---

[13] Formal censorship of literature and the press by the *Glavlit* office was different from the informal practices of overseeing newspaper content by party organizations to which various newspapers "belonged." During the Stalinist period, the press content had to be verified both by the *Glavlit* and by the newspaper's overseeing party organization *before* publication. In the late Soviet period, the party and Komsomol oversight of the press shifted into a postfactum mode, allowing journalists and editors much more room to maneuver.

[14] See Wolfe (2006: 126–142) and Huxtable (2012: 124–139) on journalists, editors, and readers complaining about the poor quality of news reporting in the Soviet Union during the Khrushchev and Brezhnev periods, with journalism reformers advocating a faster-paced, Western-style, event-driven approach to news.

departments specializing in youth and Komsomol life, culture, science, legal affairs, readers' letters, and so on). The news department in *LS*, headed by Valentina Buzmakova, did have a dedicated "news hole" on the front page of the paper, but it was filled rather infrequently – on average, once or twice a week (and even less often when Buzmakova was on vacation).

Due to this rather low status of news reporting as a genre, some practices and attitudes were tolerated in Soviet editorial offices that would be strongly disapproved of by Western journalists. Among those practices was manufacturing of citizens' *otkliki* ("comments and reactions") to various official events, including party plenums, resolutions, and decrees. Most Soviet journalists saw the manufacturing of citizens' *otkliki* as menial busywork. For some inexplicable reason, citizens' *otkliki* had to appear the day after the party resolution or decree had been published in the newspaper, which was the butt of constant newsroom jokes as newspaper staff searched for real people willing to go on the record praising the new resolution. Not surprisingly, many *otkliki* were simply made up, which did not seem to bother anyone, including the party: officials themselves, I was told, wanted quick *otkiliki*, rebuffing journalists' arguments about shortage of time with, "Well, make them up then! You think we don't know how you do it?" (*My chto, ne znajem, kak eto u vas delayetsia?*).[15] Journalists would call people they knew – often protagonists from earlier stories – and ask them whether they minded if a letter "from them" would appear in the newspaper the next day welcoming this or that resolution or decree. Protagonists would usually agree, and with that, the issue would go to print.

Other practices professional journalists in liberal democracies would disapprove of had to do with various narrative techniques bordering on fiction that Soviet journalists employed.[16] Some techniques were tolerated; others encouraged. They included guesswork (*domysel*) and even fabrication of details (*vymysel*) in descriptions of emotional states and qualities of characters; use of direct quotes reconstructed from memory; generous use of epithets and other forms of narrative

---

[15] For an example of how an entire interview with a high-ranking party official could be made up, see Wolfe (2006: 124).

[16] Recent reevaluations of narrative devices as a component of professional journalistic practice include Aucoin (2001), Underwood (2008), Whitt (2008), Sims (2008), and Zdovc (2009). Earlier attempts, of course, include the New Journalism movement in the United States in the 1960s and 1970s.

enhancement; journalists' subjective judgments of events and persons; and journalists' reflexive commentary on their own thought process that took place during the researching and writing of the story.[17] It is difficult to determine how much those techniques were derivative of the broader emphasis in Soviet journalism on matters of morality rather than on facts and to what extent those techniques might have been a creative response to censorship limitations described earlier. It is likely the two were connected, and taking an explicitly moral turn on a story helped Soviet journalists accomplish several things at once: it helped them circumvent censorship restrictions on newsgathering, it gave them ammunition in political arguments with their party overseers, and it allowed them to reaffirm their cultural authority as storytellers and defenders of the "little guy" with their readers.

Some of those attempts to shift gears into the moral plane inevitably fell flat and appeared naive or moralizing or both because some of the stories had *not* been carefully researched in the first place (and, as a result, lacked moral sophistication). It was thus still very important for journalists in the late Soviet period to take the time to research their stories: it was expected that a journalist might take weeks, sometimes months to work on a single story (in *LS*, journalists were expected to spend around a third of their time in the field, gathering material for stories; in *LG*, many *ocherk* writers published no more than one or two essays a year).[18] Memoirs of prominent Soviet journalists are full of recollections of how long it took to gather all the relevant details for a story and how long it took to figure out what the story was really "about."[19] Recalls Inna Rudenko (2005), a leading *ocherkist* for *KP* in the 1970s and 1980s:

I was never interested in exotic places, but in people's lives, their passions. The protagonists of my stories must have felt that sincere interest when

---

[17] Space limitations prevent me from offering a detailed examination of reflexivity in Soviet journalism (which I identified in the Introduction as one of the qualities of speech aiming at truth). For an excellent treatment of the subject, see Wolfe (2006: 71–103).

[18] Otto Latsis, who worked primarily for *Izvestia*, recalls how Anatoly Agranovsky sometimes had "300 pages of field notes for a 12 page essay" (Latsis, quoted in Bogdanov and Zassoursky 1998: 66).

[19] This is very similar to the process of data collection and conceptualization in ethnographic fieldwork. On the convergence of "slow journalism" and qualitative research in the social sciences, see Zelizer (2004), Bacon (2006), Boyer and Hannerz (2006), and Bird (2009).

This is ethnography → for paper?

I interviewed them. Gosh, what interviews? I lived their lives with them – went to work with them, visited their friends with them, got to know their relatives, we drank tea together, went to theater together. Maybe that is why they still remember me ... I would collect so much material that I could write a novel out of it. But I had to write an *ocherk*. Around a theme. And with a clear purpose. It was tantalizing to sit in front of a blank sheet of paper ... And another thing I want to add: I worked very hard to create real and vivid portraits of my protagonists [*tak vykovyrivala svoikh geroyev, tak dolgo s nimi vozilas'*]. I always brought back so many small details, subtle things [about the protagonists]. I never made anything up. On principle. Some colleagues said, "You can't have a feature story without a made-up detail." But I made up nothing. Nothing. Believe me.

That some of Rudenko's colleagues were less scrupulous in data gathering illustrates that fidelity to facts on the ground was indeed not the most pressing concern for Soviet journalists. I was often told that it came down to being a matter of individual conscience (and talent) and to whether or not journalists were willing to work hard (or to cut corners) in drawing believable portraits of their protagonists. In a widely circulated textbook published in 1978, Valery Agranovsky, a *KP ocherkist* (and the brother of the famous Anatoly Agranovsky), offered his thoughts on the allowable degree of *domysel* ("guesswork") and *vymysel* ("fabrication of detail") in a feature story:

It is important *not* to break yourself from reality so much that it would lead to an averaging of an image, to stereotypical descriptions. This would harm the truth and truthfulness [*vredit pravde i dostovernosti*] [of the story] ... But thinking up additional detail does not mean lying: it does *not* mean that you can marry an unmarried man, kill the living and resurrect the dead. Fabrication of additional detail [*vymysel*] and guesswork [*domysel*] manifest themselves primarily in the selection of material, in the conceptualization of the event, in the attitude of the author, in the position he takes ... Yes, [the journalist] has a right to *vymysel* and *domysel* – to exaggeration based, if you will, on intuition ... But one has to guess [*domyslivat'*] truthfully,[20] so as not to arouse doubt in the reader. This is not an easy thing to do; it is directly connected with the sense of balance, with self-discipline, and with the ability of the author to exercise restraint. (V. Agranovsky [1978] 1999, emphasis added)

---

[20] No Western journalist would likely put "guess" and "truthfully" in the same sentence! I thank one of the book's anonymous reviewers for bringing this to my attention.

Valery Agranovsky's more famous brother, Anatoly Agranovsky (probably still the most revered Soviet journalist), was stricter on *vymysel* ("fabrication of detail") but more lenient on *domysel* ("guesswork"). In the Preface to a collection of his *ocherki* that had first been published in *Izvestia*, he writes:

And what about the right to guesswork [*pravo na domysel*]? There have been many arguments about "the allowable degree of artistic generalization" [*khudozhestvennoe obobshchenie*] among literary scholars. Well, I think, in an *ocherk*, that degree can be any. In this book – I warn readers in advance – I did not aim to blindly follow the facts no matter what [*ne stremilsia vo chto by to ni stalo tupo sledovat' za faktom*]. But there should never be any deceit, any confusion. One should never pass off *vymysel* for truth, or call facts *vymysel*. In a book by P. P. Vershygora titled *People with Clean Conscience*, there was a reconnaissance man who always divided his reports into three categories: "I saw it myself. I heard it. I suppose." That is more or less how we should work. (A. Agranovsky 1968: 8)

The reason why both Agranovskys are able to discuss *domysel* ("guesswork, suppositions") in conjunction with truthfulness is because they operate with a concept of artistic truth, or the truth of meanings (*pravda smyslov*) as opposed to strict documentary truth, or the truth of facts (cf. Aucoin 2001). This distinction was first made by Aristotle in *Poetics*, where, in response to Plato, Aristotle argued that poetry and art in general do not mimic reality but *contain* it by working in the register of "what could happen" instead of "what happened" (Lambek 2000). Poetry is believable and therefore true when it captures universal or typical aspects of human experience; this is the power of artistic generalization. Paradoxically, the Agranovsky brothers argue, sometimes this level of generalization can *only* be reached through scrupulous attention to some unique, individual detail that cannot, and must not, be fabricated. Anatoly Agranovsky again writes:

I am not a theorist, but I have long been convinced of the following: the more precise, the more penetrating the detail with which a particular case is described, the stronger what is typical for all people and places will manifest itself ... This means that we, the newspapermen, must dig around for detail [*kovyriat'sia v detaliakh*], go further and deeper rather than wider, to investigate the particulars. It is difficult, it is not always safe, but after all, we all choose our own paths. (Quoted in Bogdanov 1998: 135)

✳ Important

Working in the moral register, using narrative tools of literature to do it, and reaching for artistic rather than documentary truth were thus ways for Soviet journalists to maintain a commitment to truthfulness in circumstances when they could not organize their value system around truth digging of a documentary kind. As we see from the preceding quote, Soviet journalists still valued getting to the bottom of things in the face of obstacles, limitations, or dangers, similar to the way Western journalists do it. For the Soviet journalists, this meant finding the detail "that no one else had noticed," finding "the fact that no one else had found before," and especially coming up with "a thought that was new and original" (A. Agranovsky, quoted in Bogdanov 1998: 135).

This focus on unique detail, revealing the typical through the individual, turned out to have unexpected complications of its own in Soviet journalism – and in the most interesting of ways. Because of their moral angle and literary devices, many of the stories, particularly critical ones, would come off as hinting that a particular transgression at hand was not an isolated occurrence but was, in fact, a feature of the entire Soviet order. Newspapers' party overseers would often become paranoid and start to see denunciations of the whole Soviet way of life behind every text *despite* those texts' explicit assurances to the contrary (Soviet journalists who wrote critical pieces would often make sure to say that what was being described was an isolated occurrence and was *not* characteristic of Soviet industry, agriculture, education, or some other aspect of Soviet life more broadly). Journalists could not do very much about this ambiguity: it was their narrative devices, especially their attention to subtle detail, that had the power to give that impression. Knowing this, many journalists took pleasure in exploiting that ambiguity, working even harder at finding unique details that could signal how typical a particular case of corruption or stupidity might have been beyond the particulars of the story at hand. Censors and chief editors could not do very much about this unexpected effect of *ocherk* either: they could edit out some typifying details but not all of them; they could prevent the publication of some *ocherki* but not all of them.

Arkady Vaksberg, a legal scholar by training and one of the best known *ocherkists* at *LG*, describes this predicament especially well. The newspaper's party overseers could not help but notice the high degree of generalization in the *ocherki* published in *LG*, even though nowhere were those generalizations explicit (Vaksberg 2011). As a result, the party overseers could not find specific fault with the writing itself, but they could not leave those *ocherki* without any kind of intervention either (because that would have sent the signal that the party condones such potentially subversive practices). So a decision was found: every *ocherk* was to be accompanied by an insert that "warned the injudicious reader that he [or she] is about to read about a very 'stand-alone', 'isolated incident,' by no means typical, but on the contrary, very exceptional, one could even say unique" (Vaksberg 2011). Needless to say, the effect of such inserts was exactly the opposite. The party overseers "truly must have lost their mind," quips Vaksberg, "to act so clumsily and crudely [*toporno*], illustrating so perfectly that the guilty mind is never at ease [*na vore i shapka gorit*]" (Vaksberg 2011). Vaksberg recalls one of the thousands of letters he received after an *ocherk* of his was published:

"Are you not ashamed of yourself," the letter writer reproached me, "lying to us that the case you described is so absolutely unique? The whole time I was reading your *ocherk*, I was thinking, this is written about our factory, point for point!" I replied to the reader and said, "Dear so-and-so, if you interpreted the *ocherk* to be written about your factory – that is indeed the case then [*znachit, v ocherke tak i napisano*]. How I managed to do that is my personal journalistic secret." Several days later a telegram arrived: "All understood eagerly await new *ocherki* about exceptional cases." And that is how we communicated with our readers ... Typological characters, recognizable situations – all of this guaranteed that the *ocherki* were "co-authored" with our readers.[21]

Once Vaksberg and other feature writers at *LG* became nationally known for their *ocherki*, it became more difficult for them to conduct investigations in different cities following up on readers' complaints. Whenever complained-about officials heard the journalists' names, they would torpedo any of their investigative efforts. *LG* found a solution: it

---

[21] Russian journalist Nadezhda Azhgikhina offers her own thoughts on what gave *ocherk* its power as a genre: "The *ocherk* lived ... keeping its ancestral connection with prose, on the one hand, while remaining a 'bell' to civic action, on the other ... *Ocherki* combined the elegant elements of literature with ardent elements of *publicistika* – whether about the 'singular' cases of corruption [or] novel educational methods ... those were the texts that excited the minds and vexed the souls, forming the dispositions that would guide perestroika ... [In *ocherk*] there was also a traditionally careful – that is, compassionate and interested – attitude to the protagonist. [His or her] lineaments, gestures, mistakes and naïve dreams were probably the most effective contrast to the monotony and dreariness of the official ideological landscape that surrounded us. Even criminals, whom the authors seemingly condemned, emerged in the aureole of contradictory stories. Psychology, detail, vagaries of fate and fortune – all of that became an alternative to the official ideological 'shell'" (Azhgikhina 2004: 94–95).

would send in lesser known investigators [*razrabotchiki*] first, whose names were not associated with any high-profile exposés.[22] Among those investigators, Vaksberg (2011) says, were extremely competent people, including retired procuracy, police, and even KGB workers. A careful tactic for their behavior would be developed in advance. Often these investigators would give the illusion that they were coming "simply" to check on a "probably false" complaint that the newspaper had received. "The guilty parties would actively begin to unmask 'the libel' [*lzhivyi donos*] and, in the process, would unmask themselves" (Vaksberg 2011).

In addition to collecting a slew of documents, those "reconnaissance" men and women would prepare the ground for interviews that the *ocherkist* would then conduct with all involved parties, including "the protagonists, the anti-heroes, their relatives, acquaintances, friends, enemies, witnesses, sincere fighters for justice, informers, whisperers, and so on and so forth" (Vaksberg 2011). This once again demonstrates the thoroughness with which the best of Soviet journalists collected material for their stories, despite the limitations on newsgathering and the low professional status of news reporting. The care that many of them took to get to the bottom of the story, the doggedness with which they searched for the details of the story that could not have possibly been made up and that lifted the story to the level of generalization – all of these efforts served as invitations to readers to trust the journalist, even as the journalist was often limited in what he or she could say in print.

Words That Bind

establishing relationship with readers

As mentioned earlier in this chapter, Soviet journalists understood their political and moral tasks in a much broader fashion than their colleagues in liberal democracies. The Soviet political system explicitly called on journalists to govern – and they did so visibly, in open view. This created an opportunity for a particular kind of link between publicity and truthfulness to be activated, as discussed in the Introduction. Publicity helps to keep people in check because they act in front of many others, putting their honor and dignity on the line. To be clear, I am not arguing that whenever people speak and act in public, their words will be perceived as legitimate and truthful. No one can make

---

[22] For more on the work of *razrabotchiki* for *LG*, see Gamayunov (2009a).

such a guarantee; rather, publicity is an important condition that *can* help words and deeds aim at truth, in Williams' (2002) phrase.

As also discussed in the Introduction, there are at least two ways publicity can help to establish moral certainty. One is through face-to-face interactions, when speakers can test for themselves each other's human and moral worth. The other is publicly committing (and watching others commit) to a set of moral coordinates and seeing that this commitment is followed through. This is what anthropologists of ethics understand as the "truth-producing feature" of ritual: promises made in public help to lay the ground for people to trust one another, helping to clarify (if only temporarily) the obscurities and uncertainties of the world with which people must deal (Lambek 2010; Rappaport 1979, 1999). Anthropologist Talal Asad (2003) is right to insist that in liberal democracies, the truth-producing power of ritual is exercised primarily in the legal sphere. There is no other dimension of secular life that is simultaneously so public, so procedural, and with such profound consequences for one's life as its legal dimension.

In the Soviet Union, the legal system is known to have been much less autonomous from the other branches of government compared with its liberal-democratic counterpart.[23] Still, to maintain legitimacy, the party-state could not afford to *be seen as* openly flaunting its own principles of rationality, fairness, and justice. *In public*, the Soviet state needed to be seen as binding itself to those declared moral coordinates. Journalists became the representatives of the state whose task was to do just that: to continuously show that the Soviet state was ready to stand by its own words, as it were.[24] In that position, journalists were at arm's length from power – close and connected but not subsumed by it. This is commonly the social position that the category of the sacred occupies in a culture – as the sustainer of profane power

---

[23]   Even in liberal democracies, though, the higher up the judge sits in the judicial hierarchy, the more political his or her decisions become (Scheppele 1996).

[24]   Many aspects of Soviet legal practice were actually not devoid of what Parsons, translating Weber, called rational-legal authority (see Roudakova, n.d.). Additionally, the Soviet legal system was permeable to moral pressures, sometimes mounted by journalists. *Literaturnaya Gazeta*'s legal essays (*sudebnye ocherki*) played an important role in that regard as Vaksberg and other journalists used the press's "pulpit" to push for changes in Soviet law. For more on the sometimes tense relationship between Soviet journalism and law, see Huxtable 2012: 68–72.

the press maintains/upholds morality in USSR

but also as the very locus from which profane power can be challenged on moral grounds (Durkheim 1915; Lambek 2000: 312).

With organized religion thoroughly marginalized in the USSR, journalism, perhaps more so than any other cultural institution, became the agent to whom the state gave the tools to work this "territory of the sacred." The state repeatedly called on the press to be a people's press, a truthful press, open to criticism and self-criticism, one that helped Soviet society to maintain a high moral bar. This position toward the press was constantly reiterated in various party plenums and resolutions; additionally, in April of 1968, the Supreme Soviet Presidium issued a decree that legally obligated journalists to respond to and deal with every valid complaint they received from citizens (Hopkins 1970: 303; see also Boim 1974). This put journalists in a curious bind. On the one hand, they were explicitly encouraged to stand up for every person unjustly wronged by the government; on the other hand, drawing public attention to the problems uncovered through citizens' complaints was inevitably obstructed by Soviet authorities who preferred to keep things swept under the rug. Still, the authorities could not afford to be seen as ignoring citizens' complaints; this gave journalists the moral certainty with which to persevere.[25]

paradox

Being responsive to readers' complaints and, overall, maintaining a close connection with readers became Soviet journalists' "Holy Grail." That close connection with readers was also journalists' most powerful argument when they needed to defend themselves in front of their party overseers. This happened relatively often. Party officials tended to react extremely nervously to critical articles and would regularly call on journalists to "explain themselves" or face disciplinary

---

[25] Early Soviet leaders treated citizens' complaints as a preferred form of political control from below – preferred for its flexibility compared with what was understood as the legal red tape of bourgeois states (Boim 1974). Lenin apparently tried to set up an example there, regularly and personally handling a high volume of complaints from citizens (Boim 1974: 515). Alex Inkeles (1950: 219–220) suggests that such criticism from below worked "as a functional substitute for a system of free elections in that it provide[d] a roughly equivalent restraining influence on administrative officials." Inkeles further suggests that this form of public control must have provided "the citizenry with the satisfaction of at least feeling that it exercises some public control over those officials." Russian sociologist Elena Bogadnova makes a similar point, arguing that the opportunity to file a complaint against a bureaucracy and knowing that something will be done about it "were, in effect, the only civil right Soviet citizens consciously possessed" (Bogdanova 2005).

sanctions. Journalists (usually editors) would arrive at meetings with their party overseers armed with heaps of readers' letters praising journalists' work and giving additional examples of official negligence, corruption, bungled planning, or whatever the problem was that had been raised in the critical article (see Syrokomsky 2001; Shchekhochikhin 2003a; Loginova 1992; and many others). This often (but not always) put the party overseers in an awkward position of having to back down under the moral pressure from journalists (Huxtable 2012). In Foucault's (1997b: 292) terms, those would be the moments when power, as distinct from domination, was made "mobile, reversible, [and] unstable" because it was permeable to ethics.

power is permeable to ethics

Interviews, memoirs, and archival data all show that Soviet journalists understood the imperative to maintain a close connection with readers as a moral obligation. Keeping that relationship with readers active was as significant as keeping a promise. Readers knew it: if they brought a valid complaint to the attention of a newspaper, they were guaranteed a response (which was not the case with other branches of Soviet bureaucracy). It was also expected that if a problem had been written about in the newspaper, measures would be taken to correct it, and often quickly. Such *inevitability* of the response (journalists bound to respond to readers; officials bound to respond to newspaper criticism) is *the* foundation of lasting moral orders for Durkheim and other theorists of moral obligation. It is what sociologist Douglas Challenger (1994) has called the nonnegotiable or noncontractual elements of contract on which meaningful social life depends.

In his discussion of moral facts, Durkheim makes an important point that is relevant here: when people act in accordance with moral laws, they experience it as a combination of duty and pleasure. In their interviews and memoirs, Soviet journalists recall the imperative of working closely with readers in exactly those terms. One of *LG*'s leading feature writers, Yuri Shchekhochikhin (2003a) put it this way, for instance: "Working with readers' letters taught me one thing – that our profession is insanely difficult. You bear colossal responsibility for what you do ... It is hard everyday work ... But it is also very fulfilling."[26]

---

[26] There is some tradition of studying readers' letters to newspapers and radio programs in Western media studies. See, for instance, Katz (2012), Schultz (2000), and Wahl-Jorgensen (2002). There is also Ron McKay's (1991) collection of letters from citizens (translated verbatim) received by the Soviet weekly called *Argumenty i Fakty* during perestroika.

What *were* the social and discursive practices that sustained this relationship of obligation – this cultural contract between journalists and readers, as it were? How did journalists communicate to their readers that they were on their readers' side? As mentioned in the Introduction, Soviet newspaper offices in many ways were public places. Readers could get in touch with a journalist by writing letters, they could telephone the editorial office, or they could come in person and expect to be treated with dignity and respect.[27] Editors at *LS* in Gorky put these expectations into writing in an internal document titled, "The Laws of *LS*" (*Zakony LS*):

Every day, hundreds of people visit and telephone our editorial offices. Many of them have urgent and important questions, with which they trust our journalists. *LS* journalist must warrant this trust with sensitivity [*chutkost'yu*], responsiveness [*vnimaniem*], constant readiness to help any person who came into the editorial office. Any hint of callousness [*cherstvost'*], arrogance [*vysokomerie*], indifference [*bezdushnost'*] among the *LS* collective must be cut short by taking the most serious measures. Our reader has a right to count on us, to know that if he came to our editorial office on a work day, he will, as a rule, find people in every department [of the newspaper]. (GOPANO Archive, f. 7792, op. 10, d. 12)

Former *LG* journalists similarly recall how their editorial offices were full of visitors, sometimes to the point that people would queue up in front of some journalists' offices.[28] Many visitors would arrive from out of town and would wait for hours to tell the journalist their story of having been wronged and having failed to find redress elsewhere. Known for its incisive *ocherki* discussed earlier and having a circulation of over 6 million, *LG* was at the top of many readers' list when it came to searching for justice, especially if one was unfairly demoted, fired, or expelled from university, Komsomol, or the party, especially for having criticized one's superiors. Another variety of

---

[27] In addition to every local newspaper being open to visitors, there were public complaints offices (*obshchestvennye priyomnye*) around the country associated with major national newspapers as well. Those associated with *Izvestia* were set up by Alexei Adzhubei, Khrushchev's son-in-law, and one of the Soviet Union's most famous newspaper editors (Wolfe 2006). By the time Adzhubei, like his father-in-law, was removed from power, twenty-five complaint offices associated with *Izvestia* had been set up across the Soviet Union. Almost all continued to operate through the 1980s (Mamleev 2003).

[28] See Gamayunov 2009a, 2000b; Loginova 1992; Kozhevnikova 2001.

complaints *LG* journalists frequently dealt with was negligence and lack of professionalism in the Soviet legal system and efforts to cover it up by the authorities. In those cases, the newspaper literally became the justice seeker's last resort.

Other, more common kinds of complaints journalists dealt with had to do with the authorities' failure to provide citizens with what had been promised to them – apartments, benefits, pensions, college stipends, guaranteed job placements, day-care spots for children, hospital and rehabilitation care, and so on. Many other complaints dealt with malfunctioning infrastructure – public transportation overcrowded or not running on time, construction sites abandoned, sports facilities closed during working hours, low-quality food served in cafeterias, recycling centers turning people away, and so on. Still other complaints were classic whistle-blower signals about cases of workplace corruption, including tip-offs about goods being siphoned off from factories and warehouses for private use, or complaints about tyrannical bosses making the lives of their subordinates unbearable.

Because the range of complaints was so wide, there was no standard response to them. A substantial number of complaint letters were published, especially if they were deemed typical, to draw public attention to an issue. Such letters would be accompanied by a note from the editors warning that the newspaper is expecting a response from the relevant officials or organizations in whose power it was to fix the problem causing the complaint. If the response was not received in a timely manner or was unsatisfactory, journalists would publicly shame the officials or the organization and repeat their demand that measures be taken; then they would report on the (usually positive) outcome.[29] Other complaints or requests for help were dealt with behind the scenes – that is, without the story making it to print (Roudakova 2009). This would happen if a reader's complaint or request was too specific to warrant publication, or if the issue had just been written about in the newspaper, or if the journalist was certain that such a letter would be turned down by the editor, the censors, or the newspaper's party overseers. In these cases, journalists took an active role and became readers' moral and sometimes even

---

[29] In most cases, Soviet officials did respond to newspaper criticism in a timely manner. Those who did not risked attracting attention not only from the newspaper but also from the party authorities, which had more serious consequences for the official's career.

legal representatives before other Soviet bureaucracies. They would write letters, make phone calls, and even make personal visits to relevant organizations on behalf of the reader until the reader's problem was resolved – all without the story ever making it into print.[30]

Whether the complaint from a citizen arrived by mail, by phone, or in person, it had to be registered by a department of letters – usually the largest department in every newspaper.[31] The procedure involved in keeping written track of citizens' "signals from below" was elaborate and illustrates better than anything else that the Soviet press in many ways functioned as a genuine government bureaucracy (cf. Gupta 2012). Once again, the editors of *LS*, in an internal document from 1984, spelled out the rules according to which the letters (and signals from readers arriving by other means) were to be handled:

Every letter that arrives to the newspaper is to receive a response within ten days regardless of whether it is going to be published, forwarded for an investigation, used in a story by a correspondent, or turned over to the archives ... In cases where the decision on the letter might take longer than ten days (but no longer than a month), a preliminary response is to be sent to the author of the letter. Letters from military personnel and their families are to be examined immediately, and no longer than seven days from the day the letter arrived ... If a letter is to be forwarded for an investigation [to an organization higher up], such investigation is to be placed under special control. It is explicitly forbidden to forward readers' letters to organizations and officials whose actions constitute the subject of the complaint ... Letters forwarded for an investigation are to be accompanied by a note signed by the head of the relevant department [of the newspaper] (or by the chief editor in especially important cases), and to be put under the department head's control. A proper note of this is to be made in "the warehouse book" [*v ambarnoi knige*]. The same concerns all critical publications (accountability! [*uchet!*]). All responses received from officials and organizations are to be recorded. The relevant department must know at any particular time what kind of critique has taken place, and what is being

---

[30] For an extended example of this, see Roudakova (2007: 132–134). Some readers apparently resented it if the journalist did not deal with their issue in person. Yuri Shchekhochikhin of *LG* recalls: "Probably, like many of my colleagues, many a time have I been called a 'bureaucrat' and other such things. Why, [readers] would tell me, 'are you forwarding my letters [to organizations] – we asked you to come in person'. So I had to explain long and hard that the newspaper is not a prosecutor's office or a judge" (Shchekhochikhin 2003a).

[31] At one point, *Izvestia*'s department of letters employed seventy people (Mamleev 2003: 185).

done about it . . . [Once the wrongdoing is resolved] the department head is to inform the letter-writer of the measures taken, in writing or orally. (GOPANO Archive, f. 7792, op. 10, d. 12)[32]

Staff working in departments of letters dealt with the original welter of mail, dividing letters into different categories based on their topic, urgency, and newsworthiness. Many letters were classic letters to the editor, expressing an attitude toward an article that had been published in the newspaper.[33] Others wanted journalists to answer a question or provide information on a subject. In the pre-Internet age, Soviet journalists thus ended up working as search engines for their communities. In almost every issue, *LS* was answering some inquiries from readers: where to return defective goods, where to learn a particular skill, which factories were offering summer jobs, where to find lyrics for a popular song, where to fix a particular piece of equipment, and so on. In their memoirs and interviews, journalists recall working with readers' letters as a big bureaucratic burden but also as a source of professional satisfaction. Every week, *LS* proudly reported how many letters it had received the previous week (ranging from a few hundred to 2,000).[34] It would then devote at least one full page a week to publishing some letters and responding to others. Sometimes readers' responses to one another would be published around a particular thread. Additionally, there was a weekly telephone hot line for readers' questions and a yearly "*LS* Questionnaire" (*Anketa LS*), where journalists asked readers' advice on how to improve the newspaper for the following year.

According to Inna Rudenko, a veteran *Komsomolskaya Pravda* journalist mentioned earlier in this chapter, it was shameful not to take your readers seriously. "There were different kinds of journalists,"

---

[32] Concluding the section on the rules governing the handling of letters, there is an interesting note in the document that gives a sense of the human relations among journalists in *LS*: "Letters and packages addressed to individual journalists are not to be opened by the letter department, but to be handed personally to journalists. If the letter or package turns out to be work related, the recipient must register them in the book of incoming correspondence" (GOPANO, f. 7792, op. 10, d. 12).

[33] According to Yuri Shchekhochikhin (2003a) of *LG*, "some letters had two, three hundred signatures. People wrote not because they wanted to see their name in the paper, but to say that they were behind us in [our] investigation[s]."

[34] The newspaper's circulation fluctuated between 120,000 and 140,000 copies, serving about 3 million inhabitants of the Gorky region.

Rudenko said in a recent interview, "but to publicly flaunt your cynicism – that was impossible" (Rudenko 2005). Vsevolod Bogdanov, head of Russia's Union of Journalists since 1992, recalls how much importance Soviet newspapers placed on earning readers' trust. "I remember watching an episode in some Western movie where a journalist is handed a stack of letters that came in response to a high-profile story. And I remember my horror when I saw him laugh and throw those letters into garbage! We read every letter, kept track of it, many letters were published if they developed a particular theme. When I came to work the next morning, I could not calm myself down: what cynicism, how can one behave like that!" (Bogdanov 1998: 79–80).

Trying to leave no complaint or inquiry unanswered, drawing public *[Developing]* attention to problems, demanding a response from officials, and sham- *[relations]* ing the guilty were all important ways for Soviet journalists to develop *[with]* ties that bound them to their readers and their readers to them. But *[readers]* there were also other ways. They involved face-to-face interactions between journalists and readers and were established when readers came to look in on and to partake in the process of newspaper production. This made Soviet editorial offices public in yet another important way. Every former *LS* journalist I spoke with recalled that, especially in the evenings, *LS* editorial offices were swarming with visitors. Young and not so young people came in on specific days of the week when a particular club was in session – the club of high school correspondents, of college student correspondents, of working youth correspondents, of film lovers, of cartoonists, and, in the 1980s, simply the club of "friends of *LS*."[35] Any reader "who had interesting ideas" was invited (via the newspaper pages) to join those gatherings, *LS* journalists took turns chairing them, and commonly those meetings turned into writing and reporting workshops. *LS* journalist Galina Shcherbo[36] conveyed the general feel of those gatherings: "On those evenings when a din can be heard from the [newspaper's] Department of Student Life, it is a sure sign that the members of the club [for high school correspondents] are once again arguing about something. Each visitor is able to state their most fantastic suggestions and nobody will dismiss them because they may give rise to great ideas. Youths come to the club both

---

[35] On the work of such clubs in *KP* (which often served as an inspiration for *LS*) in the 1960s, see Huxtable 2012: 243–261.
[36] *LS*, January 24, 1985, p. 3.

with interesting news items and with their resentments and complaints, because it is important for them not only to get their name in the paper but simply to talk with their peers and to receive advice."[37]

One explanation for this range of activities is the following: like all Soviet newspapers, *LS* had a mandate (and an obligation) to be a people's paper. That literally meant that people other than journalists had to be represented on newspaper pages.[38] The internal document I have been quoting from, "The Laws of *LS*," and all of *LS* journalists I spoke with were explicit about this: every staff writer had a monthly minimum of 1,000 "lines" (*stroki*) of newspaper text that they had to have published, but everyone was also responsible for an additional minimum – of 1,600 "lines" – that were to come from nonstaffers (*neshtatnye avtory, avtorskie stroki*). In practice, this quota was not strictly maintained: some nonstaffers were not very good writers, so journalists ended up heavily editing or simply rewriting some of the nonstaffers' prose. Nevertheless, it was important to *be seen* as someone who was constantly on the lookout for new nonstaff talent and worked closely with those people on their writing skills. "The Laws of *LS*" is categorical about this: "If you are not bringing up [your own] young non-staffers – that means you are afraid of competition [*esli ne rastish' molodykh neshtatnyh avtorov – znachit boishsia konkurent-sii*]" (GOPANO, f. 7792, op. 10, d. 12).[39]

Another explanation for the inclusion of readers in the editorial process was the mandate (and obligation) for every Soviet newspaper to serve as a "collective organizer." To put it less formally and in the

[37] Nadezhda Azhgikhina (2005: 58) recalls a similar spirit in the offices of *KP* in the 1980s: "It was in the air, at least in the air of two or three of the most interesting rooms in the old *KP* that were frequented by all manner of interesting people – young poets and innovative teachers, unrecognized scientific geniuses and eccentric geeks. In those offices, it quickly became clear what was good and what was shameful; what was important, and what one should never do no matter how many blessings the editors might bestow upon you."

[38] The active involvement of Soviet readers and nonstaffers in the production of newspaper content resonates with decades of research and debates in media studies on active audiences (Radway 1991; Morley 1992; Abercrombie and Longhurst 1998), audience participation (Schultz 2000; Bruns 2005; Lowrey 2006; Livingstone 2013), public journalism (Merritt 1998; Glasser 1999), citizen journalism (Allan and Thorsen 2009), and conversationalization of the media (Kunelius 2001; Gillmor 2004; Peters 2005).

[39] For a detailed account of how *KP* journalists worked with their nonstaff authors, see Huxtable (2012: 143–278).

way *LS* journalists actually understood it, *LS* was to serve as a kind of clearinghouse for various community activities. Although not advertised, *LS* weekly editorial meetings were open to the public. "It is advisable," wrote the editors in "The Laws of *LS*," "that specialists, interesting people, and story protagonists be invited to the editorial meetings."[40] Several times a year *LS* would hold open editorial meetings (*vyezdnye letuchki*) in various public places – in large community centers or "palaces of culture" as they were known in the Soviet Union, in theaters, in parks in the summer, or in meeting halls of large industrial factories (there were especially many of those in the Gorky region – one of the reasons the city was closed off to foreigners). Sometimes instead of (or in addition to) open editorial meetings, *LS* journalists would hold question-and-answer sessions with readers (*vstrechi s chitateliami*). Those meetings tended to be very well attended.[41]

Finally, *LS* editorial offices served as a space where members of the various clubs maintained by the newspaper could meet local dignitaries. The city's artists, writers, scientists, and other intellectuals who liked the newspaper and enjoyed speaking to a young audience were often invited by *LS* for an informal conversation with readers "over tea." Sometimes it was people known nationally who were passing through and who had agreed to an interview with *LS*. Reports about those conversations, written up by one of the nonstaffers, would later appear in *LS* under the "Living Room Dialogues" rubric. It is probably fair to say that the majority of Gorky's residents in their teens and twenties with an inkling for writing or for community engagement had at least tried one of the *LS* clubs during the 1970s and 1980s when those clubs were most active.

Parrhesia in the Late Soviet Press

In this final section I want to examine what the practice of *parrhesia* – of speaking candidly and courageously – looked like in Soviet newspapers and editorial offices. In particular, I want to advance the

---

[40] It appears that various "interesting people" did indeed spend substantial time at the newspaper. Another "law of *LS*" says, "Conversations and personal meetings with friends and acquaintances in the workplace must not get in the way of the work of your comrades" (GOPANO, f. 7792, op. 10, d. 12).

[41] Igor Gamayunov (2009a) from *LG* recalls that meetings with readers similar to these were regularly held by *LG*.

argument, briefly sketched by historian Stephen Kotkin, that as a cultural and ethical practice, parrhesia belongs to the genealogy of socialism as well as liberalism. Understood as a moral duty and delivered at the risk of angering more powerful interlocutors, parrhesia was part and parcel of "speaking Bolshevik," as Kotkin (1995) demonstrated for the Stalinist period. The Soviet Union simply would not have lasted as long as it did if people could not, in some fundamental way, engage with its political project on the level of ethics. In this section I want to show how during the Brezhnev era as well, taking a risk to speak frankly and openly was part of the ethical repertoire (Rogers 2009) that was available to Soviet citizens, particularly journalists. The famous Twentieth Party Congress of 1956, where Nikita Khrushchev denounced Stalin's crimes, emboldened many journalists to attempt to practice parrhesia without the fear of persecution. Drawing on the data I collected and on recent histories of journalism in the late Soviet period (Wolfe 2006; Huxtable 2012), I argue here that parrhesiastic speech exerted a strong ethical pull on journalists in late socialism, remaining their key professional value and grounding their identities as intellectuals and truth seekers on behalf of the public.

Historians and Sovietologists have usually treated the critical component of the Soviet press under the rubric of *kritika* and *samokritika* – Lenin's idea of "criticism and self-criticism," which he understood to be a distinguishing feature of socialism as a superior form of political organization. As discussed in the Introduction, Lenin tasked the entire society and especially the press with *samokritika*, and scholars have focused on the official treatment of so-called signals from below – complaints from citizens – as evidence of *samokritika*. Western scholarly focus has been on the limited scope of such complaints, on the responses to them by the press and the party, and on the role this form of political communication played in maintaining socialism's legitimacy.[42] Scholars concur that for most of the Soviet Union's existence, some topics were far too sensitive and could not appear in the press under any circumstances. They included questioning the party's leading role in society, the lives of Soviet leaders, the country's foreign

---

[42] See Hopkins 1970; Inkeles 1950; Remington 1988; see also Boim 1974; Fitzpatrick 1996; V. Kozlov 1996.

policy, operations of the Soviet military-industrial complex, the cost of the country's victory in World War II, and similar topics. Raising questions about more mundane matters was not, however, off limits, as demonstrated earlier in this chapter. Citizens were encouraged to complain to the press about the day-to-day workings of Soviet industry, agriculture, infrastructure, education, medicine, and so on; the press was obligated to investigate those complaints; and state bureaucracies were obligated to respond. *Flow of information*

As discussed in the Introduction, during the Stalinist period, some of the most common signals from below that journalists worked with involved (1) complaints about industrial sabotage and negligence among factory workers and (2) complaints about malfeasance, misappropriation of funds, suppression of criticism, and other abuses of power among factory and farm managers. As historians of Soviet journalism have argued, this form of Stalinist-era *samokritika* was driven primarily by the party – rather than journalists.[43] A key task for the Stalinist press was to mobilize people for the building of communism, and one way to do that was by identifying specific *individuals* who stood in the way of social progress. Drawing on citizens' complaints, journalists and worker and peasant correspondents were encouraged to identify such individuals and to expose their progress-impeding behaviors. Even at the height of Stalinism, though, there were journalists (war veterans in particular) who had their own ideas of what social criticism should look like – ideas that did not always dovetail with the party's expectations.[44] Nevertheless, generating one's own critical leads was risky for journalists under Stalin because punishment for editorial "errors" could be severe and could result in a prison sentence.

After Stalin's death in 1953, and especially after the Twentieth Party Congress of 1956, the tone and scope of newspaper criticism began to shift (Wolfe 2006; Huxtable 2012, 2014). Khrushchev's revelatory speech at the Congress "unleashed a torrent of discussion" and a round of soul-searching among journalists (Huxtable 2014: 210). An important change also took place in censorship practices: newspapers began to be verified by the party *after* publication rather than

---

[43] Huxtable 2012, 2014; Wolfe 2006; see also Brooks 2000; Lenoe 2004.
[44] See Hopkins 1970: 95–96; Huxtable 2014; Wolfe 2006: 31–32; Brooks 2000: 160. See also Weiner 2001.

before, as was the case under Stalin.[45] As Huxtable (2016) explains it, "[O]nce editors gained the censor's trust, they were expected to exercise their own judgment over the suitability of an article, knowing that if the *vertushka* [the party's internal phone line] didn't ring before 11 am, the previous day's paper had passed muster with the Politburo."

Encouraged by the party to effectively partake in the governing of society, journalists began to understand themselves as social critics *in their own right.* They started to take a more activist civic stance, reminiscent of their nineteenth-century predecessors, seeing themselves as the party's intellectual and moral avant-garde rather than its "transmission belt" (in Stalin's famous phrase). Instead of following the party's lead and identifying specific individuals who were impeding communism building, Khrushchev-era journalists began to formulate societal problems as they saw them and to put pressure on authorities to eliminate them (Huxtable 2012: 96–8).[46] Those newly identified problems began to include bungled planning, inefficiencies and ineffectiveness of management, environmental degradation, and poor customer service. Understanding themselves as "social researchers" (*obshchestvovedy*) as well as opinion leaders, journalists started to aim for a degree social analysis and generalization in their work (Huxtable 2012; Volkov 2000; Wolfe 2006).

Journalists' interest in social analysis dovetailed with the emergence of sociology as an academic discipline in the late 1950s and early 1960s. Especially throughout the 1960s, journalism and sociology became closely aligned, given their shared interest in public opinion formation (Firsov 2008; Kon 1999; Shlapentokh 2000). This was aided in large part by the pioneering work of sociologist Boris Grushin, who ended up heading *Komsomolskaya Pravda*'s Department of Propaganda in the 1960s. Based in that department, Grushin founded the Institute of

---

[45] This did not extend to the continuing proscription by the *Glavlit* office against the publication of state secrets and other especially sensitive topics that would have been considered anti-Soviet propaganda by the *Glavlit* (casting doubt on the ideological monopoly of the party, the desirability of communism, Soviet foreign policy, and so on). For the most part, journalists censored *themselves* on these topics until perestroika.

[46] The late 1950s and 1960s were also a period of journalism's rapid professionalization in the USSR. Schools of Journalism were opening in many universities (e.g., Azhgikhina 2005), the first Union of Journalists was formed (French 2014), and a liberal, reform-minded editor (Yegor Yakovlev) took the helm of a monthly publication for journalists (*Zhurnalist*), transforming it into a lively professional discussion forum.

Public Opinion – the first organization for the study of public opinion in the Soviet Union (Firsov 2008; Grushin 2000; Huxtable 2012: 189–233). *KP* began canvassing readers' views on a wide range of topics; and many other publications, including regional newspapers like *LS* in Gorky, followed suit. Popular works by sociologists began to appear in major Soviet newspapers and magazines (Kon 1999, 2000).[47]

After Khrushchev's ouster from power in 1964, and especially after the Prague spring crackdown in 1968, the relationship between the journalists and the party began to sour. The kinds of social analysis and criticism journalists were practicing in the 1950s and 1960s began to make party officials extremely nervous (Huxtable 2012; 2014; Wolfe 2006). The party began to argue that too much *kritika* and *samokritika* was "fowling one's own nest," giving solace to the enemy, and fomenting internal discord. At times, it seemed that the party still wanted journalists *paradox* to keep identifying social problems, but it did not want those problems publicized. "Why did you publish that article?" a high-ranking official berated a *KP* journalist in 1964, for instance, after the latter revealed sloppy workmanship and safety hazards at Moscow's newly built Luzhniki stadium. "I wish you'd come to me and talked about it [instead]. We know that there are a lot of faults at the Luzhniki" (Huxtable 2014: 214–15). As Huxtable (2012: 96) puts it, whatever desire the regime still may have had at that point to rid of society's shortcomings *in general*, it did not seem to want to deal with them *in particular*. *micro vs macro*

At other times, it was clear that the regime – meaning the high-ranking party and state officials – was no longer interested in socialism's improvement but instead in protecting its political fiefdoms. Especially after 1968 and until perestroika, journalists and officials ended up engaging in what Huxtable (2016) calls a "low-level battle" with journalists "attempting to sneak critical materials into the paper and [officials] trying to keep them out – sometimes successfully, sometimes not, and, most of the time, somewhere in-between." Former editor of *KP* Boris Pankin described this battle as "the game of cat

---

[47] According to Vladimir Shlapentokh (2000), who had worked with Grushin, the journalists and the sociologists during the 1950s and 1960s were united in their reformist and progressive sensibilities. "All of us," Shlapentokh (2000: 116) recalls, "even the non-party members like myself, not to mention Grushin [and others] – all of us wanted to help the party to govern society effectively . . . None of us were fighting with the system – we wanted to modernize it, to improve it." Yegor Yakovlev, former editor of *Zhurnalist*, expressed the exact same sentiment (quoted in Bogdanov and Zassoursky 1998: 25).

and mouse" journalists played with their "high-ranking readers" (Huxtable 2014: 218). Journalists would publish a critical article, "officials would accept its conclusions" with the caveat that "certain of those conclusions were inaccurate, or overstated" (Huxtable 2014: 218). Based on those "inaccuracies," and enlisting the support of some high-ranking party members, the criticized would try to discredit the article and the journalists who wrote it. Sometimes those attempts would fail because *other* high-ranking officials would speak up for the journalists (who would defend themselves with additional facts, readers' letters, and informal shaming of officials for the suppression of criticism). At other times, the attempts by the criticized to discredit the article would succeed, and the editor would be sanctioned. In the late Soviet period, the most common type of sanction was an official "reprimand." Multiple reprimands eventually led to the editor's demotion or transfer – to another paper, to party and government work, and, in some cases, to "exile" as a foreign correspondent abroad. *Ha!*

Between Khrushchev and perestroika

Such were the uncertain rules of the game that journalists and party officials settled into toward the end of the Khrushchev period and continued until perestroika. Importantly, as part of that game, "one never knew in advance whether the regime would react [to criticism] with approbation or opprobrium" (Huxtable 2014: 218). This uncertainty, combined with the fact that journalists felt more secure after the Twentieth Party Congress, created the moral space from which they could occasionally take the risk to speak openly and candidly – the mode of speech Foucault identified as parrhesia. As both Wolfe (2006) and Huxtable (2012) conclude, the underlying journalistic sentiment during the Brezhnev period was the realization that journalism was still a force *for* socialism but increasingly *against* the ailing party. Brezhnev-era journalists came to see the party as marred in collective power grabbing, back scratching, heel digging, and other woeful elements of what Russians call *krugovaya poruka* (see Ledeneva 2006). As Wolfe (2006:122) put it, by the 1970s and 1980s, Soviet journalists "had the best seats to witness the party's creeping sclerosis, and this gave journalists and editors who shared a sense of disappointment at the fate of the Soviet sixties a kind of license, for they knew that the party could not very well renounce the work of journalistic investigation into the shortcomings of Soviet society, even as they had no real use for it." It is of course this very license journalists and editors tapped into as they enthusiastically embraced Mikhail Gorbachev's glasnost and perestroika.

So how did parrhesia look in Soviet newspapers and editorial offices? What kinds of people were recognized as parrhesiastes, and how? To recall, for Michel Foucault (2010, 2011), parrhesia was a way of speaking that was clear and direct, with nothing left to interpretation. It was also based in conviction and experienced as a moral duty. Finally, parrhesia always involved speaking from a position of less power. Effectively, it was about those rare moments, and those moments only, when one spoke *to* power as an equal (cf. Arendt 1958). Because parrhesia risked the ire of the more powerful interlocutor, it built one's character, which is probably why Foucault was particularly interested in it. Classic examples of parrhesia would include a student challenging the teacher, a philosopher shaming a tyrant, and a citizen criticizing the majority.

As both Wolfe (2006) and Huxtable (2012) note, and as memoir data and my conversations with former *LS* staff show, most journalists from the Brezhnev period have at least a few stories about a conflict they entered into with their party overseers over a critical piece they published (or attempted to publish). As discussed earlier in this chapter, to an important degree these are self-gratifying and in some cases self-expiating memories, where journalists want to remember themselves as having been on the right side of history. What is more interesting, though, and in the end more valid, I think, is that in addition to recalling their own brave acts, journalists usually remember a colleague or two whose integrity they admired and whom they considered their moral and professional inspiration. Those colleagues are remembered as people who were not afraid to speak up – at editorial meetings, on newspaper pages, and in conversations with party officials – while others hesitated. For the quality Soviet newspapers I have been examining, the same names of exemplary journalists usually came up. For Brezhnev-era *Izvestia*, it was almost always Anatoly Agranovsky, discussed earlier; for *KP*, it was often Inna Rudenko, also discussed earlier; for *LG*, it was Yuri Shchekhochikhin (to be discussed below); and for *LS* in Gorky, it was often Galina Shagiyeva (also to be discussed below). Here, for instance, is how a former colleague remembers Inna Rudenko at *KP*:

And then there was another Rudenko lesson. She was "the critic on duty" [*dezhurnym kritikom*] for the editorial meeting [*letuchka*] that week. It was the late seventies, the heat of [Brezhnev's] stagnation, and the apogee of a creeping rehabilitation of Stalin. So, she got up and began speaking in her quiet voice about Stalin – about his monstrous crimes and about the *nomenklatura* cravings for a strong leader. She spoke firmly and fearlessly, even though out there in the world, one could once again be persecuted – for reading Solzhenitsyn, for instance. She spoke quietly, but it is as if she had a megaphone in her hands: the entire *letuchka* turned into a speechless rock, cowering in fear and delight, feeling small from her gall and courage.

And then, every one of her publications was a lesson. "Duty," for instance – the *ocherk* where she spoke up for a young man who was shot in the spine in Afghanistan. She was the first to say out loud that there was a real war going on there; she was the first to demand that the authorities take responsibility for the men mutilated by that war. They [the authorities] might not have forgiven her for it, but they did not dare – she had the support of the Afghan war veterans ... Even if she had not written anything else before or since, she would have already made history. (Lepsky 2014)

At *LG*, it was Yuri Shchekhochikhin, head of the department of investigations, who stood out to colleagues for his moral and professional integrity. Investigative journalism was Shchekhochikhin's calling – his *ocherki* at *LG* and later at *Novaya Gazeta* (where Anna Politkovskaya also worked) were the most daring. He was the first Soviet journalist to speak about the existence of drug dealers (in 1987) and of organized crime (in 1988) in the Soviet Union. He continued with his investigative work after he became a member of the last Soviet and then the new Russian Parliament. He died a sudden and mysterious death in 2003 after what many believe was a toxic poisoning. His last investigation was into corruption at the office of the Prosecutor General of the Russian Federation.

Shchekhochikhin is a particularly good example of a Soviet-era *parrhesiaste* for our purposes because he is remembered not only for speaking frankly and openly himself but also for encouraging others – readers and colleagues – to do the same. He came to *LG* from *KP* in 1980. One of his first investigations at *LG* was a story about a Naval Academy graduate in the city of Odessa in Ukraine, Nikolai Rozovaykin, who attempted to blow the whistle on a series of financial machinations he had witnessed at his former alma mater ("After the Storm," *LG*, January 19, 1983). Rather than following Rozovaykin's lead, the criminal justice system in Odessa turned against Rozovaykin himself. He was stripped of his professional qualifications, his party and Komsomol membership were revoked, and he was barred from working as anything but a janitor for a total of five years. During those years, he spent twenty months behind bars on trumped-up charges of "social parasitism" (*tuneyadstvo*), "hooliganism," and slander. To defend himself, Rozovaykin kept writing to, calling, and visiting as many naval, judicial, Komsomol, and party bureaucracies as he could, to no avail. Eventually, his letters reached *LG*, where Shchekhochikhin began working on his story. In a 1984 interview Shchekhochikhin gave to *Zhurnalist* in the aftermath of the story's publication, he talked about why he took up Rozovaykin's case.[48] "The letters Rozovaykin wrote to *LG* did not just interest me – I was drawn to them," Shchekochikhin (2003a) explained. "Rozovaykin's position was close to mine, personally. It was a natural, normal position [of a truth and justice seeker]. The kind of position that is absolutely necessary for the development of society ... My protagonist drew on the strength of the law. He was a fighter. He was socially active, and that was the most important thing ... That is why I felt this story needed to reach public domain."

Rozovaykin's story indeed powerfully resonated with *LG* readers. *LG* received over 2,600 letters in response to the *ocherk*. "Readers supported in all seriousness the stance Rozovaykin took – the stance that was also the newspaper's stance – to actively intervene in life," Shchekhochikhin (2003a) explained. "Many letters came from people who found themselves in situations analogous to what was happening in Odessa. Those were difficult letters to answer." Many readers worried about Shchekhochikhin after publication of the *ocherk* and demanded reassurances from *LG* that he was doing well. A telegram from the city of Norilsk in the far north of Siberia read, for instance: "Rumors abound here that Shchekhochikhin lost his job [after the *ocherk*]. Is that so? Please have Shchekhochikhin himself respond" (Shchekhochikhin 2003a).

---

[48] The interview was recorded in 1984 and remained unpublished until Shchekhochikhin's death in 2003. It had been approved by *Zhurnalist*'s editorial board and had been put into publication plan. But the chief editor must have decided to run it by the censors "just in case." "Too much of an extolment [*eto vse-taki panegyrik*]" was the censor's verdict, scribbled across the archival copy of the interview. "There were two spelling errors in '*panegyrik*,'" quipped *Zhurnalist* in 2003, hinting at the low education level of the censor. See Shchekhochikhin 2003a.

At least part of the story's resonance had to do with Shchekhochikhin's rather daring style of writing, especially by Soviet standards. For instance, Shchekhochikhin describes the pressure that he and his editor were under as he worked on the story. That pressure, he writes, stalled the publication of the *ocherk* for many months. By the time the *ocherk* finally came out, Rozovaykin's professional qualifications and party status had been restored – but, Shchekhochikhin woefully remarks in the conclusion to the *ocherk*, nobody from the police or the prosecutor's office in Odessa lost their jobs. On the contrary, some of the officials involved in persecuting Rozovaykin were promoted to leadership positions. Shchekhochikhin is also doubtful whether there is enough political will in Odessa to bring anyone to justice for the corruption at the Naval Academy – the original reason for Rozovaykin's quest.[49] Still, Shchekhochikhin considers the story very significant. The story needed be told, he writes in the *ocherk*, because it is about the importance – for society – of seeking truth *in the open*. "Truth only becomes truth when one risks their life to find it. Truth needs to be sought after openly, or we will lose it. If we quietly tolerate a thousand small things, they will add up to one intolerable condition."[50]

Through *ocherki* like this, Shchekhochikhin was in effect pushing for glasnost (openness) before that concept became synonymous with perestroika under Gorbachev. It was not often that such *ocherki* appeared in late Soviet press, but they appeared often enough, helping to maintain readers' trust in journalists. Such *ocherki* were more common in *LG*[51] and in publications like *KP* and *LS* that were geared toward Soviet youth. In the unofficial hierarchy of Soviet media outlets, newspapers for the young were generally afforded more room for experimentation and criticism than their adult counterparts. This, I was told, was because the press's party overseers understood that people in their teens and twenties are at a period in their lives when they intensely search for answers, ask more questions, are less

---

[49] Shchekhochikhin was right – in the years following the publication of "After the Storm," the case looking into corruption at the Naval Academy fell apart. Instead, the law enforcement officials who attempted to conduct that investigation were themselves convicted and put behind bars, once again on trumped-up charges. It was only after Shchekhochikhin's follow-up *ocherk* in 1989 that those convictions were overturned.

[50] Quoting from Shchekhochikhin (2010: 66).

[51] For more on the uniqueness of *LG*, see Dzirkals et al. 1982: 115–130.

compromising and more easily feel betrayed by insincerity, and are less tolerant of hypocrisy.[52] One of the former readers of *KP* and *LG* wrote, for instance, "I did not know [Shchekhochikhin] personally. I only read his articles. But every time I read them, I was struck by the sense that this was a person who looks at the world the way I do. He was angry at the things that angered me; and he was joyous about the things that brought me joy as well" (Ryabinina 2003).

In addition to pushing for honesty and openness in his writing, Shchekhochikhin is remembered for his candor in his relations with editors, colleagues, and the nonstaffers he worked with both at *KP* and *LG*. At *KP* he headed "The Scarlet Sail" – a youth club that taught teenagers how to write (similar to the clubs ran by *LS* journalists discussed earlier).[53] Here is how one Scarlet Sail regular recalls the atmosphere created there by Shcheckhochikhin in the 1970s:

He always said, "Do it in a way that interests you. So that you are not ashamed of yourself later. Do it the way you think is right" ... Hoards of teenagers came to him, the captain of the Scarlet Sail. I was among them. For some reason, we were interesting to him. He did not teach us anything. He talked to us. One more time: This famous journalist talked to us, teenagers. He listened to us. We could even argue with him.

The Scarlet Sail was the first national scream by teenagers. The scream was not for help, but for understanding. Shchekhochikhin, the captain, was responsible for that scream – before everybody, including the stern [party] bosses ...

He created the atmosphere. In that smoke-filled room where the Scarlet Sail met, only one thing was not allowed – to ask adults for writing leads. Instead, other things were encouraged, like coming up with your own ideas, however improbable. We were allowed to be clever! To show off, to fantasize. And we were taken seriously. Nobody laughed at us. It is only much later that I understood what Shchekhochikhin wanted to teach us. He wanted to teach us how to think freely. (Maximov 2003)

At *LG*, colleagues remember Shchekhochikhin as someone who spoke frankly and openly at editorial meetings, particularly when

---

[52] Journalists knew that, and many of them preferred to work in outlets for the young until retirement, despite the official expectation that one would move on to an "adult" newspaper once they reached their late thirties. Readers also knew that, and quality youth newspapers such as *KP* and *LS* maintained large audiences in part because they included many older readers (noticeable through readers' letters).

[53] For more on the Scarlet Sail, see Huxtable (2012: 243–250).

addressing *LG*'s bosses. Igor Gamayunov, a former colleague at *LG*, recalls an editorial meeting in early 1988, for instance, where Shchekhochikhin openly rebuked *LG*'s editorial board and especially *LG*'s powerful editor, Alexander Chakovsky, for blocking the publication, at the last minute, of a small story Shchekhochikhin had prepared:

> As a journalist, I am really hurt [*bol'no ranit kak zhurnalista*] to see that the editorial board seem to treat us as mere clerks who should be following their instructions. It was painful for me to find out that the small text that I had prepared was thrown out at the last minute and did not make it to the most recent issue. As always, it was thrown out without any warning ... It was a letter from the workers at the Prosecutor's Office in Kharkov who wrote in support of a monument to the victims of Stalin's Purges ... Why was the story taken off the page after the galley proofs were already signed? How did that happen? And how did it happen that [another *LG* journalist] could not publish his article in *LG* and had to take it to *Moskovskie Novosti*? ... This sense of the newspaper that has ceased to be my "own" [*svoei*], it stands in the way of my writing. This is really painful for me personally [*mne lichno tiazhelo*]. I forgot when was the last time that [the editors] came to our floor talk to us [the writers] ... Killing a text without any warning to the author is unethical. (Quoted in Gamayunov 2009b)

LG's chief editor, Alexander Chakovsky, evidently felt compelled to respond. Chakovsky, who continuously edited *LG* from 1962 to 1988, was more of a suave politician than an editor (Dzirkals et al. 1982; Izyumov 2011). In many ways he was the perfect Soviet editor-in-chief. He knew how to maintain political capital with party overseers while keeping a creative, free-spoken atmosphere in the newspaper he headed. That atmosphere nurtured the work of *LG*'s more venturous *ocherkists* on whom the popularity of *LG* depended.[54] So Chakovsky

---

[54] After interviewing two of *LS*'s former editors, Georgy Rabkov and Vladimir Lapyrin, I was left with a similar impression. Both seemed to me like people who were intelligent, who cared about their journalists, who were cautious enough in their judgments, and yet who had not been blindly subservient to the party. Most of the time, former *LS* journalists told me, their editors stood up for them when the paper was criticized by their Komsomol overseers in Gorky. In Vladimir Lapyrin's case, he was able to defuse many tense situations through humor. In other newspapers, editors did contradictory things like accepting the reprimand from party officials while simultaneously rewarding the journalist for quality work. Former *KP* editor Boris Pankin recalls, for instance, how, during his first several years at *KP* as a young reporter, he came to admire the balancing act of his then editor-in-chief. Young Pankin remembers a day when his editor-in-chief came back from a scathing visit to his party overseers with a "severe reprimand"

stood up and began to speak – in a conciliatory tone. He started off by saying that "our newspaper was always strong on sincerity"[55] and that "it is important that we stand together in these difficult moments" (Gamayunov 2009b). He then explained that the reason he took out Shchekhochikhin's text was that there had been too many articles about Stalin in *LG* recently showing him to be "a terrorist, a despot, a tyrant" and that Shchekhochikhin's text would have been one too many. Chakovsky then went on to speak long and candidly about his personal relations with various Soviet leaders, from Khrushchev to Gorbachev, implying that there are nuances to every leader's personality. Seeming a little embarrassed toward the end, he added: "Perhaps I spoke of too much here [today]. [But the main thing] I ask of you – please, treat me with the same openness, the same honesty, the same trust that I have for you. Let us be truthful to one another, and let us keep comradely relations amongst ourselves!" (Gamayunov 2009b).

As a particular kind of address *to* the powerful, parrhesiastic speech like Shchekhochikhin's has a specific goal: to bring ethics back into politics. To recall, for Foucault (1997b, 2010, 2011), parrhesia is aimed at domination rather than at power per se. There is no room for ethics in domination, but there is such room with power. For Foucault, power, among other things, is about the government of others, which is done in part through ethics. When power ignores ethics, it turns into domination, becomes blocked and frozen, and loses legitimacy. Parrhesia is an attempt to unblock, or to undercut, domination by making it responsive to ethics. This is precisely the effect we see of Shchekhochikhin's speech on Chakovsky, *LG*'s well-connected editor-in-chief. Chakovsky was compelled to respond to Shchekhochikhin's rebuke, and he did so in a conciliatory tone because he must have shared at least some of the values of his free-spoken

in hand for Pankin's critical article. Nevertheless, the editor wrote up an official praise letter for Pankin's file and ordered to pay him a bonus. "And this is when I began to really respect the profession of an editor – the profession to which I later devoted many years of my life" (Pankin 2002: 7). Ninel Loginova of *LG* recalls a similar situation, when the galley proofs of her *ocherk* on the plight of the Roma in the Soviet Union were put into the publication plan several times by different managing editors, until one day they made it to the deputy chief editor, who wrote on them in big letters, "Very good. Will not work" (Loginova 1992: 21).

[55] For more on sincerity as a signal of truthfulness in Soviet journalism, see D. Kozlov (2013) and Wolfe (2006: 33–38).

colleagues.[56] For Chakovsky, to be called on his political cowardice, in the presence of other journalists, amounted to him losing face with the very people he was supposed to lead. Hence Chakovsky's (not particularly impressive) attempt to mend those relations with his creative staff – by showing to them that he, too, can speak frankly and is no stranger to their values. Whether or not those particular signals of atonement secured any "uptake" with *LG* journalists is of course impossible to know.

In their turn, parrhesiastes such as Shchekhochikhin, Rudenko, and others did not just one day wake up valuing frank speech either. They nurtured the obligation to call corruption and cowardice by their names as part of their professional identities long before perestroika, setting an example for colleagues who were more cautious.[57] Certainly, more systematic archival research needs to be conducted into the actual practices of parrhesia in Soviet editorial offices in the Brezhnev period. My goal here has been simply to gesture to the continuing *value* of those practices – for journalists, editors, and audiences – in late socialism.[58]

A final point needs to be made about the practice and value of parrhesia in late Soviet press. It is important to reiterate that I am not taking Soviet journalists to be truth seekers pure and simple. Throughout the late Soviet period, journalistic parrhesia coexisted in

---

[56] Wolfe (2006: 131–135) offers a compelling illustration of where Chakovsky's own values likely lay. In 1970, Chakovsky wrote a detailed private letter to Soviet leader Leonid Brezhnev. The letter is critical of the Bolshevik tradition in Soviet press, arguing that this tradition is failing on many fronts and is ultimately eroding people's confidence in Soviet power. The Soviet public has an intense thirst for information, Chakovsky argued, and the Soviet media are failing to satisfy that thirst due to censorship and self-censorship. Chakovsky worries that this will eventually lead to Soviet power's demise. The letter is written in the genre of a wise advisor speaking frankly but patiently to the king. The letter is not confrontational but certainly takes risks, which makes it a good example of parrhesia in itself.

[57] Shchekhochikhin says that he himself learned how to be a good journalist from his older colleagues. "I learned from Inna Rudenko, from Nelli Loginova, from the masters of Soviet journalism like Yuri Rost, Yaroslav Golovanov, Valery Agranovsky . . . The first thing I learned was not to lie to anyone and not to be afraid of anything. Second thing – to write how you feel. Your own opinion, regardless of how old you are, is very important. Third, I learned I had to write well . . . And lastly – [I learned] not to reveal my sources. Because they were always in more danger than I was" (Shchekhochikhin 2003b).

[58] For some other examples of editorial parrhesia, see Nenashev (1995: 55–56); Syrokomsky (2001); Pankin (2002: 88–90); Yakovlev and Nenashev (2003).

an uneasy tension with the more repressive elements of the Soviet political order. As described earlier, parrhesiastic speech could never be directed at socialism itself. Censorship and self-censorship made parrhesia more of an ideal than a practice. It was discouraged by the party; it was not materially rewarded. For all these reasons, it was risky and rare. Indeed, only some journalists aspired to be parrhesiastes, and only some editors tolerated it.

Still, parrhesia's cultural value remained high throughout the late Soviet period. This is illustrated particularly well by situations where journalists remember themselves as parrhesiastes even as evidence from other sources contradicts those memories. I can offer one such example here, but I am convinced there are more. The case in point involves the memories of Ilya Shatunovsky, a prominent satirist and feuilleton writer first at *KP* and then at *Pravda*. In an interview with Radio Free Europe in 2003, Shatunovsky clearly remembered himself as someone who "always stood for truth and justice" (Shatunovsky and Rykovtseva 2003). "That was my professional credo. I always considered justice to be the highest human good, and that's why I always sought it." When asked if the party ever "ordered" him to attack anyone in his feuilletons – to mock and lampoon someone to destroy their name and reputation – Shatunovsky seemed insulted by the question. "I never scoffed at the victims of the Soviet regime," he retorted. "I never wrote a single feuilleton about the dissidents, even though many times I was asked to do it and was told to do it. I never wrote a single article against the dissidents. I may not have shared all of their convictions, their positions, their programs. But never in my feuilletons. I always held on to a belief that if it were a standoff between a person and the state, I always took the position of the person. Because if the state is abusing the person, then one should not add to it. That's why I practically have none of those feuilletons" (Shatunovsky and Rykovtseva 2003).

It so happens that we have evidence very much to the contrary. Historian Benjamin Nathans (2007) discusses one of Shatunovsky's feuilletons, titled "From the Biography of a Scoundrel," which appeared in *Ogonyok* in January 1963. The feuilleton mocked Alexander Volpin – a Soviet mathematician, logician, language philosopher, and prominent member of the so-called defenders of rights movement among Soviet dissidents. Defenders of rights were engaged in what has been called radical *civil obedience* – that is, demanding that the Soviet power simply obey its own laws. After the Twentieth Party Congress made a renewed commitment to the rule of law, Volpin decided to launch "a formal appeal regarding his arrest and imprisonment in 1949 on charges of 'anti-Soviet' activities" (Nathans 2007: 650). Volpin had been amnestied in 1953, but the anti-Soviet charges themselves were never dropped. As Nathans (2007) remarks, it probably did not help that around the same time as he filed his appeal, Volpin published a selection of poems and another work titled, "Free Philosophical Tractate," with a publisher in New York.

The Soviet state responded to such "betrayal" with a full-blown campaign against Volpin. Shatunovsky's satirical feuilleton scorning Volpin crowned that campaign. Shatunovsky "denounced Volpin as a slanderer of Soviet power 'which gave him everything in life,'" calling him "an accomplice to treason ... and a currency speculator to boot" (Nathans 2007: 651). Following Shatunovsky's feuilleton, Volpin was confined to a psychiatric hospital for three months. On his release from the hospital, Volpin sued Shatunovsky and *Ogonyok* for libel. During the pretrial depositions, Volpin asked that the truthfulness of Shatunovsky's charge be evaluated – the charge that Volpin's book of poems published in New York was "anti-Soviet slander." In Volpin's opinion, only a willful misreading of that text could have produced such a charge. To Volpin's astonishment, Shatunovsky offered the court the following explanation: "From my party-minded point of view, the conventional definition of 'slander' as a deliberate falsehood is irrelevant" (Nathans 2007: 652). The court eventually dropped the case.[59]

There are several ways to interpret Shatunovsky's desire to remember himself as a justice seeker and almost a defender of dissidents, even though the historical record points to the contrary.[60] It could be a simple memory lapse on Shatunovsky's part or, more likely, we are dealing with some variant of self-deception, selective remembering, and willful forgetting. Shatunovsky's feuilletons did carry biting satire of factory managers, low-level state officials, and other offenders of public morals in some positions of authority. But, given feuilletons' intention to take someone down through mockery, and given the fact that

---

[59] On Shatunovsky as a contradictory figure, see also Huxtable (2012: 69–70).
[60] The listeners of the radio program where Shatunovsky was interviewed had mixed reactions, to say the least, to his claim that he was a justice and truth seeker (Shatunovsky and Rykovtseva 2003).

those feuilletons appeared in the country's most powerful newspaper (*Pravda*), they lacked a crucial component of parrhesia – the _risk_ associated with speaking truth to power. This is precisely the risk that Rudenko and Shchekhochikhin were willing to take in their work. Still, it is significant for our purposes that Shatunovsky remembers himself as someone who stood up to power instead being part of it. When nonparrhesiastes among the journalists remember themselves as valiant risk takers, it still points to the high *value* of courageous speech in Soviet journalism.

A Realist View of Truth

Shatunovsky's understanding of anti-Soviet slander quoted earlier offers a good entry point into the concluding section of this chapter. Shatunovsky presumably intended to say that regardless of Volpin's actual words, the *spirit* of Volpin's writings was fundamentally anti-Soviet. Shatunovsky's certainty about what Volpin's writings "really meant" was part of a broader take on knowledge we may identify as epistemological realism.[61] Rooted in a materialist understanding of history (Lenin 1909; Marx and Engels 1932), the realist approach to knowledge was a common feature of Soviet intellectual and ideological knowledge production. Historical research into the culture of knowledge production in countries that embraced the materialist understanding of history has just begun (see Glaeser 2011; Shore 1998; n.d.), so we need more data to appreciate the nuances of that process. Still, in broad strokes, Soviet intellectuals and cultural producers, including journalists, understood truth to be a real thing. It was solid and tangible rather than relative and plural. It could be hidden from sight or exist in plain view, it could be avoided or feared, other things could be masquerading for it, but its singular existence was undeniable.

Epistemological realism usually comes with the sense (and the heft) of knowing what truth looks like. It is accompanied by the urgency to seek truth and by the need to broadcast those findings to others. The more Soviet journalists saw themselves as the avant-garde of the party, the more they became convinced that they had the moral responsibility to establish what the truth of socialism looked like (cf. Shore 1998). Soviet journalism in the Khrushchev and Brezhnev periods thus

---

[61] I thank Chandra Mukerji for bringing this to my attention.

became a profoundly moral project: journalists came to believe it was them, and not the ailing party, who should have the final say in how society should be governed (Wolfe 2006). This understanding was shared by propagandists and intellectuals alike and by people like Shatunovsky who fell somewhere in-between. As a result, all these cultural actors were making claims to the *same* solid truth of socialism, whereas their counterparts in liberal democracies might have allowed for greater epistemological relativity (different groups and individuals pursuing their different truths). Even the defenders of rights among the Soviet dissidents arguably shared in the same culture of epistemological realism as did Soviet journalists. After all, the dissidents' campaign of radical civil obedience demanded none other than the Soviet authorities obeying their own laws. It is not unlikely that Alexander Volpin, for instance, had the same kind of certainty as did Shatunovsky that the truth was on his side. This is what made the practice of truth and justice seeking in the Soviet Union complicated and historically specific.

Let me illustrate this point with a story from *LS* in Gorky, this time with the added benefit of hindsight. As mentioned earlier, Galina Shagiyeva was a journalist at *LS* who is remembered today by her colleagues as a particular kind of parrhesiaste akin to Rudenko and Shchekhochikhin at *KP* and *LG*. Colleagues today remember Shagiyeva as someone who continuously had to "make trips to *Obkom*" (*LS*'s overseeing organization) to resolve conflicts over her critical publications. When I interviewed Shagiyeva in 2000, I was impressed by her intelligence, her commitment to the profession, and the degree of reflexivity in her thinking. At *LS*, Shagiyeva headed a club for college student correspondents called *Yabloko* ("The Apple") that was very popular among Gorky youth, resembling (and probably modeling) the Scarlet Sail that Yuri Shchekhochikhin headed at *KP*. Unlike many of her colleagues at *LS*, Shagiyeva was a committed party member. Her "beat" was postsecondary education and the life of college-age youth, so many of her *ocherki* began as grievances or requests for help from college-age students.

Shagiyeva was the kind of journalist who was the first among her colleagues to embrace glasnost encouraged by Mikhail Gorbachev. As mentioned earlier, this was not uncommon for the parrhesiastes among the journalists. They were striving for candor and openness long before perestroika, and it made sense that they were the ones most invested in promoting glasnost. At *LS*, Shagiyeva was the first to write about the effect of Stalinism on generations of Soviet citizens – particularly on their propensity to conformism and their fear of speaking up. In an *ocherk* published on September 1, 1988, Shagiyeva wrote about a class of 1938 that met to celebrate the fiftieth anniversary of their high school graduation. Shagiyeva writes movingly about the joy these elderly people felt at the sight of one another. At the same time, Shagiyeva is bothered by the lack of conversation among them on the topic she thinks should be on everyone's mind – the experience of graduating high school at the height of Stalin's Great Purges. Now that glasnost is encouraging everyone to reexamine the dark corners of Soviet history, would not reflecting on the experience of living through the Purges be a most appropriate topic for discussion, she asks? After all, several teachers of that graduating class lost their lives in the Purges, as did many relatives and neighbors.

Shagiyeva is bewildered by the seeming lack of interest among the members of the 1938 class to ask themselves the difficult questions about their fateful past and their role in it. Naming some of the graduates (and two of their teachers who also came to the celebration), Shagiyeva ends up implicitly reproaching these old people for their unwillingness to think, for "looking the other way," and for making compromises with their conscience. Indirectly, Shagiyeva questions these people's moral integrity, admonishing them for their lack of dignity, courage, and self-respect. "After that *ocherk*, I felt like such a heroine," Shagiyeva recalled to me in an interview in 2000. "For a long time afterward, I felt like a real journalist. My colleagues were proud of me." However, twelve years after the publication of her *ocherk*, Shagiyeva felt very different. "These days I go back to that story in my mind and I feel ashamed, I feel scared," she admitted to me in her 2000 interview. "Why did I attack those people? Those were elderly people who had lived their difficult lives. They lived them as best they could. Who was I to judge them?! ... The only thing that consoles me is that nobody died or had a heart attack or something as a result of that publication."

Shagiyeva's *ocherk* and her own evolving professional and moral evaluation of it show very poignantly the beginning of the breakdown of epistemological realism in Soviet journalism. As Shagiyeva herself explains:

The Soviet system was very powerful. The reader existed in that system as a reader, but also as a citizen. The system encouraged readers to think, to educate themselves. Everything in that system was tight, coherent, logically consistent; everything was understandable; you could even say it was comfortable. The system was logical and smart. Journalists felt right at home in that system. We were educated in that system. We were propagandists – but that propaganda was genuine, humane ... And then, abruptly, everyone's eyes were opened. And we were on our own. It was difficult to go from a coherent system into a wide-open field. All of a sudden, you are told – okay, you are on your own now. Go figure out on your own where right and wrong is. Decide for yourself now what to do.

For Shagiyeva, among other things, the breakdown of this system amounted to learning how to think in more relative terms about people's motivations and their personal and historical truths. Living and working through the fall of the Soviet Union had the effect of making Shagiyeva's stories less uncompromising and more nuanced. As mentioned earlier, I found her reflexivity arresting and her explanations of the transformation she and her colleagues went through particularly insightful. In contrast to Shatunovsky, for instance, she was willing to ask *herself* the difficult questions that she wanted – and expected – others to contemplate as well.

To conclude, this chapter made two main arguments. One is that journalists in the late Soviet period developed a particular set of *social* relations with their audiences – relations that were aimed at maintaining their audiences' trust. To do so, Soviet journalists wrote and acted in ways that one might tacitly recognize as aiming at truth. Those efforts included journalists striving for descriptive accuracy, sincerity, and reflexivity; they also included showing to readers that journalists were willing to stand up for the readers in cases of conflict with Soviet bureaucracies. The other argument this chapter made was about a particular understanding of truth that was built into the Soviet governmental project, of which journalism was part. Owing to Marxism as a form of philosophical materialism, this view of truth was realist rather than relativist, singular rather than plural. It is precisely this take on truth that began to break down with the fall of the Soviet Union.

The broader aim of this chapter has been to argue for a view of Soviet journalists as simultaneously political and *moral* actors who occupied an ambivalent space within the Soviet governmental project, particularly in the late Soviet period. As discussed in the Introduction, morality and ethics are a dimension of human life that fundamentally deals with the uncertainty of human experience and with the need to act in the face of that uncertainty. To the degree that acting in the face of uncertainty involves making choices informed by conscious reflection, there is an ontological connection between ethics and freedom (Foucault 1997b; Laidlaw 2014). Admittedly, this freedom is not absolute but "of a definite, historically produced kind" (Laidlaw 2002: 323), but it is freedom nonetheless.[62] This is why it is not uncommon to see occasional references to "internal freedom" among former Soviet journalists.[63] "Freedom is in your character, your gut, your willpower, your ability to absorb the punches without backing down," Mikhail Nenashev (2004: 11), a prominent former Soviet editor, has stated, for instance. "We have as much freedom as we can take onto ourselves. Those concepts – of freedom, of independence – are personalized, intimate concepts. The journalist is always as free as his [or her] ability to carry the burden of freedom" (Nenashev 2004: 11). Paradoxically, journalism's capacity to withstand that burden declined sharply *after* the fall of the Soviet Union. Chapter 2 will now delve into what allowed this to happen.

capitalism

---

[62] This point has often been lost in anthropology and other social sciences due to the influence of Durkheim and Marx (Laidlaw 2002, 2014).
[63] See Rudenko (2005), Agranovsky (Wolfe 2006: 101), Nikitinsky (2006), Shatunovsky (2003b), and others.

2 | *Journalism and Capitalism*
The First Encounter

Press freedom is commonly thought of as media's ability to disseminate information to large audiences without interference from the state. The fact of private media ownership is implied in this understanding of press freedom but is usually not highlighted. When transitions to democracy in Eastern Europe and the former Soviet Union are discussed, Western commentators usually want to know whether the state is still pressuring the media rather than what shape private media ownership has taken in the region and how it has affected the practice of journalism. Such questions are crucial to ask in a postsocialist context, though, because relations of private media ownership had to be created anew and under specific historical circumstances, and the meanings and practices of journalism were profoundly affected by that process. This is a distinctive feature of post-Soviet media transitions: in Latin America, East Asia, and Southern Europe, media transitions away from authoritarianism were arguably less dramatic because they were occurring on top of already existing relations of capitalist media ownership (Voltmer 2013).

Scholars studying media institutions in the former Soviet bloc began to examine this relationship between journalism and capitalism after 1989. In particular, we know that immediately prior to and after the fall of state socialism in Eastern Europe, many editors rushed to launch their own private media outlets, straddling the roles of editor and owner. Few of those outlets survived past the first few years of the transition, though, because consumer advertising – the main economic engine of private media – was in short supply after the collapse of planned economies across the region. German, Swiss, and Scandinavian media conglomerates saw this situation as a unique investment opportunity. They quickly moved into emergent media markets in Eastern Europe and the Baltic countries, more or less dividing those markets among themselves – to the point that in some of those countries, up to 80 percent of national print output and up to

75 percent of national television market share were captured by foreign-owned companies by the mid-1990s (Gulyas 1999, 2003; Perusko and Popovic 2008; Voltmer 2013).

West European media conglomerates brought with them certain rules of engagement about how a successful capitalist media enterprise operates and what kind of journalism it relies on. Business, financial, and consumer-oriented press represented one kind of model of media entrepreneurship that was successfully transplanted eastward; tabloid press was another (Gulyas 2000). Business and tabloid media are generally two of the most efficient ways to make money through the mass media: the former sells quality news to wealthier audiences and charges top dollar for it; the latter sells a cheap news product in high demand to large audiences.

For those privately owned outlets in the former Soviet bloc that were not bought up by Western European media conglomerates and that continued to make ends meet amid the economic collapse of the early 1990s, minimizing production costs wherever possible was a top priority. For general-interest publications, this meant relying on the feed from news agencies, on press releases, on reprints from other publications, and on punditry and opinion pieces, all of which were inexpensive to produce compared with the investments required for quality investigative reporting or in-house research projects (Balcytiene 2008; Voltmer 2013). "Advertorials" – promotional pieces masquerading as editorial opinion or news produced by advertisers – were, and continue to be, yet another way to quickly generate media revenue across the former Soviet bloc (Erjaevic and Kovacic 2010; Ornebring 2012).

As such, these money-making and cost-cutting trends in news production are not particularly unique to Eastern Europe or to Russia. Since the late 1980s, journalism scholars and practitioners in the United States and elsewhere have been documenting how the increased pressure for profits, coming from stockholders of media companies, has been eroding journalistic professionalism in favor of market-driven journalism where "MBAs rule the newsroom" (McManus 1994; Underwood 1993). Yet journalism's encounter with capitalism in the former Soviet bloc in the early 1990s was in many ways *un*like what was going on in newsrooms in the United States and elsewhere in the West. The sheer extent of "checkbook," or paid, journalism in Eastern Europe and Russia and the speed with which it became the norm in many outlets have taken observers and researchers aback (Voltmer

2013: 207–216). Moreover, much of the advertising masquerading as news has been negative political advertising aimed at discrediting or damaging political opponents – a genre recognized across Eastern Europe by the Russian word *kompromat* (Ornebring 2012). What is particularly disconcerting about *kompromat* is that it does not seem to matter to any of the parties involved whether or not *kompromat* is factually correct. *Kompromat* can be fabricated, mixing fact, opinion, and fiction; journalists may be forced to produce it; it can be blocked from publication for an additional fee; and it can have a "paid by" notation next to it – all of this while having the rhetorical trappings of a muckraking report (Koltsova 2006; Ledeneva 2006: 28–90).

What is going on here? What sense are we to make of these practices? I do not see the wide spread of paid journalism in Russia and Eastern Europe as simply an extension of the profit-maximization imperative that has been gradually taking over newsrooms worldwide. Something else is surely going on. As this and Chapter 3 will argue, what we observe in Eastern Europe, but especially in Russia, following the privatization of the media is a full-blown deprofessionalization of journalism as an occupation. In the sociology of professions, professionalism and capitalism are usually seen as closely linked: Professional groups are understood to have been formed by first creating and then monopolizing the markets for professional services – by turning professional knowledge into a standardized, recognizable commodity, distinct and identifiable by potential consumers (Larson 1977). What we see with the introduction of capitalism *after* socialism, I will argue, is a reverse trend, at least when it comes to journalism. Capitalist relations of production broke open the meanings of public and private from which journalism as a collective project takes its bearings – both in state socialism and in liberal democracy. This sudden erosion of meanings of public and private left many journalists uncertain as to who they were representing, to whom they owed their labor, and what should be the relationship between information and money. This uncertainty undercut the opportunity for journalists to develop new, post-Soviet forms of professional solidarity, leaving many of them – as this and Chapter 3 will show – estranged from one another and feeling that they are "on their own" and working primarily "for themselves."

Why do I believe that deprofessionalization of journalism has been especially pronounced in Russia compared with countries in Central and Eastern Europe and the Baltic states? More comparative work needs to be done to conclude that with certainty, of course, but I do think that the early and massive entry of foreign capital onto the scene in Eastern Europe played one important role in stabilizing not only the media ownership structures in those countries but also, to some extent, the professional routines and practices of journalism as well. EU accession requirements such as the passing of requisite freedom-of-information laws and other EU-mandated media regulations must have additionally helped to forestall a full fragmentation of journalism's "cognitive core" in Eastern European countries. Neither of those conditions were present in Russia. As this chapter will show, at least throughout the 1990s, Russian journalism was pulled in multiple directions by a variety of social forces that prevented any sort of professional stabilization. To back up my claim – that the beginning of journalism's defragmentation in Russia is to be found, in part, in the absence of the stabilizing force of foreign media ownership – let us examine what those early practices and relations of private media ownership in Russia looked like, what historical forces fueled their formation, and what those practices and relations of ownership meant for Russian journalism in the immediate post-Soviet period.

Where Do Private Media Come From?

In the summer of 1990, the first law on the press was passed in the Soviet Union. The law forbade media censorship and removed party and state monopoly on media ownership.[1] Although the law did not contain any provisions for the transfer of assets (office buildings, printing presses, or national distribution networks) to journalists, it was still greeted with euphoria in editorial offices across the Soviet Union. Many groups of journalists quickly asserted their newfound independence by reregistering their media outlets as owned by journalists themselves. Many new outlets sprang up as a result of internal conflicts within existing editorial collectives, when a group of journalists, led by an enterprising member of the editorial board, would split off to launch a new outlet. Other, less entrepreneurial editors began steering their outlets toward hybrid forms of ownership where the

---

[1] The law legalized the tendencies that had already been underway in the Soviet Union for some time: the Party had effectively relinquished press censorship by 1989–1990, and private media outlets had begun to appear before the law was passed.

outlet would be jointly owned by journalists and a governmental or a commercial entity. These included democratically elected parliaments and city councils and newly set up private banks, stock exchanges, and other businesses whose founders also wanted to try their hand in media entrepreneurship.

The reason why teaming up with a governmental or commercial body seemed like an attractive option to groups of journalists in the early 1990s was an important provision written into the new law on the press. Motivated by the desire to protect journalists' independence not only from government officials but also from private media owners as well, the authors of the law gave groups of journalists the right to keep their own accounting even when their outlet was co-owned by a governmental or commercial body.[2] That is, the editorial staff (*redaktsia*) of a media outlet were given the status of an *independent legal entity* with the capacity to engage in commercial transactions separately from the outlet's external co-owners. As Mikhail Fedotov (2002), one of the authors of that law, explains, the framers of the law intended to give journalists the best of both worlds with this arrangement. On the one hand, external co-owners would presumably contribute the startup capital to the media outlet as a condition of becoming that outlet's co-owner. On the other hand, the journalists were given the option of earning money on their own so that they could keep enough distance between themselves and their co-owners in cases of editorial conflict.

In fact, the term *media owner* did not even appear anywhere in the law; the statute spoke more euphemistically of "media founders" (*uchrediteli*) instead. Such cautious wording was a testament to the public discomfort surrounding the notion of private media ownership in Russia in the late 1980s and early 1990s. Like journalists, the authors of the law welcomed the revocation of state monopoly on media ownership. At the same time, many people, including the authors of the law, were uncomfortable with some of the connotations of *private media ownership* – particularly the idea that private individuals could in principle do whatever they please with an institution as fundamentally public as the mass media.[3] The euphemism *media founder* seemed like a good compromise. As the meaning of the term

---

[2] For more on the blurred boundary between private and state ownership of the media in 1990s Russia, see Koltsova (2006: 73–85) and Roudakova (2008).

[3] For an example of that discomfort, see the work of Slovenian media scholar Slavko Splichal (1992, 1994).

suggests, founders were imagined as people or entities who would contribute assets to help launch independent media outlets off the ground and who would enjoy the prestige of having their name associated with a media outlet. This, the authors of the law estimated, would give groups of editors and journalists some space in which to breathe and to learn how to make money on their own.

The vagueness of this legal arrangement meant that the rights and responsibilities of media owners vis-à-vis journalists were left unspecified, and this ambiguity turned out to be a mixed blessing. On the one hand, it indeed gave more entrepreneurial journalists a unique opportunity to both draw startup capital from co-owners *and* to maintain some distance from those co-owners through a separate stream of revenue. On the other hand, the limits this arrangement placed on the power of media owners discouraged systematic financial investments into media outlets on the part of co-owners, leaving many groups of journalists severely strapped for cash and unable to hire additional personnel to take over the business side of operations. The arrangement also bred an understanding among existing and potential media owners that media property was different from other forms of property in that the co-owner had no obligation to bankroll the media outlet when it was of no strategic or tactical use because journalists could "just as well" earn their salaries themselves. Finally, this arrangement created a valve through which the external co-owner could effectively control the editorial policy of the outlet despite the law's guarantee of editorial independence: if journalists were unable to make money on their own, the co-owner could manipulate the disbursement of donations to the outlet depending on whether the editorial line was to the co-owner's satisfaction.

Despite these entanglements, and despite rising prices on paper, the years 1990 and 1991 were still relatively favorable for press freedom in Russia. Importantly, during those years, the new Russian government, quickly gaining in stature over the ailing Soviet power, offered periodic bail-out packages as a sign of its commitment to democracy to publications on the brink of financial trouble without asking for much, if anything, in return (Zasursky 2004). Russia's first post-Soviet Minister of Information, Mikhail Poltoranin, himself a former journalist, was behind the idea of targeted state subsidies to the press, arguing that press freedom required both editorial independence and financial solvency and that the young Russian state had an obligation to support the media in achieving both goals at once (Poltoranin 1990, 1994).

So between the passing of the first law on the press in the summer of 1990 and the onset of neoliberal reforms in early 1992, the majority of Russian media outlets, while practicing a variety of relations of ownership, managed to remain fairly independent editorially and stay afloat financially through a combination of subscription, newsstand sales, government subsidies, some advertising, and some private sponsorship, all in an atmosphere where public demand for and trust in the printed word remained exceptionally high. Journalists' reputations soared, sometimes nearing that of national heroes. Without fail, journalists across the post-Soviet space remember that short period with fondness and nostalgia as the time when they were truly free and extremely influential at the same time.[4] At least in part, that sense of political agency and potency was nurtured by the discourse of the Fourth Estate that perestroika-era journalists eagerly embraced – a discourse that merged together classic liberal caveats about freedom of speech and expression, an Enlightenment view of men of letters as *telos*-setting intellectuals (Carlyle 1849); the outgrowth of US constitutional theory where the media are seen as the "fourth branch of government" working closely with the other branches (Cater 1959), and a historically specific yet internationally mobile discourse of journalists as government adversaries. A 1990 editorial in *Zhurnalist*, appropriately titled, "What Are We to Be Called Now?," captures this awesome moment:

These days, it is not only an organization or a group of persons, but also an individual citizen who can launch their own newspaper or magazine. This right gives our press, our culture a chance to produce exceptional public figures, wielders of societal thought of Herzen's magnitude[5] ... The citizen who starts his own newspaper takes on the highest kind of responsibility before society – because he is not sharing it with anyone ... Instead, he has the courage to speak as an individual thinker [*imeyet muzhestvo govorit' iskliuchitel'no ot sobstvennogo imeni*]. (Zhurnalist Editorial 1990)

In line with their newly understood roles, many former Soviet journalists ran for public office, participated in the drafting of legal codes, and

---

[4] For a similar sentiment among East German journalists, see Boyer (2005: 220–225).

[5] Alexander Herzen (1812–1870) was one of Russia's most prominent political writers and philosophers of the nineteenth century.

launched new social and political movements, all the while continuing with their editorial and entrepreneurial duties.

Unfortunately, this relative equilibrium when the Fourth Estate seemed to rule side-by-side with the other branches of government while enjoying an unprecedented credit of trust with the broader public did not last past 1992 as a cluster of factors quickly began to undermine it. General price liberalization launched by President Yeltsin's economic team in January 1992 led to a steep hike in the prices of paper and printing services, which led to drops in the production of paper and newsprint while the demand for them remained high, which, in turn, disrupted the production cycles of many newly launched outlets. An even greater blow, however, was delivered by inflation, which began to spiral out of control soon after prices were freed. During the late Soviet period and especially during perestroika, most Russians were avid media consumers: members of an average household subscribed to several publications and regularly bought several more at newsstands. Starting in 1992, shrinking incomes and fast-disappearing life savings of the majority of Russians meant that the consumption of printed matter began to drop sharply precisely at the moment when the number of media outlets continued to grow as more and more editors were putting their entrepreneurial ambitions to the test.

Spiraling hyperinflation also brought a severe restriction in cash flow across the entire economy, paralyzing the operation of many of its sectors, including the mass media, and forcing many businesses to turn to barter instead of cash (Humphrey 2002; Woodruff 1999). Barter deals for advertising space became common in the first half of the 1990s, with media managers scrambling to convert barter into products and services that would be of use to the outlet. As one regional editor put it at the time, "barter is when advertising space is exchanged for gasoline, electricity, pantyhose, chocolate, and funeral services" (Kachkaeva and Richter 1999). Even with the reliance on barter, newly launched businesses in the consumer sector were themselves struggling with price liberalization and hyperinflation to find money for advertising campaigns, so the majority of them tended to advertise selectively or not at all,[6] which further frustrated media managers who

---

[6] The businesses were also constricted by the new Russian tax code, which demanded that advertising be paid for from posttax profits. Russian lawmakers in the early 1990s had an understandable anxiety about advertising and opted for laws that restricted rather than encouraged it. This is in contrast to the way

had originally placed high hopes on commercial advertising as their major source of revenue. Finally, the government subsidies on which many outlets relied in 1990–1991 petered out throughout 1992 as state budgets at all levels became stretched extremely thin due to the epidemic noncollection of taxes – an unsurprising result of the collapse and subsequent "barterization" of the economy.

Left largely to fend for themselves and unwilling to give up, editors and publishers in the first half of the 1990s acted like most people would in highly volatile economic environments: many learned to quickly recombine their existing resources and continued to devise short-term strategies to stay afloat. In addition to skillful use of barter, they sublet[7] parts of their offices to commercial firms, launched parallel businesses such as real estate or marriage agencies, and applied for Western aid, if knowledgeable in English and the discourses of press freedom. Starting in 1993–1994 and increasingly afterwards, most media executives also began to rely on regular influxes of electoral cash to keep their outlets afloat.

For a dramatic illustration of these processes, consider the post-Soviet fortunes of *Leninskaya Smena* (*LS*), the popular regional youth daily published in Gorky (now Nizhny Novgorod) discussed in Chapter 1. After the law on the press was passed, *LS* journalists reregistered the newspaper as solely owned by the newspaper's editorial collective (*redaktsia*) – thus becoming formally independent from their Soviet-era Komsomol overseers. Soon, however, several leading journalists left *LS* – some to join new business-oriented media ventures in what was now Nizhny Novgorod, others to launch an independent news agency, and still others to work for regional television and new opportunities there. Those who stayed behind and those who newly joined them began to navigate the uncharted waters of private media entrepreneurship as best they could. Responding to hyperinflation and price hikes on paper and printing services, *LS* tripled its yearly subscription price in the fall of 1991 and then dramatically raised it again several months later, recanting on its contract with subscribers and

---

advertising is treated in the majority of Western countries: it is defined as a "business expense" and is entirely tax exempt. The clause obligating businesses to pay for advertising from posttax profits was finally dropped from the books in 2002.

[7] Many newly independent editorial collectives were now renting their offices from the government organizations of which they were part prior to 1990.

angering and losing many of its readers. Instead of closing down the newspaper, asking for governmental subsidies, or inviting a commercial entity to become the newspaper's co-owner, the chief editor of *LS* at the time, Igor Kryzhkov, urged journalists to search even harder for commercial advertising and to absorb some of the production costs by accepting drastically reduced salaries. According to his former editorial staff with whom I spoke, the chief editor did not have an entrepreneurial streak, could not think commercially, and did not understand the importance of investing in the business side of operations. Instead, the chief editor believed that the prestige of the *LS* brand – its reputation as the most trusted newspaper in the region – was going to be enough to pull the newspaper through, sooner or later generating enough sales and advertising income to keep it afloat.

A profound crisis of governance within *LS* staff ensued. In the winter of 1993, yet another large group of journalists, led by deputy chief editor Alexander Volkov,[8] left *LS* to start a new outlet; many remaining journalists took to the bottle. Igor Kryzhkov himself left in 1994. Despite all of this, *LS* continued to be published through 1995, turning into a tabloid to sell more copies through newsstands. Remarkably, during this period, *LS* still managed to produce some good journalism, including some of the better regional coverage of the Russian-Chechen war, sending its own correspondents to Chechnya. Financial woes continued to plague the newspaper, though, contributing to journalists' growing demoralization. In late 1995, the newspaper finally stopped coming out, but some journalists continued to show up at work for a few more months anyway out of habit.

A striking document I found in one of Nizhny Novgorod's archives illustrates the extent to which *LS* journalists' professional lives had unraveled by then. On January 24, 1996, after *LS*'s rental agreement with the city had run out (recall that the privatization of *LS* meant only the transfer of the *LS* trademark to journalists, not the transfer of assets), officials from the municipal property fund visited *LS* offices and conducted a property inventory of the building. They wrote up their report as follows:

Most of the rooms were locked and could not be inventoried ... Six rooms were open. In the rooms, there is old furniture, sacks of flammable debris, baskets full of trash; the rooms are dirty, the doors are broken ... Several of

---

[8] A pseudonym.

the rooms do not have central heating. It was not possible to speak with Y. V. Kozonin, the [new] editor, because he was asleep in his office during work hours (at 3:30 PM). In the same room with him was [the head of the news department] O. V. Kapitanov and several strangers (*postoronnie*). They were sitting around the [editor's] table amidst open vodka bottles and chasers. The editorial staff of *LS* was requested to hand over their keys to the building. (GOPANO f. 8892, op. 10, ed. khr. 40)

If this story represents the nadir of Russia's transition to a privately owned press in the early and mid-1990s, then another story can stand for a more successful but still problematic version of the transition. This is the story of *The Sentinel*,[9] a private newspaper launched by Alexander Volkov, *LS*'s former deputy editor. In early 1993, Volkov convinced about a dozen of his colleagues to quit *LS* and join him at his new publication, *The Sentinel*, with him as the editor and publisher. To fund this new enterprise, Volkov told me, he had first contemplated a parallel launch of "some sort of commercial firm that would support the newspaper" but eventually settled on co-ownership of his new outlet with an acquaintance of his, a founder of one of the first stock exchanges in the city, who provided Volkov with initial capital to start. As Daria Moskvina,[10] who worked for Volkov's *Sentinel* in the first half of the 1990s, speculated to me, the new co-owner of *The Sentinel* must have been "a bit of an idealist, had ambitions to become a public figure, and Alex [Volkov] must have convinced him that investing in his paper was the best way to gain the public stature the guy had hoped for." Daria's husband, however, who had also worked in the paper in the early to mid-1990s, speculated that the reason behind the new co-owner's investment in Volkov's paper was the possibility of "negative PR" against the region's then young and charismatic governor, Boris Nemtsov, and the business interests allied with him.

One way or another, the new co-owner was shot and critically wounded about four months into the operation of the new outlet and decided to quit business and politics, leaving *The Sentinel* to fend for itself. "I felt responsible for the people who were working under me," Volkov recalled to me in an interview in 2000:

And I didn't want to give up. It was 1993, the year of hyperinflation. Every month I was getting telegrams that would categorically inform me that the cost of paper is going up by 200 percent this month, or that the cost of ink or

[9] A pseudonym. [10] A pseudonym.

whatever is going up 100 percent next month, or that our rent will increase five times, and so on. I had to hustle unbelievably. Once we had no money left to pay for the print-run – so I went to the director of the printing plant and told him, "Take some of our shares!" And he did, so we did not pay for print for the next eight months, and I was instead able to pay journalists their salaries. Then the next time I ran out of cash I went to a bank to ask for a loan, telling them that we'd pay back the interest in advertisements. They agreed, and we eventually made enough to pay back the loan. Then another time I went to the director of the printing house to barter a high-speed copier for free print. High-speed copiers were still rare, and I had promised free advertisement to the company that sold those copiers in exchange for one of them. And then there was a moment when I had exhausted my resources and still could not come up with cash to pay the journalists that month. So I went to this other businessman, and told him: if you place your advertisement with us right now, I'll be able to pay people their salaries this month. And that worked, too … Only through all of this I realized that the newspaper is a *commodity* – a very specific one, but still a commodity.

What Alexander Volkov only hints at here (via the reference to the newspaper as a commodity), and what becomes clear from conversations with journalists who had worked for his paper in the first half of the 1990s, is that the largest share of *The Sentinel*'s revenues by 1994 came from electoral campaign contributions. Unlike the initial wave of democratic elections and referenda in Russia in 1989–1991, the second wave of electioneering, which began in October of 1993 (and, for Nizhny Novgorod, continued through 1994 and 1995), attracted much larger pools of electoral cash from the region's newly minted capitalists. In December of 1993, Nizhny Novgorod was electing six representatives to the new Russian parliament (Duma), and immediately afterwards, three other campaigns were being launched, to culminate on March 27, 1994, in the Nizhny Novgorod regional legislative assembly, the Nizhny Novgorod city council, and a direct plebiscite for the position of the city's mayor.

Like many other media executives in the city, Alexander Volkov was quick to realize that this train of elections, and the large number of candidates hoping to fill those positions, was an opportunity not to be missed. Importantly, until 2002, there was no comprehensive attempt at a legal definition of political advertising, so almost any kind of electoral coverage that seemed favorable to a candidate or unfavorable to his or her political opponents could, in principle, be interpreted as positive or negative advertising by media managers and could be charged as such. This opened a major loophole for the monetization of electoral coverage in the absence of media outlets' other reliable sources of income. This, in turn, set in motion a process of moral and professional unraveling of journalism – the process that would be complete by the late 1990s and early 2000s.

Monetization of Electoral Coverage

The first campaign in which electoral coverage was successfully monetized in Nizhny Novgorod was the mayoral campaign of 1994. That campaign was the first in a series of especially fierce battles among the city's new political-economic elites, battles that ended up pulling most journalists into their vortex and pulling them apart. Like many political conflicts in Russia's regional centers in the early 1990s, this particular conflict was a contestation over spheres of influence between the governor of the Nizhny Novgorod region (which is home to about 3 million people) and the mayor of the city itself, which is the capital of the region (and is home to about a million and a half of those 3 million people).

The governor of the Nizhny Novgorod region at the time was Boris Nemtsov. Until his assassination in February 2015, Nemtsov was a prominent figure in Russia's opposition movement, but in 1994 he was a charismatic thirty-four-year-old favorite of President Yeltsin and was known for his swift neoliberal policies in the Nizhny Novgorod region (which, among other things, earned him the praise of Margaret Thatcher who visited the region in 1993). The incumbent mayor of the city of Nizhny Novgorod, who crossed paths with Nemtsov, was a former lawyer named Dmitry Bedniakov. Bedniakov had been appointed mayor of the city in 1991 and now wanted to be democratically elected. A few weeks before the election, Bedniakov had proposed that, on election day, the city also vote on a city charter, which, if passed, would have strengthened the position of the mayor and the city council and would have taken some power away from the regional authorities, including, of course, the region's governor. The governor, Boris Nemtsov, did not want to cede power to the city and did not want the city charter to pass. Instead, the governor wanted his protégé, the speaker of the regional parliament, a man named Yevgeny Krestianinov, to be elected mayor instead.

A few months prior to the election, both candidates for the mayor's seat launched their election campaigns. Two other candidates entered the race, but as the campaign picked up momentum, it became clear that the incumbent mayor and the speaker of the regional parliament were the two candidates most likely to win the election. Businessmen across the city began to fund those two campaigns, knowing that supporting the mayor-to-be meant having privileged access to lucrative government contracts, difficult-to-obtain construction permits, and new opportunities for the privatization of municipal property that was in full swing. Now, for journalists, this was an exciting time as well. This was the first time the city was electing a mayor, and for journalists it was a chance to partake in the shaping of the future of the city in a way they had not done before. So most journalists approached the campaign as community activists who believed their active stance in the campaign was instrumental to the future well-being of the city. And for the city's newly minted publishers and broadcasters, who were desperate to make ends meet in the absence of commercial advertising, the campaign was a golden opportunity to earn much-needed income for their outlets. In a few years, journalists would begin to refer to the months and weeks prior to election as a "harvest yield" (*strada*) that their outlets would rely on during the barren periods in-between campaigns.

Consider the stories of these three journalists who were actively involved in the coverage of the 1994 mayoral campaign. Two of them worked for *The Sentinel*, Alexander Volkov's publication. In the political conflict between the governor and the incumbent mayor, Volkov decided to side his paper with the governor and his protégé rather than with the mayor, in exchange for some funding for his paper. Volkov told his journalists that he would not force them to write anything they did not want to, but if any of them had anything positive to say about the governor or his protégé or anything negative to say about the incumbent mayor, they were free to put their talents to use, in exchange for some extra pay. Svetlana Bulgakova[11] was one of the journalists who had generally been a supporter of Nemtsov and his neoliberal economic policies. So she became one of the journalists who took up Volkov's call to take the side of the governor and his protégé in that

---

[11] A pseudonym.

campaign. For her, this was a win-win situation where she got to channel her political sympathies in exchange for additional pay.

Another journalist, Daria Moskvina, mentioned earlier, was among Volkov's employees at *The Sentinel* as well. Daria expressed no interest in supporting the governor or his protégé in her writing. She was not a fan of either the governor or the mayor. Her journalistic convictions had been shaped instead by a combination of a watchdog stance vis-à-vis all holders of power and by a late-Soviet understanding of journalists as public intellectuals. It so happened that by the time the campaign rolled around, Daria had been working on a story investigating the incumbent mayor's preference for foreign investors at the expense of encouraging local entrepreneurship. Daria did not plan her article as part of the mayor-bashing campaign that was picking up in multiple outlets across the city, including her own. But once Daria's article was published, it made a big splash and *was* quickly perceived to be part of the media attack against the mayor. Many of Daria's colleagues across the city were now discussing her article in their columns, suggesting that her investigation might have been ordered and paid for by Krestianinov, the governor's protégé. Without Daria's consent, the article was then made the centerpiece of promotional materials mailed to every household in Nizhny Novgorod as part of Krestianinov's campaign. The article became so well known that for many years it was taught in one local university as a classic text of negative political advertising.

My third story is of Yelena Yakovleva,[12] at the time a political correspondent for a local broadcasting station (NNTV). The station was founded right before the fall of the Soviet Union by the Nizhny Novgorod region's first democratically elected parliament. Because NNTV was not only founded but also funded by the regional parliament, and because the speaker of that parliament, Krestianinov, was now running for mayor, journalists working for the station were expected to lend their support to the speaker's campaign. Yelena disliked the speaker and had no intention of supporting him. She did not feel strongly about the incumbent mayor either, so at the beginning of the campaign she had decided to be as detached in her reporting as possible. As the campaign gained momentum, however, Yelena realized that the two opponents were on unequal footing and that the

---

[12] A pseudonym.

speaker, with the governor behind him, commanded much greater political and media resources than the incumbent mayor. This made her rethink her role in the campaign. Reluctantly, and guided in part by her understanding of balance and fairness, Yelena began to lend some additional publicity to the incumbent mayor – by interviewing him in her programs and offering him a platform to express his views. The moment she did that, she discovered, she began to be perceived as one who sided *with* the mayor and *against* the governor and who might have even been paid by the mayor's campaign headquarters to offer him additional publicity.

The campaign had an unexpected and inglorious ending. Four days prior to election day, the governor (Nemtsov) annulled the incumbent mayor's initiative to hold the referendum on the city charter. Bedniakov, the incumbent mayor, disobeyed the decree and ordered the preparations for the referendum to continue. The next day the governor convinced his protégé to withdraw his candidacy from the mayoral race. This prompted the local elections commission to cancel the elections. Finally, two days later, President Yeltsin (who was known to support Governor Nemtsov) issued a decree dismissing Bedniakov from his post as mayor of Nizhny Novgorod.[13] Journalists who supported Bedniakov were livid at the campaign's outcome; journalists who supported governor Nemtsov and his protégé Krestianinov were ashamed and perplexed; and journalists who tried to keep their distance, like Daria and Yelena, were perturbed by the ease with which they were pulled into the campaign against their choosing.

Journalism's Fragmentation

What I would like to highlight here is a number of unintended consequences that journalists' participation in that campaign brought about. Throughout the 1990s, those consequences would take on a life of their own as social forces fueling journalism's fragmentation. First, the initial encounter of journalism with money resulted in a substantial blurring of the boundaries between news and advertising via the notion of publicity that could refer to both. As mentioned earlier, until 2002, Russia had no comprehensive legal definition of

---

[13] In 1998, Boris Yeltsin annulled the decree as erroneous.

political advertising. From the word's common usage in Russian, *advertising* could mean "copy paid for by the client," or it could simply mean "favorable publicity." This ambiguity meant that during election campaigns, media managers could capitalize on candidates' need for publicity by construing just about any mention of a candidate in press or appearance on air as advertising. Like Volkov's *Sentinel* and many other outlets across the city, the broadcasting station where Yelena Yakovleva worked (NNTV) invited mayoral candidates to sign advertising contracts for the duration of the campaign. Because the definition of advertising could be stretched widely, the contracts did not stipulate in any precise terms what media outlets were, in fact, promising to candidates. Not surprisingly, this introduced tensions into relations between journalists and NNTV's management, but perhaps more important, it made many journalists doubt themselves as to whether they were, in fact, offering "free advertising" to candidates and, if so, what they could or should do about it.

The incumbent mayor did not sign an advertising contract with NNTV because he was initially reluctant to pay for political advertising on television altogether. But NNTV expected *all* candidates to sign advertising contracts with them; in fact, NNTV's director, Olga Noskova, admitted as much into Yelena's camera in a documentary film Yelena produced about the election. After it became clear that the mayor did not intend to pay NNTV for his electoral promotion, the director of NNTV signaled to journalists that any neutral or positive coverage of the mayor during the campaign was to be brought to a minimum, because it would count as advertising that he did not pay for. As a result, aside from Yelena Yakovleva's reporting, NNTV's coverage of municipal issues during the campaign more or less came to a halt. The mayor began to be mentioned primarily in the context of media attacks against him by Governor Nemtsov and his protégé. It is at this moment that Yelena rethought her role in the campaign and began to offer additional publicity to the mayor by interviewing him against her boss's injunctions.

Yet even Yelena was uncertain as to whether she was doing the right thing in those circumstances. Her documentary about the elections, titled "The Fourth Power," betrays this uncertainty. In an interview with the mayor on the eve of the election, Yelena asked him, "How do you explain the fact that a number of journalists are openly agitating (*angazhirovany*) in your favor?" The subtext of this question is, "Are you paying those journalists to promote your positions?" Mayor Bedniakov responded:

Okay, as far as journalists' engagement [*angazhement*] is concerned. Indeed, we have signed a contract with one federal channel to increase the coverage of the city's problems because I've been virtually shunned from the other channels. But if you analyze the programs on that channel in which I took part before I registered as a candidate, you will not find a single program where I promoted my electoral platform or where I spoke about my preparation for the elections.

A lawyer by training, Bedniakov seems to be putting forward a definition of (political) advertising here as media content that promotes a candidate's electoral platform – but only after the candidate has been registered as such. Whether or not such content is paid for by the candidate is secondary in this logic. Bedniakov did admit paying for the promotion of his platform (for "increased coverage of the city's problems," as he put it) but he made it clear that he was forced to do so. In an ideal world, according to Bedniakov, candidates should not pay for the promotion of their electoral platforms: the media should provide candidates space to do so for free.[14]

Yelena Yakovleva was suspicious of the distinctions Bedniakov was trying to draw, so she asked a clarifying question: "But [the mere fact of] your appearance on the screen is already political advertisement in your favor, is it not?" This question speaks volumes about the confusion and uncertainty of political journalists in Russia in the early 1990s. The view that any electoral publicity is already advertising is the view Yelena's management would have liked her to adopt so that the station could collect enough advertising income to last until the next campaign. Yelena was suspicious of that view, but she was equally suspicious of Bedniakov's perspective, where journalists hand the control over the message to the candidates themselves and do so "for free." It seems to me that Yelena found herself in a "lose-lose" situation professionally – caught between what the politicians wanted, on the one hand, and what media managers wanted, on the other. We could also interpret Yelena's question to the mayor as a throwing in the towel of sorts – as a turning of the issue of what separates news and advertising into a *public* matter in the face of journalism's seeming inability to

---

[14] This is in fact the principle behind the prohibition of paid political advertising in a number of Western European democracies.

make those distinctions on its own. Mayor Bedniakov snapped back: "Well, you know, if we follow this logic [where any publicity equals advertising] then I should just leave this place, forget about all of the city's problems, stop talking to the press, to anyone, because my onscreen appearance in conjunction with housing issues, with social issues can always be interpreted as political sympathies on the part of journalists and as electoral advertising on my part."

It is ironic that of all the players in this drama, it was the incumbent mayor who came closest to articulating a view about the porous border between news coverage and electoral publicity that journalists in Western democracies have long come to accept as a matter of fact. To Western journalists, political campaigns are inevitably periods when candidates try and often succeed in using journalists instrumentally. To counteract that, journalists in the United States and elsewhere have come up with ways of covering electoral politics that are intended to put journalists back in the driver's seat – by framing elections as strategy and tactics, discussing candidates' image-making efforts, assessing the accuracy of candidates' claims, and so on (Hallin 1994: 133–152). Beyond the free publicity they receive in the news, candidates may or may not be able to pay for additional publicity depending on what lawmakers in a particular country have decided is in the public interest. In the early post-Soviet environment, though, where the meanings of public and private and the relations between information and money were not yet stabilized, none of this was apparent. Defining advertising "simply" as that which the client pays for seemed unsatisfactory to many parties, including journalists such as Yelena. It also continued to be unsatisfactory to public officials working in Russia's regulatory agencies. Russia's advertising regulator, for instance, had issued several clarifications on the subject, specifying that "payability" does *not* constitute a valid criterion of advertising.[15]

The first law on advertising passed in Russia in 1995 did introduce the concept of political advertising (*politicheskaya reklama*), but it did not develop it. It was not until 2002 that a more comprehensive legal distinction between informing citizens about elections, and political campaigning for or against candidates (*predvybornaya agitatsia*) was spelled out in Russian electoral law. The problem in 2002 was that the

---

[15] For the latest clarification, see www.fas.gov.ru/clarifications/clarifica tions_30337.html (accessed February 4, 2014).

lawmakers more or less wrote journalists out of election law. Journalists were left with the responsibility for informing citizens about elections but were proscribed from engaging in political campaigning without explicitly marking it as such. Political campaigning was defined extremely broadly – as "activity aiding to create a positive or a negative impression of a candidate among voters" rather than as promotion of a particular platform or as copy paid for by the candidate. Under such broad definition of political campaigning, editorials and political commentary during election campaigns had to move into the advertising segments of newspapers and broadcast programs, which further shifted the control over the message to the candidates and away from journalists (see Chapter 3). Thus what started as media managers wrestling the right to make news judgments away from journalists during election campaigns turned into the perceived inability of the media on the whole to regulate themselves. With that perception in mind, the lawmakers stepped in, effectively weighing in on the side of media managers and candidates and against journalists.

Another unintended but long-term consequence of the 1994 campaign in Nizhny Novgorod was the emergence of real fault lines among journalists across the city, who only a short few years prior to that thought that they were in this together. Journalists' embroilment in electoral politics introduced a real sense of estrangement among them and a perception that there may be as many journalisms as there are journalists.

The documentary about the 1994 mayoral elections produced by Yelena Yakovleva and aired on NNTV a few weeks after the failed election conveys that estrangement particularly well. Yakovleva interviewed editors, publishers, prominent journalists, and her own boss, the director of NNTV, to get a sense of the effect the mayoral campaign had on the profession. The topic was obviously a sensitive one because interviewees shifted in their seats, sighed, and paused between sentences. A local correspondent for a national television channel, Nina Zvereva, who was a particularly ardent supporter of the governor during the campaign, admitted that she lost objectivity in her coverage of the election and proceeded to rationalize and justify her actions. A former *LS* editor, Vladimir Lapyrin, who became a publisher of a business weekly, said that he did not feel sorry for colleagues such as Zvereva – because "no one [was] forcing us to stay in this profession: we [could] always quit." Another former *LS* journalist, Valery

Semisalov, a columnist at an evening daily in Nizhny Novgorod at the time, expressed disbelief at the ease with which his colleagues across the city seemed to be "ready to sell not only their pens, but their souls." A colleague of his at the same paper shamed Daria Moskvina for having tainted her reputation by associating her name with the media attack against the incumbent mayor. "She is a young journalist – how is she going to live with this reputation?!" Alexander Volkov, editor and publisher of *The Sentinel*, however, was unapologetic. He claimed that he knew which media outlet was financed by whom during these elections, and he saw nothing wrong with it. When political advertising is the only game in town, Volkov said, media managers cannot afford to ignore it.

By the time I was conducting fieldwork in Nizhny Novgorod in 2001–2002, the rift among journalists that began with the mayoral campaign of 1994 graduated to entrenched animosities. By the early 2000s, there was a discomfiting history of acrid public fallouts between former colleagues, to the point that some were publishing *kompromat* against one another. Many journalists who worked during perestroika and the early post-Soviet years left the profession by the end of the 1990s, or like Daria and Yelena, they left political journalism in favor of business and financial reporting or consumer-oriented "news you can use."

Finally, yet another unintended outcome of the mayoral campaign, which would intensify with each subsequent set of elections throughout the 1990s and early 2000s, was readers' and viewers' growing distrust of journalists as people who have the public's best interest in mind. The fact that candidates were paying for coverage of their campaigns was not lost on anyone: as journalists supported "their" candidates and criticized, denounced, or shamed others, it became less and less clear to anyone watching the campaign whose civic-political ardor was genuine and whose was "bought" and "paid for." To most observers, campaign contributions flowing into media outlets during "harvest" periods cast a long shadow of moral doubt over the sincerity of journalists' rhetoric, no matter how independently arrived at that rhetoric might have been.

Yelena Yakovleva's documentary captured the beginning of this process, giving a glimpse of what Nizhny Novgorod dwellers thought about the press during the mayoral campaign of 1994. On the eve of the election, Yakovleva conducted about a dozen street interviews with people of various walks of life, all of whom turned out to be bitterly disappointed by what they were observing:

YELENA YAKOVLEVA (Y.Y.):	Who are you going to vote for, Bedniakov or Krestianinov?
VARIOUS PASSERS-BY:	No one! There is too much prattling, babbling, lying on television – we stopped believing what journalists have to say!
Y.Y.:	Do you think there is press freedom in Nizhny Novgorod today?
VARIOUS PASSERS-BY:	No way! Journalists are unfree like everyone else; they depend, like all of us, on their bosses, holding on to their jobs.
	Journalists used to be dependent on the Party before; today they depend on the ruble.
	Here, I am a university professor. My salary is 800 rubles [about $27 a month at the time]. How much is yours?
Y.Y.:	A little more.
VARIOUS PASSERS-BY:	A little more, hah? And who pays you?
Y.Y.:	The state [NNTV is funded by the regional parliament].
VARIOUS PASSERS-BY:	The state … So it buys you! The state buys you!

My goal in offering these historical and ethnographic vignettes has been to give an account of the economic, political, and cultural forces that worked together to produce new relations and practices of private media ownership in Russia in the early 1990s, which, in turn, had a profound effect on how journalism continued to be practiced and understood. As mentioned at the beginning of this chapter, my hunch is that in Russia these historical forces were operating in a social space characterized by much greater uncertainty than in countries in Eastern Europe and the Baltic region. Culturally, the postsocialist transition in those countries was broadly perceived as "a return to Europe," which was not the case in Russia. "A return to Europe" frame meant fewer reservations on the part of East European elites to imitate and, in some cases, to seek absorption by political, economic, legal, and cultural institutions of Western Europe. This imitative and absorptive logic extended fully into the domain of the mass media (Splichal 2001). Foreign capital was invited to enter East European media markets early on and with very few restrictions.

Unfortunately, there is very little ethnographic work that examined this process in Eastern Europe in greater detail. Dominic Boyer's (2005) ethnography of the absorption of the East German media system by its West German counterpart in the early 1990s remains the most insightful examination to date of how relations of private media ownership and the new practices of journalism were historically and culturally produced in a post-Soviet context with the advent of foreign capital. Admittedly, the German case is an extreme one: media institutions in East Germany went through a drastic top-down restructuring during the reunification process. The vast majority of journalists over the age of fifty were let go; many outlets were simply closed down; and control over others was turned over to media managers, editors, and owners appointed specifically for those jobs from West Germany.

Still, the process of media transformation in East Germany documented by Boyer (2005) is helpful for getting a general sense of what the initial encounter between journalism and capitalism looked like on the ground in the context of foreign media ownership. West Germans, Boyer (2005: 190) notes, acted as the "adults" of the transition: East Germans were understood as in need of guidance, seen as not quite capable of executing the transition on their own. The shift to West German ownership brought about "an immediate shift in organizational management to install what were described as 'western standards of democratic journalism'" (Boyer 2005: 190). Aside from replacing almost everyone in senior editorial positions, new owners "hired consultants to determine which former GDR journalists should be retained and which should be laid off or sent into early retirement" (Boyer 2005: 191). Some of the criteria for the layoffs included older age, lack of enthusiasm toward the transition, combative attitudes toward the new management, a lack of competitiveness, an inability to work under time pressure, and so on. Many of those who were retained or hired anew went through retraining seminars and paid internships at Western media organizations.

Western owners and consultants also had some say in editorial matters. Boyer (2005: 192) describes a case where the conservative media conglomerate Axel Springer acquired a regional daily newspaper in East Germany and sent a consultant to oversee the transition to new ownership. The consultant "informed the chief editor . . . that he should discontinue covering media politics: 'No one is interested in this. Put more information in . . . about the soaps and other TV series.' That command ended the only systematic coverage of the unfolding East German broadcasting politics within the east press" (Boyer 2005: 192). All the leftist journalists were soon let go; the reform-era chief editor himself was also fired, with the explanation that "he wasn't a 'newspaper man'" (Boyer 2005: 192). Not infrequently, Boyer's East German interlocutors commented to him that going through the transition made them acutely aware that West German journalism, too, represented a "System" – that is, a set of ideologies and disciplining practices of its own. Many journalists noted that people who seemed best adjusted to this new "System" were, in fact, the "Yes men and women" of the socialist period, whereas their more outspoken colleagues tended to be dismissed by the new management (Boyer 2005: 192).

Foreign ownership also meant the ability of unprofitable media outlets to absorb losses. Many foreign-owned outlets in Eastern Europe were able to remain unprofitable for a substantial period of time while the retraining of journalists – and the training of advertising and marketing personnel – continued. Unlike their Russian colleagues, journalists working for those outlets did not have to search for advertising on their own under the continual threat of losing their income. The fact that foreign-owned outlets set up advertising departments as distinct from news operations must have also helped to formally separate news and advertising, sparing many journalists in Eastern Europe the uncertainty of telling the two apart experienced by their Russian colleagues. It is also likely that the new managers of foreign-owned outlets brought with them specific criteria on evaluating and pricing journalistic labor. In the Russian context, in comparison, the question of who owed what to whom and what moral and human rules were to govern the practice of buying and selling journalistic labor and judging its value remained open for negotiation and contestation throughout the 1990s and into the early 2000s.

This is not to say that the unfolding dynamics of private media ownership I described for Russia were absent in Eastern Europe. After all, many of the historical forces that propelled the formation of private media ownership in Russia were present throughout the former Soviet bloc. Intrabureaucratic battles over the spheres of influence that involved the media, like the conflict between the mayor and the governor of Nizhny Novgorod region described earlier, were a common feature of the postsocialist landscape where the state was in the process of de- and recomposition. Economic destitution of newly private media outlets was certainly another historical condition shared across the region, as was media proprietors' reliance on politically motivated capital to keep their outlets afloat (Splichal 1994, 2001). A regulatory vacuum that resulted from the delayed passing of relevant media legislation was another common feature of the postsocialist media landscape (Voltmer 2013: 136). Finally, there is similarity across the former Soviet bloc in how journalists continued to understand their societal role and mission. The idea of journalistic objectivity, or the separation of fact and value, has always had little traction in Russia and Eastern Europe – before, during, and after the demise of socialism. Journalists' understanding of themselves as public intellectuals has often translated into their willingness to openly take sides in political conflicts. It may have also meant that compared with their Western colleagues, Russian and Eastern European journalists were less queasy about the presence of politically motivated capital in their media outlets.

Nevertheless, the substantial presence of foreign capital in Eastern European media markets, the shorter period of regulatory vacuum before the requisite media laws were passed, and the overall cultural frame of "a return to Europe" – all these forces worked together to create a centripetal pull that helped to standardize journalists' encounter with capitalism in Eastern Europe. In Russia, however, the unprecedented level of uncertainty that characterized journalism's encounter with capitalism in the early 1990s created a strong centrifugal push, splitting journalism into bits and pieces and sending them in multiple directions. Early post-Soviet journalism became a personal rather than a collective project. As many of my interlocutors pointed out in the early 2000s, whoever did not leave the profession by the mid-1990s now felt that they were "on their own" and working primarily "for themselves."

The claim I am making here – that there were few, if any, centripetal forces to counteract the fragmentation of journalism in Russia during the 1990s – can also be illustrated by another fieldwork finding of mine. I discovered that while there was at least some agreement (among the journalists I worked with) on what constituted egregious violations of journalistic behavior, I found that there was no corresponding position of journalistic virtue on which they could collectively agree. Instead, one had plenty of opportunities to witness mutual accusations among journalists in unprofessionalism, irresponsibility, disrespect for the audience, abuse of press freedom, selling out, and other journalistic sins. These accusations were compounded by the breakdown of the Soviet system of on-the-job mentorship and peer control among journalists, by fast spread of behind-closed-doors appraisals of journalistic labor by private employers, by fast turnover of personnel, by a sharp loss of occupational solidarity and prestige, and by an understanding that journalism ethics was now a deeply personal rather than collective matter.

To make sense of such fragmentation of a profession, I find it useful to talk about the *privatization of journalism* after the fall of the Soviet Union. Privatization is usually thought about in economic and legal terms as a change from public (state) to private ownership, accompanied by legal mechanisms to support the new economic forms. But as scholars of postsocialism (Dunn 2004; Humphrey 2002; Verdery 1996, 2003) and neoliberalism (Barry et al. 1996; Ferguson 2006; Hibou 2004) have amply documented, privatization is never only a shift in forms of ownership: it has a profound effect on the state itself, transforming practices of governance, and on the public and social realms, reconfiguring people's senses of solidarity, obligation, and commitment. Privatization does this by prying open and letting loose the meanings and structures of public and private, creating unexpected and often confusing spaces for political, economic, and moral actions. Individual actions gain special importance during such transitional moments – as nodes around which the newly reconfigured structures of public and private take shape.

Following Beatrice Hibou (2004: 15–18), we can view the process that unfolded in and around journalism after socialism as a case of private actors treading public territory in the atmosphere of continuing moral and institutional uncertainty and volatility unleashed by privatization. If we think of Soviet journalism as public (state) territory that journalists occupied as public (state) actors, then the various forms of hustling in and around the media we observed in the 1990s can be seen precisely as a case of private actors treading formerly public territory. It is important, Hibou (2004) emphasizes, that we do not reduce this process merely to corruption or adulteration of a public domain by private interest. Rather, Hibou suggests, *both* public and private domains go through a metamorphosis as a result of such encounters: the public domain experiences a degree of devolution, while private actors arrogate new public roles, infusing the public domain with new logics. What this new and substantially devolved public domain ended up looking like in Russia in the late 1990s and early 2000s is the subject of Chapter 3.

3 | From the Fourth Estate to the Second Oldest Profession

The public rejection of journalism that began in Russia in 1993–1995 accelerated through Boris Yeltsin's reelection campaign of 1996, peaking in the late 1990s and early 2000s when nationally known journalists became the public faces of information wars among the new Russian oligarchs and other powerful political players. Russian media scholars usually point to those information wars as evidence of media ownership concentration and of media instrumentalization by Russia's power-holders in the first decade after the fall of the Soviet Union (Koltsova 2006; Mickiewicz 1999; Oates 2006; Voltmer 2013). Very little, however, has been written on the cultural fallout of those information wars – that is, on the lasting effects of routinely treating the media as a weapon and a war zone – for journalism and for society at large.

This chapter fills this important gap, asking what happens to the need to seek truth and to speak it to power – arguably the kernel of journalism as a profession with a public mission – under the circumstances of rapid and full-blown instrumentalization of the media. This chapter is based on eleven months of ethnographic fieldwork in newsrooms in Nizhny Novgorod in 2001–2002. During this period, the city of Nizhny Novgorod and the region surrounding it lived through two rounds of elections – for a gubernatorial and a mayoral seat. Those elections are widely considered to have been the most manipulative in Nizhny Novgorod's recent history due to an unprecedented degree of smear campaigning that was employed. Those campaigns quickly gained nationwide notoriety, speeding up the passage of Russia's restrictive election law of 2002 (SMI-NN.RU 2002). As noted in Chapter 2, the intention of the 2002 law was to rid election coverage of promotional content; in reality, lawmakers ended up severely restricting what journalists could in fact say during an election season without it counting as electoral advertising and needing it to be marked and paid for as such.

Changing Patterns of Media Ownership

After the fall of the Soviet Union, as discussed in Chapter 2, the majority of newly private media outlets in Nizhny Novgorod were still owned by their initial founders, often former Soviet journalists. Recall how Alexander Volkov, for instance, was the primary owner of *The Sentinel* and remained in control of its editorial policy despite the fact that his newspaper was struggling and he was desperate to do almost anything to keep it in business. Volkov ended up staying afloat throughout the mid-1990s by retailing his journalists' labor to politicians and entrepreneurs seeking publicity without needing to sell *The Sentinel* to more powerful players eager to acquire media resources of their own.

This is precisely what changed by the early 2000s, a decade after the fall of the Soviet Union. By then, most media outlets in Nizhny Novgorod came to be formally or informally controlled by what Russian sociologist Olessia Koltsova (2006) called "cross-institutional groups." Cross-institutional groups (CIGs) emerged in Russia in the late 1990s and early 2000s where, in circumstances of "state capture" or "state failure," groups of individuals from different social institutions would pool together resources to jointly struggle for and wield power. Such groups included financiers, businesspeople, state agents (particularly those with access to the distribution of public resources, such as governors or mayors of large cities), and representatives of security agencies acting in a private capacity (Koltsova 2006: 18; Volkov 2002). CIGs could be understood as proto-state structures that took shape in the post-Soviet period when the state was still in the process of de- and recomposition. Vladimir Putin's rise to power in the early 2000s can be understood in those terms – as one CIG, comprised of economic, financial, government, and security agents loyal to Putin, eventually taking over competing CIGs.

By the late 1990s nationally and by the early 2000s regionally, most CIGs made it a priority to add media to their arsenal of resources with which to struggle for and wield power. Thus began the process of media ownership concentration, with the concomitant transfer of editorial control from individual media managers to representatives of CIGs. In Nizhny Novgorod, this process can once again be illustrated by the story of *The Sentinel*, Alexander Volkov's newspaper. *The Sentinel* began as a privately owned, individually run publication, yet by 1999 it became part of an unofficial media conglomerate controlled by a powerful CIG. Two CIGs were particularly prominent in the Nizhny Novgorod region at the time: one was forming around a local businessman and politician named Dmitri Saveliev and the other around a presidential envoy to the region named Sergei Kirienko.[1] Former allies, Saveliev and Kirienko made their initial careers in oil-related business in Nizhny Novgorod in the mid-1990s. By the late 1990s, Saveliev had become the head of Russia's oil-transporting monopoly and a Member of the Duma, while Kirienko enjoyed brief stints as Minister of Energy and as Russia's Prime Minister (it was under his premiership in 1998 that Russia defaulted on its loans and sharply devalued its currency).

By 2000, both men had lost some of their standing in Moscow and returned to Nizhny Novgorod, their base. No longer allies but adversaries, they were now competing for the political domination of the region and were concentrating resources toward that goal. In addition to courting regional businesspeople, Saveliev (the oil magnate turned Member of the Duma) allied himself with the incumbent mayor of Nizhny Novgorod, Yuri Lebedev. Sergei Kirienko (the Prime Minister turned presidential envoy), in his turn, recruited the allegiance of the incumbent governor, Ivan Skliarov. Both the mayor and the governor were nearing the end of their terms, though, and would soon have to fight for reelection: the new gubernatorial election was set for 2001 and the new mayoral election for 2002. To fight those and other electoral battles, the CIGs led by Saveliev and Kirienko set about buying or otherwise establishing control over as many influential media outlets in Nizhny Novgorod as they could.

The CIG controlled by Sergei Kirienko ended up assuming formal or informal ownership of a local television station, a regional news agency, a radio station, and several newspapers.[2] Volkov's *Sentinel* – by now a popular political tabloid – was initially on the list of media assets that the Kirienko-controlled CIG was intent on acquiring. However, Volkov did not want to sell his newspaper to Kirienko's group, he told me in an interview in the summer of 2000, because he

---

[1] Kirienko is currently serving as First Deputy Chief of Staff in Putin's presidential administration. Between 2005 and 2016, he was the head of Rosatom, Russia's state nuclear energy corporation.

[2] On the porous boundaries between media owners, sponsors, and advertisers in late 1990s and early 2000s Russia, see Koltsova (2006: 73–85).

did not trust that the new owners would continue to fund the newspaper once the elections were over. Additionally, he disliked the aggressiveness with which representatives of Kirienko's CIG pursued *The Sentinel*, to the point of threatening Volkov if he continued to resist the selling of his newspaper. This prompted Volkov to turn to Kirienko's rival, Saveliev (the oil magnate turned Member of the Duma). Eventually, Volkov pulled a complicated business maneuver. Caving in to the threats coming from Kirienko's CIG, Volkov did agree to sell *The Sentinel* to that CIG. At the same time, he convinced the entire staff of *The Sentinel* to quit and to join him in launching a new publication, where he would hold 51 percent of the shares, with the remaining shares held by Dmitri Saveliev, the leader of the rival CIG. To add insult to injury, Volkov's new publication kept the format and style of the old *Sentinel*, adding *Novyi* ("New") before the title. Volkov and Saveliev must have gotten along because *The New Sentinel*[3] became one of the key publications in Saveliev's media holdings, with whose help Saveliev won his seat in the Russian Duma in December 1999 and fought many other battles in 2000–2002. By 2000, Saveliev's media conglomerate also included two local television stations, a regional news agency, and several other newspapers, including *Leninskaya Smena Plus* (*LS Plus*), a brand-new tabloid launched in hopes of capitalizing on the reputation of the Soviet-era *LS*.

While Saveliev's media holdings were comprised of more recognizable brands on the Nizhny Novgorod media scene, it was Sergei Kirienko's CIG that was in fact more powerful because of Kirienko's connections all the way to the Kremlin. This was the main reason why I wanted to study an outlet controlled by that CIG. As is always the case with ethnographic work, it took me several months to build trust with editors, publishers, and journalists in Nizhny Novgorod who could then vouch for me to their colleagues working in media outlets controlled by Kirienko.[4] The private newspaper where I ended up conducting several months of fieldwork was called *The Observer*.[5] It was founded in 1996 by a local entrepreneur named Andrey Portnoy,[6]

---

[3] A pseudonym.

[4] It also meant that for editors and journalists in the Saveliev media holdings, I was seen as someone who sympathized with their rivals. Alexander Volkov and another editor from the Saveliev media holdings declined to meet with me until the electioneering for the mayor's seat in 2002 was over.

[5] A pseudonym.   [6] A pseudonym.

who originally envisioned *The Observer* as a business weekly that he felt Nizhny Novgorod was still lacking. And, indeed, for the first few years of its existence, *The Observer* stayed away from open politicking, concentrating on economic and consumer trends in the region. Things changed dramatically when Sergei Kirienko, the Prime Minister turned presidential envoy, returned to Nizhny Novgorod and became intent on concentrating media resources with which to wage electoral and other battles. It so happened that Kirienko's media man, a Russian "Karl Rove" named Maxim Rybak,[7] who had followed Kirienko to and from Moscow, had been one of *The Observer's* original shareholders. Until 1999, Maxim Rybak had little interest in what was going on at *The Observer*, allowing Portnoy, the main owner, to run the newspaper as he saw fit. Once Kirienko and Rybak returned to Nizhny Novgorod, though, Rybak assumed a much tighter control over *The Observer*, with Portnoy apparently going along with it. The previous editor of *The Observer* was let go, and a new editor answering directly to Rybak was put in his place. The new editor did not last very long and was replaced by another and then yet another a year later.

Further Deprofessionalization of Journalism

The way its last editor, Alina Narinskaya,[8] ran *The Observer* was in stark contrast to what I had witnessed at a publishing house in Nizhny Novgorod called *Birzha* ("Stock Exchange"), where I conducted initial fieldwork and acquired contacts before moving on to *The Observer*.[9] To begin with, *Birzha* allowed me to come and go as I pleased. I was let in on both the editorial meetings and discussions of *Birzha*'s financial and management matters. Nothing of this sort was the case at *The Observer*, which remained a secretive operation. Every time I came in, I had to obtain permission from the editor to enter the building, which often took up to an hour. I was never able to meet the owners themselves. At *Birzha*, the editorial meetings were quite open: journalists were encouraged to invite to those meetings acquaintances or people they had written about as representatives of *Birzha*'s

---

[7] A pseudonym.   [8] A pseudonym.
[9] The *Birzha* publishing house was an exception on Nizhny Novgorod media scene, while publications such as *The Sentinel* and *The Observer* were the norm.

target audience. *Birzha*'s publisher and chief editor, a former *LS* editor Vladimir Lapyrin, introduced in Chapter 1, kept the editorial meetings long, in line with the Soviet practice. During those meetings, staff journalists took turns discussing and evaluating one another's work, voted on the best story of the issue (month, year), and planned the next issue. In contrast, at *The Observer*, the editorial meetings were infrequent and short and consisted mostly of Narinskaya, the editor, assigning stories and topics to reporters and specifying the angles from which the event or the topic should be covered. There was no pitching of stories by rank-and-file reporters to the editor and no peer evaluation of one another's work at *The Observer*. Senior journalists did sometimes pitch stories to Narinskaya, but always in private, never during staff meetings.

One of the most common concerns of journalists that I heard at *The Observer* was whether a topic, an angle on a story, the choice of experts for commentaries, or the simple mentioning of someone by name was "cleared" (*soglasovano*) with the outlet's owners and political patrons. On a wall in the newsroom, there was a typed-up sheet with a list of about two dozen names, members of Nizhny Novgorod's political, economic, and cultural elite. Those names were *not* to be mentioned in *The Observer*'s publications under any circumstances. However, some of the names were crossed out, and others had been added by hand, which suggested that the blacklist was not cut in stone but continued to shift as political circumstances changed. When I asked journalists about the list, they said that it was drafted a while ago and many things have changed since then, but they still sometimes consulted it to guide their writing. When the editor was not around to clarify whether something or someone had been cleared for publication, senior journalists, more privy to *The Observer*'s politics, filled in for the editor. But when the editor was present, everyone, including senior journalists, kept checking with the editor if a particular detail in the text they were working on might run counter to the interests of the owners and sponsors. No one, it seemed, wanted to make the mistake of submitting a piece that did not agree with the paper's party line both in spirit and in detail. There had been too many times, I was told, when a story or a commentary was killed because the political wind changed too quickly for the journalist to catch, and the journalist was left without an honorarium for the story.

Journalists thus were placed in starkly subordinate positions vis-à-vis the editor, owners, patrons, and sponsors of *The Observer*. The degree of subordination, I came to believe, was greater than in the early 1990s, when journalists still exercised some limited freedom of judgment in their coverage of regional politics despite the dire economic conditions their outlets were in. Recall from Chapter 2 how during the mayoral campaign of 1994, Alexander Volkov, editor and publisher of *The Sentinel*, did not force his journalists to take editorial positions favorable toward Governor Nemtsov and his protégé running for mayor. This was despite the fact that Nemtsov and his protégé were effectively providing a financial bailout package to Volkov's newspaper with their electoral funds – which meant that they could, in principle, attach any conditions they wanted to those funds.[10] Recall also how Yelena Yakovleva, a political journalist for NNTV, a local broadcasting station, acted on her understanding of balance and fairness when she decided to provide the incumbent mayor, Dmitry Bedniakov, with free electoral publicity despite her boss's injunctions. Yakovleva did *not* lose her job after disobeying her boss who had instructed NNTV staff to starve the mayor of electoral publicity because he did not intend to pay for it. In fact, there is a scene in Yakovleva's documentary, aired on NNTV after the failed elections, where Yakovleva and her boss, Olga Noskova, take turns interviewing one another about the media's role in the campaign. Yakovleva stands by her decision to provide the mayor with free publicity in the run-up to the elections, citing the importance of striving for balance in representing all sides of the electoral conflict. Noskova defends her view – that all candidates should expect to pay for publicity during an election season. Both views are thus equally represented on air despite the fact that one comes from a journalist and the other from the director of the station.

By the time I was conducting fieldwork at *The Observer* in 2002, there was hardly any room for journalists to make individual news judgments. Many aspects of journalists' work looked like wage labor to me: their work was highly supervised; there was no mentorship, no peer control of the quality of work, and little solidarity with colleagues in

---

[10] It helped that Governor Nemtsov was known as a liberal figure and a champion of press freedom in the region. Naturally charismatic, he preferred political spin to outright pressure on media outlets to get his message across.

other outlets. Their workload was irregular and commonly determined by editorial fiat, and instead of a salary, their earnings were piecemeal, privately negotiated, and off the books, which created room for arbitrary decisions by the management about who gets to be paid when and in what amount. During the several months I spent at *The Observer*, journalists' paychecks (or rather cash payments) were routinely delayed weeks at a time, which everyone was very unhappy about, openly at editorial meetings and in private conversations. Alina Narinskaya, *The Observer*'s editor, kept citing "financial difficulties" with advertisers and sponsors and repeatedly asked journalists to "wait a couple more weeks." Once in a while, a rumor would spread that the money finally came through, and indeed, Narinskaya would announce that the money was on its way. However, the first ones to receive anything would be the senior journalists, while everyone else would be routinely asked to wait a little more.

Not surprisingly, such working conditions resulted in a very high turnover of personnel. At the time I was visiting *The Observer*, only the senior journalists (including Svetlana Bulgakova, introduced in Chapter 2) had been working there for more than a year; everyone else was new. The rank-and-file writers were young and inexperienced. As mentioned in Chapter 2, more experienced journalists had left the profession by the late 1990s or left political journalism in favor of business and consumer reporting or public relations jobs. Some of the younger journalists I talked with at *The Observer* told me that they were there for the expressed purpose of earning some cash from election campaigns; journalism itself was not their passion, and they did not plan to stay in the profession for long. In addition to working at *The Observer*, some of them simultaneously moonlighted at other candidates' campaign headquarters or wrote advertising copy under pseudonyms – both for *The Observer* and on the side.

Needless to say, these working conditions were detrimental to journalists' morale, weakening their professional identification with one another and lessening their collective-bargaining power vis-à-vis their employers, all of which was made easier amid the continuing confusion about the relationship between publicity and money. Spending some time with entry-level reporters at *The Observer*, I was struck by how their primary identification seemed to be with the owners and patrons of *The Observer* rather than with their colleagues across the city – a fact to which they did not seem to give much thought. One day I asked them to explain to me "who was whom" on the blacklist mentioned earlier that had been casually hung above one of the reporter's desks. One of the people on the list was Valentina Buzmakova, a former *LS* journalist who was considered to be one of the best news reporters in Gorky during the Soviet years. Buzmakova established her own news agency in the 1990s and was fiercely trying to remain an independent player on the Nizhny Novgorod media scene in the early 2000s. Her twenty-minute question-and-answer program of political interviews would be picked up by one local television channel after another, only to be canceled on every channel because of Buzmakova's criticism of those channels' owners and sponsors. "So how did Buzmakova make it onto this list?" I asked this group of reporters at *The Observer*. "It's interesting, actually," one of them volunteered an explanation. "I think everyone here knows that we are supposed to dislike Buzmakova, but no one really knows why" – a remark that must have struck home because it elicited a unanimous chuckle. Another time I asked a reporter why journalists at *The Observer* had not formed a union to better protect their interests. "We don't need a union," the reporter replied, "Alina [Narinskaya, the *Observer*'s editor] is our union. If we need something, we ask her."

A sense of alienation from colleagues across the city was even more palpable among senior journalists at *The Observer*. This was not especially surprising because many senior journalists across Nizhny Novgorod became the public faces of the information war the two most powerful CIGs in the region were waging against one another. "There are caste-like divisions today among us," Svetlana Bulgakova, a leading writer for *The Observer* at the time, told me in response to my question about journalistic solidarity. "We used to all hang out together, us and people from the [rival] media conglomerate, used to joke about how things are on the other side of the frontlines. That is gone now; things are more serious today." One of the reasons for this chill in relations was surely the publication of a regular column in *The Observer* titled, "The Department of Morals" (*Otdel nravov*). The column (believed by some to have been written by Bulgakova) came out regularly throughout 2001 and contained flat-out *kompromat* – disparaging accusations and spiteful gossip that may or may not have been true – about various public figures in Nizhny Novgorod who for one reason or another crossed paths with *The Observer*'s owners and their political allies. The column was never discussed in editorial meetings. It was published unsigned, inviting wide speculation as to who was really behind it. The very first dose of *kompromat* released by "The Department of Morals" targeted Alexander Rezontov, head of news division at Volga TV, a regional television station controlled at the time by Dmitry Saveliev's CIG. At least another half a dozen character assassination pieces targeting other journalists working for media outlets controlled by Saveliev followed. Saveliev's media managers did not hesitate to strike back. A brand-new tabloid called *Leninskaya Smena Plus* (*LS Plus*) was created for the express purpose of partaking in the *kompromat* wars between the two rival CIGs. *LS Plus* became the mirror image of "The Department of Morals" column in *The Observer*. Now it was journalists at *The Observer* such as Bulgakova who became the targets of vituperative media attacks in *LS Plus* and elsewhere.[11]

Even when journalists were not the direct object of attack in the press, they operated in an atmosphere poisoned by the spiteful discourse of their colleagues that often translated into personal animosities. On one occasion, I was visiting *Nizhegorodskie Novosti* (*Nizhny Novgorod News*), a daily newspaper that was not part of either of the media conglomerates dominating the city's media scene in 2001–2002. *Nizhegorodskie Novosti* had been founded by the regional parliament and thus was technically a government-owned newspaper. The parliament (filled primarily by regional businessmen) and its speaker were trying to play their own political game but were increasingly coming under the influence of Sergei Kirienko, the presidential envoy with connections to the Kremlin. This meant that *Nizhegorodskie Novosti* was increasingly controlled by Kirienko's media team, which was starting to show in the selection of stories and frames. When I visited journalists at *Nizhegorodskie Novosti*, they were working on promotional materials for a mayoral candidate running as a red herring to deflect votes from the incumbent mayor, Yuri Lebedev. Lebedev's reelection campaign was backed by Dmitry Saveliev, the oil magnate turned Member of the Duma and leader of the rival CIG. When I asked the journalists about their relations with colleagues working for the Saveliev media holdings, their stark reaction startled me:

[11] The wide spread of *kompromat* in the late 1990s and early 2000s was no doubt aided by the difficulty of putting an end to it through legal channels. As Koltsova (2006: 108) explains, the lack of independence of Russia's courts, their slow work, and the difficulty of proving that the journalist had libelous intentions all aided in the proliferation of *kompromat*. When the courts did find journalists guilty, the gains to media organizations of having published *kompromat* were usually greater than the fines journalists were ordered to pay to plaintiffs.

The journalists who work there, who work for Saveliev, for Lebedev [the incumbent mayor backed by Saveliev] – they are just scum. It is they who produce that vile little election paper [a short-lived pamphlet rumored to be produced by journalists at *The Sentinel* in support of Lebedev's reelection campaign]. You can easily tell who writes those texts – it is [X] who does it, and you can see, she does it with great pleasure, in that jeering tone of hers. Those people, that "team of journalists" wants to get back at us for something, they are pouring all sorts of filth and mud on us, mangling our names by making their pseudonyms out of them. They must be expecting that there will be some sort of response from us – but they wait in vain. We do not react to filth and mud. (Author's field notes, June 2002)

As I contemplated this answer, a passage from Alexander Volkov's 2000 interview came to mind. "I do not believe in journalistic solidarity," he asserted to me. "If the interests of my investor contradict the interests of another investor, the investors will collide, and the journalists will be pushed against one another. What journalistic solidarity are you talking about? It was during the 1980s that journalists were united. Today everyone is on their own."

The Naked Truth about Journalism

As mentioned at the beginning of this chapter, these information wars between rival political groups are usually interpreted as evidence of full-scale instrumentalization of the media by Russian power-holders by the end of the first post-Soviet decade. According to sociologist Alena Ledeneva (2006: 70), for instance, the main purpose of *kompromat* is "not to discover the truth" but to put pressure on political opponents and business competitors. In this sense, *kompromat* can be seen as the purest form of media instrumentalization. Ledeneva (2006) sees continuity between post-Soviet *kompromat* and other extralegal practices in Russia, such as blackmail and what is known in Russia as *krugovaya poruka*, or controlling the behavior of others through mutual restraint and suspended punishment. This is why, Ledeneva (2006) explains, it often does not matter whether or not *kompromat* is factually accurate: made-up accusations can produce as strong of an effect on the target of *kompromat* as would truthful revelations.

As important as these perspectives are, they remain inattentive to the effects media instrumentalization has had on journalism as a cultural institution with a public mission. Journalists who are forced to or who choose to produce *kompromat* do so not as automatons but as social actors with their own understanding of what they are doing. As journalists act on those understandings in specific circumstances, they produce new meanings of what counts as normal or appropriate journalistic behavior in the public realm. Those new meanings, in turn, may have an effect on how journalism is experienced as a forum for truth-seeking and truth-telling – both within the profession and outside of it. This and the next section seek to capture this dynamic.

As discussed in Chapter 1, Soviet journalists understood themselves as representatives of the state, as coparticipants in the Soviet governing project. At the same time, particularly in the late Soviet period, journalists saw themselves and were widely seen as "the most humane leg" of Soviet power, to which the average citizen, unjustly wronged by other bureaucracies, could turn for help. Siding with the "little man" (*chelovek*) against the offending bureaucracies and underscoring the average person's humanity were an important frame through which journalists in the late Soviet period understood their role and mission. During perestroika and the early 1990s, as discussed in Chapter 2, Russia's journalists embraced a different metaphor for the role of the press – that of the Fourth Estate. In the perestroika context, the Fourth Estate symbolism was particularly apt because it combined classic liberal caveats about freedom of speech with a socially progressive view of journalists as *telos*-setting public intellectuals.

By the end of the 1990s, yet another metaphor emerged – that of the second oldest profession – through which journalism in Russia began to be talked about and understood. Discussions of journalism as "selling out" began to pick up in Russia in the mid-1990s: we saw an early instance of that discourse in street interviews recorded by Yelena Yakovleva in Chapter 2. When I arrived in Nizhny Novgorod for an extended period of fieldwork in 2001, references to journalism as political prostitution were everywhere in public culture,[12] so I wanted to know whether and how this metaphor resonated with journalists themselves. Perhaps not surprisingly, I found many journalists struggling with it, especially in reference to themselves. At the same time,

---

[12] The Google Ngram Viewer (https://books.google.com/ngrams) makes it possible to search for the incidence of the term *second oldest profession* (*vtoraya drevneishaya professia*) from hundreds of years ago up through 2008 in a large corpus of Russian books. It shows that this term was almost nonexistent prior to 1990 but started rising sharply in 1993, reaching an eventual peak in 2003.

there was clearly some relaxing into the metaphor going on, especially when it was invoked in reference to colleagues or to the profession as a whole.[13]

At *The Observer* and elsewhere, I encountered a rich vocabulary through which the "second oldest profession" was experienced in daily practice. Journalists spoke about having to "spread themselves under" a politician or a businessman (*lozhit'sia pod politika*), about being expected to "lick all over" their sponsors and clients (*oblizyvat'*), and about living with the sense of being bought (*oshchushchenie kuplennosti*). Some, disturbingly, invoked the rape metaphor, claiming that "if you can't do anything about it, you should try to relax and enjoy it." If or when given a choice of whom to "spread themselves under," journalists spoke about choosing a politician or a businessman they found "least disgusting" (*naimenee protiven*) or someone they personally liked. At the same time, journalists were aware of the importance of keeping some emotional distance from their patrons and sponsors. They spoke about the danger of developing "a crush" (*prikipet'*) or getting "all pumped up" (*kolotit'sia*) about a political figure to the point of becoming too attached to him or her and later unable to find work, if need be, at a rival media holding. This tension – between doing it "for money" and "out of love" – was made especially obvious to me one day when I overheard Alina Narinskaya, *The Observer*'s editor, tell one of her employees: "Cover it up with a little journalistic opinion, or it looks too much like barefaced advertisement [*golimaya reklama*]!"

As already mentioned, there was a big difference between how entry-level and senior journalists were treated at *The Observer*. In addition to the differences in how these two groups were assigned tasks and were paid, the distinction manifested in the amount of room for maneuvering each group was given in the handling of the most unpleasant of tasks. Senior journalists, for instance, could avoid praising owners and sponsors or could stay away from producing particularly distasteful *kompromat* against political rivals, whereas their less experienced colleagues did not have that luxury. "The management does not force me to write the most blatant orders [*otkrovennuyu zakazukhu*]," said

---

[13] This is similar to how people related to the phenomenon of *blat*, or the use of personal connections for private gain, studied by Alena Ledeneva (1998). Ledeneva notes that few of her interlocutors admitted to using *blat* themselves but asserted that others use *blat* all the time.

Sergei Khralamov,[14] one of the senior journalists at *The Observer*. "I mostly edit them. It is the girls who come here from the streets [*s ulitsy*] who end up writing those. They all have families to feed, so they are trying to make a little money here."

How did one become one of the select few at *The Observer*?, I wondered. Through conversations with journalists who had left the newspaper and via observations of daily routines there, I concluded that in order to move up *The Observer*'s hierarchy, one had to write well, get along with management, understand how regional politics works, develop a voice of one's own so as to maintain some critical distance from political patrons and sponsors, but at the same time be willing to do dirty work for one's employers at least once in a while. In Sergei Kharlamov's case, it turned out that he had been the editor of the notorious "Department of Morals" column at *The Observer*. He told me that he disliked editing the column but did it anyway until he was permitted to close it down. The orders for the column, the people to attack, and the substance of the "revelations" came from the very top of the media holding. Kharlamov did write some of the entries himself, attacking the character of fellow journalists working for rival media holdings. He justified it by writing only about men but not women – that was the line he decided he would not cross. Later he ran into one of the men he had written about – a local journalist who himself had the reputation of a media assassin. The two men apparently understood one another, agreeing that they were little more than pawns in the political game played by the owners of their outlets.[15]

Rationalization was by far the most common reaction I encountered when interviewing political journalists about what they thought they were doing at *The Observer* and beyond. Because of the topic's sensitivity, I did not consider it appropriate to ask my interlocutors directly whether they felt they were "prostituting" themselves in their work. How journalists navigated their moral worlds needed to be studied indirectly, I decided, through observations and interview questions that

[14] A pseudonym.
[15] Kharlamov was frank and straightforward but not cynical, unlike some of the other journalists I interviewed. Leaning toward the extreme left of the political spectrum, he was disgusted by the poverty to which both Yeltsin's and Putin's governments subjected the majority of Russia's citizens, but he saw no way out of it. He was grateful to me for a number of Western antiglobalization articles, both scholarly and lay, that I pulled up, having learned of his interest in the topic.

would probe my interlocutors' relationship with their conscience without me coming across as condescending. To have the conversations I wanted, I asked journalists about their personal histories of working on the campaign trail or writing on order, the demands such work entailed, the payments it brought, and the level of "psychological discomfort," as I put it, that such work generated. I would ask whether they felt they could refuse to write on order and how they negotiated for themselves the lines they would and would not cross. I would also probe their relationship with the prostitution metaphor by asking whether they ever had to act against their conscience (*krivit' dushoi*), to "step over themselves" (*perestupat' cherez sebia*), and how that made them feel.

Having framed my inquiries in this way, I ended up placing my interlocutors in positions where they were especially likely to offer rationalizations of behaviors they might have been ambivalent about or even ashamed of. "I do not consider myself a servant [*ja ne derzhu sebia za obslugu*]," Svetlana Bulgakova of *The Observer* told me. "But I *can* write something 'on order' if it coincides with my personal beliefs. I can also turn it down if I am not interested in it. What makes it harder for me is that a lot of people depend on the money I bring into the newspaper [as a leading columnist]. I guess I am a team player." What about the journalist's responsibility to the audience?, I asked. "I try to remain an active player," Bulgakova answered with some hesitation. "If it were all up to me, I would have probably 'drowned' [*potopila*] most of [the city's politicians] a long time ago," she smiled. Bulgakova's colleague at *The Observer*, a young but talented journalist named Kira Tarasova,[16] quickly becoming one of the select few, echoed this sentiment. "I do not hold anyone up as my [political] idols, maybe only as friends, as acquaintances," Kira said to me. "Even if they come visit our home, I am not constrained in what I can write about them the next day. It's very important to me that I'm able to write what I consider important. Crudely put, I like to strip power holders in public."

Being a team player or a friend, writing out of convictions rather than on order, setting the terms of the game, maintaining an adversarial position toward all power-holders – these are all positive moral categories by which many Nizhny Novgorod journalists portrayed to me what they understood themselves to be doing. "I can say no if I want

---

[16] A pseudonym.

to," "I myself decide which politician I will work for," "I try to maneuver as much as I can," and "There are lines I will not cross" were common responses during my interviews. Again, observations of everyday work routines rounded out the picture emerging from the interviews, suggesting greater moral discomfort and anxiety on the part of journalists but also, paradoxically, a certain relaxing into the prostitution metaphor as time went on.

The *Observer* was a weekly newspaper, so on days when the new issue had just come out and the pace of work was slower, one could discern a more irreverent and facetious attitude toward politicians and other VIPs in the *Observer*'s newsroom. Regardless of their cross-institutional affiliation, key regional political players were often referred to by diminutive nicknames journalists had created for them. "Every one of us here has their own 'kitty,'" another up-and-coming journalist at *The Observer*, Lilia Sadykova,[17] told me. "My favorite is Kitty [*kiska*] Senturin [deputy governor of Nizhny Novgorod region at the time, running in the mayoral race of 2002]. Svetlana [Bulgakova]'s favorite is Kitty Dikin [deputy head of the regional parliament at the time and another mayoral candidate during the 2002 campaign]." Indeed, a large portrait of the photogenic Mikhail Dikin (courtesy of his electoral campaign headquarters) adorned one of the walls of the room where *The Observer*'s journalists worked, but instead of just hanging there, Dikin's portrait had been touched up by a thick black marker with a moustache, beard, horns, and a pair of large earrings added to Dikin's picture-perfect face. On his cheeks, someone left fat lipstick marks in the shape of a kiss. "They are going to completely destroy this poster while I am on vacation," complained Svetlana Bulgakova, half-joking, half-serious. "I'll probably have to bring another one from home when I get back."

This ambivalent dynamic where a journalist's subordinate position toward power-holders coexisted with a jeering, irreverent attitude toward them was also captured by the use of multiple pseudonyms widespread at *The Observer*. When I had just begun getting to know the journalists there, I was often confused as to which names stood for real persons and which were fictitious. Different journalists gave me different reasons for why their material appeared under multiple pseudonyms. "It is so that the same journalist can write on different topics,"

---

[17] A pseudonym.

said Zoya Miloslavskaya.[18] Zoya was an entry-level journalist who was responsible for writing many of the more openly promotional materials for *The Observer*. "Because it doesn't look very respectable [*nesolidno*] if the same person is writing about, say, air-conditioners today and about the mayoral campaign tomorrow." "[Pseudonyms] are there in case someone [in Kirienko's circle] doesn't like an article and orders a journalist fired," said Sergei Kharlamov. "Then we can tell him that we fired that journalist, whereas we, in fact, simply 'fired' the pseudonym." "Pseudonyms are there for articles you don't feel like writing," volunteered Kirill Bubnov,[19] somewhere in the middle of the labor hierarchy at *The Observer*. "Maybe you feel that you're wrong, maybe you feel remorseful – then you can hide behind a pseudonym." "[Pseudonyms] are for those times when the piece just doesn't feel right," echoed Lilia Sadykova. "And it is for the times when you feel like fooling around and being naughty," added Kira Tarasova, "when you don't want a certain label to be stuck with you."

A key fieldwork moment eventually made clear to me why the prostitution metaphor made so much sense to my interlocutors. One day I was sitting in the room where *The Observer* journalists worked on their texts, chatting with a reporter in the corner. When I asked him, "What do you think journalists are for these days?," recalling the title of a book by Jay Rosen (2001), a public journalism advocate in the United States, my interviewee turned around and shouted across the room, "Hey, Lilia, what do you think journalists are for?" Without a blink, thirty-something Lilia shot back, "For all-around brain-fucking, of course! [*dlia vseobshchego mozgoebatel'stva*]." "What do you mean?" I mumbled. "Well," she paused for a second, clearly enjoying my bewilderment, "politicians are fucking with us, we are fucking with the readers, and the readers don't give a fuck about what we do!"

This use of explicit sexual imagery to speak about journalism's role and mission, I eventually realized, taps into the intersection of power, morality, and affect as they are paraded in front of the public eye. As communication scholar John Durham Peters (1995) pointedly observed, the term *prostitute*, in fact, comes from the Latin meaning "to stand in public." "Things exhibited before the public eye carry shame and glory," Peters (1995: 7) reminded us. "Only highly valenced

---

[18] A pseudonym.   [19] A pseudonym.

objects are paraded before the body of the people. Already in classical antiquity, then, public is an extremely polarized concept that combines senses both of honor and its violation" (Peters 1995: 7). In other words, prostitution, like journalism, links power, honor, shame, and public exposure. As brokers of societal morality, journalists' labor is the labor of passion as much as the work of reason, and this labor is performed and judged openly, in full view. Journalists' moral predicament in the post-Soviet period, then, becomes a metaphorical fall from grace from "public men" to "public women." This prism allows journalists to maintain the symbolic continuity with Soviet journalism (by maintaining the connection between power, morality, and publicity) but reverses the moral valence of that connection: from guardians of societal virtue, journalists start to be seen as its shameful violators.

Another reason why the "second oldest profession" metaphor made sense, especially to journalists themselves, had to do with the sudden commodification of their labor following the abrupt transition to capitalism. It was, of course, Karl Marx (Marx and Engels 1978) who theorized labor as a commodity under capitalism and who did not hesitate to draw on the prostitution imagery to get his point across. For Marx, prostitution was none other than a general metaphor for wage labor, with money as "the universal pimp" mediating between "a man's life and his means of life" (Marx and Engels 1978: 102). Marx condemned money for obfuscating the social and power relations that went into the creation of its value in the first place. "He who can buy bravery is brave, though a coward. [Money] serves to exchange every property for every other, even contradictory, property and object … it is the general confounding and compounding of all things" (Marx and Engels 1978: 105). Money has an extraordinary capacity to house contradictions, Marx argued, and under advanced capitalism, these contradictions come to the fore. When laboring for wages, people's creative capacities and sensuous energy get shut down, and their labor becomes estranged, alienated, dead. But not to labor the worker cannot afford: his survival becomes dependent on the wages he or she receives in exchange for his or her dead labor. It is in this sense that money, for Marx, becomes the universal mediating pimp between people and their means of life, and prostitution becomes an extended metaphor for wage labor, with economic coercion, exploitation, and alienation underlying both.

In her analysis of employment and prostitution as forms of contract, political theorist Carole Pateman (1988) took it one step further than Marx. She argued that what unites prostitution and wage labor is not only, or necessarily, money: what connects these two phenomena (and extends to other forms of contract) are the social relations of *subordination*, which is not the same as *exploitation* on which Marx focused. Subordination can take place in the absence of monetary or commodity exchange – for instance, when protection or subsistence is delivered in exchange for conformity or obedience. In short, any time there is room for a power imbalance, there is room for subordination. With these premises in mind, Pateman (1988) turns her attention to liberal contract theory, which has long maintained the idea that contract – be it employment, marriage, prostitution, or civil-political contract – is the epitome of free agreement and voluntary commitment. Leaving the civil contract aside, Pateman focuses on the first three – employment, marriage, and prostitution contracts – all of which she finds to be crucially constituted by relations of subordination. This does not mean, Pateman hastens to add, that in every such contract subordination takes the form of overt exercise of power. We all know of marriages and employment arrangements where the husband or the employer "does not use, and would not dream of using, his remaining powers" (Pateman 1988: 158). But this is to confuse particular cases with the institution of bourgeois marriage or that of employment. Both institutions only set *limits* to the power of the employer (or the money-making husband) over the employee (or the stay-at-home wife), whereas many other aspects of employer-employee or husband-wife relations remain at the discretion of the more powerful member of the dyad. The prostitution contract follows the same logic as the other two, argues Pateman (1988), but like the marriage contract (and unlike the employment contract), it is also a sexual contract – it is about women's physical and affective labor in exchange for men's protection, money, or both.

The labor journalists exchange for money is arguably as much about passion as it is about logic and reason (Wahl-Jorgensen 2013). Journalists not only describe and analyze, they also praise and condemn, honor and "raise hell." We could say they are centrally involved in the production of what the ancient Greeks called *pathos* – public portrayal of passion, gravity, and suffering. For Aristotle, pathos was the key element connecting poetry and rhetoric. By capturing the depths of human experience, particularly the experience of suffering, pathos offers yet another way of getting at the real, complementing those of philosophy and history (Lambek 2000). Texts and performances lacking pathos fail to convince, to resonate, to be perceived as real and true. This is not to say that the presence of pathos automatically guarantees credibility to a story: *logos* (sound reasoning) and *ethos* (moral character of the speaker) are equally important. Additionally, pathos is easy to overuse to the point of falling flat, resulting in what J. L. Austin (1962) called performative "abuses." Pathos thus needs to be carefully calibrated to have a chance at securing uptake, to use Austin's language again. The production of pathos requires both talent and skill.

If we think of journalists as crucially involved in the production of pathos, then following Pateman (1988), we can see them entering employment contracts where they exchange pathos for money. The problem, as Pateman would likely see it, is that unless journalists own their means of production, they still labor under conditions of subordination to their employers. Professionalization certainly helps to mitigate that subordination – which is probably why journalists in established liberal democracies do not routinely think of themselves as members of the "second oldest profession." Drawing on Pateman's (1988) reasoning again, professional journalists could perhaps be usefully compared to stay-at-home wives in happy bourgeois marriages. The wage-earning husbands in such marriages "would not dream," as Pateman has put it, of using their remaining power over their stay-at-home wives – instead, they presumably offer their wives a large degree of autonomy (Pateman 1988: 158). Professionalization similarly creates opportunities for employees to exercise greater autonomy vis-à-vis their employers.[20] Still, the less powerful member of the dyad (the professional journalist, the stay-at-home wife) is able to enjoy his or her autonomy only as long as the more powerful member of the dyad

---

[20] Strong professional organizations can push for legislation protecting their members from employers' fiat. For instance, in many European countries there are "conscience laws," where journalists are financially compensated when they are laid off because the editorial line of their newspaper changes. Professionalization also reinforces a culture of employee solidarity, a culture in which employers' fiat is more difficult or costly to exercise. Similarly, feminism as a social movement was crucial in bringing about of a cultural change elevating the status of women in society, along with legal decisions awarding payments to stay-at-home wives following divorce from their husbands.

(the employer or the husband) maintains respect for and a commitment to that autonomy.

In a newly capitalist context of post-Soviet Russia, money boldly entered the social relations and spaces where it previously did not belong. As one of my interviewees remarked, Soviet journalists "were brought up not to think about money," but now they had to think about money all the time – whether because their salaries were paid haphazardly, or because they themselves were running their outlets and had to find sponsors, or because they were asked to actively solicit advertisement as a condition of working for an outlet, or because they sought extra sources of income to supplement their inadequate earnings. We could say that having to keep the subject of money in the front of their minds revealed for journalists the very social and power relations that Marx would say are commonly obfuscated in labor relations under capitalism. The prostitution metaphor thus allowed post-Soviet journalists to successfully *name* the predicament they were struggling with, offering a measure of moral clarity without reducing the underlying complexity at the heart of that predicament. This was, of course, possible because prostitution itself is a complex phenomenon linking power, money, morality, regulation, modernity, aspiration to autonomy, public-private distinction, and many other cultural registers.[21]

Importantly, this set of stark-naked truths about journalism (that, at bottom, journalism is a contractual relationship constituted by subordination) opened the floodgates for a more casual equation of journalism with prostitution without the overtones of moral condemnation

---

[21] Historian Ruth Rosen (1982) has argued that prostitution can emerge as a symbol of an era in historical periods characterized by rapid capitalist growth and the unsettling social and political change accompanying it. Such was the case during the Progressive Era in the United States. "Everything now has its price. This is the day of the dollar," Rosen quotes one progressive reformer. "Men barter their brains for good incomes; women trade their hospitality for social position; candidates for public office modify their principles in view of preferment. Sell out is common" (Rosen 1982: 41). It is in this discursive vein, I think, that we need to read Upton Sinclair's indictment of American journalism in *The Brass Check*, where he explicitly likens journalists to prostitutes. After all, Sinclair's revulsion extends both to the capitalist press and to prostitution proper, which he calls "the most monstrous wickedness in the world" (Sinclair 2003 [1919]: 16). The rise of muckraking and then of the objectivity norm in American journalism during the progressive era can be read as part of the same trend – as an historically specific desire to rid politics and journalism of corrupting "interest" (McCormick 1981; Schudson 1978).

implicit in the notion of "selling out." When I was conducting field-work in 2001 and 2002, I met many journalists who tried to convince me that the very notion of press freedom was flawed and naive. It would have made more sense, I thought, for this deeply cynical view to come from media owners, not journalists. Media owners did subscribe to it, to be sure,[22] but it was surprisingly widespread among journalists. Fieldwork moments like that pushed me think that the story of journalism in post-Soviet Russia is not "simply" one of media instrumentalization, that something else must be going on and that despite the short time span – a mere ten years since the fall of the Soviet Union – I was beginning to see none other than a thoroughgoing erosion around journalism's core values in Russia.

Centrally among those values is a concern with seeking truth and with speaking it to power. In addition to newsroom observations and inter-views I have been drawing on thus far, another way to document the erosion of those values would be to take a look, in the last section of this chapter, at an example of journalistic text that asks to be taken as a revelation. We could then examine whether and how a commitment to truth-seeking and truth-telling is maintained in that text. The best example of such a text from my fieldwork comes from journalists who worked for the Saveliev media conglomerate in Nizhny Novgorod – a rival organization to the one I was studying and where I was not welcome. Having spoken to several journalists in the Saveliev camp any-way, I feel confident that many aspects of news production in media outlets controlled by Dmitry Saveliev were similar to what I had witnessed at *The Observer*, so I can generalize across the two rival organizations.

Eroding the Value of Truth-Seeking and Truth-Telling

On August 24, 2002, three weeks before the mayoral election, the evening newscast on Volga TV (a popular, award-winning local televi-sion channel) opened with a story about a sensational documentary film that had been revealed at a press conference earlier that day.[23] The press

---

[22] According to Paul Klebnikov, the first editor of the Russian edition of *Forbes*, one of Russia's most powerful media proprietors in the 1990s, Boris Berezovsky, openly stated, for instance, that he "didn't believe in freedom of the press the way idealists would like to imagine this notion" (Klebnikov 2000: 226).

[23] A segment of that broadcast is available at http://youtu.be/7dnDBHMtZK0 (accessed March 28, 2014).

conference was called by Alexander Volkov, editor and publisher of *The New Sentinel*. Speaking into cameras, Volkov announced that the film had been brought to the editors of *The New Sentinel* the night before "by anonymous individuals" (*neizvestnymi*). Volkov said that he and his colleagues decided to publicize the film because they considered the information revealed there of great public importance. "Everything you are about to see," Volkov warned his audience, "could dramatically alter the political situation in the city and could fundamentally change the outcome of the elections."

The film, titled, *The Bandits of Nizhny*, contained grainy spy camera footage of alleged secret meetings between a contender for the mayoral seat, a man named Vadim Bulavinov, and some of the leaders of the city's criminal underworld. Bulavinov was at the time a successful businessman and a member of the Russian Duma. Prior to the 2002 mayoral election, he had made two unsuccessful attempts to become the governor of Nizhny Novgorod region. Now, in 2002, he was one of the frontrunners for the mayoral seat, and his candidacy was favored by the presidential envoy to the region, Sergei Kirienko.

The grainy footage in the film showed Bulavinov (or someone who looked and spoke like him and drove his car) meeting leaders of organized crime at a restaurant in Nizhny Novgorod to discuss funding for his mayoral campaign. To correct for the poor sound quality of the recording, the film offered subtitles of what was allegedly said during those meetings. Through a combination of speech and subtitles, we learn that the criminal leaders are offering Bulavinov 250,000 US dollars' worth of campaign funds in exchange for control over the city's shopping centers and marketplace areas. Bulavinov responds that this arrangement would cost 400,000 dollars instead, but assuming that those costs are met and he wins the elections, he would "absolutely" appoint whomever the criminal leaders want to take control of the city's marketplace areas.

Another piece of incriminating evidence emerges when Bulavinov's interlocutors inform him that there are plans to assassinate Andrei Klimentiev, one of Bulavinov's key contenders for the mayoral seat. Klimentiev – a popular businessman with a criminal past – had won the previous mayoral election in Nizhny Novgorod in 1998, but those election results were canceled, a criminal case against Klimentiev was reopened, and Klimentiev subsequently spent two years behind bars. Now Klimentiev was back in the game and was again a frontrunner in the mayoral race. By informing Bulavinov of plans to assassinate Klimentiev, the criminal leaders seem to be signaling to Bulavinov that he need not worry about his popular competitor because if it comes to that, the seemingly unstoppable Klimentiev can once again be taken out of the race. Finally, the footage offers evidence of Bulavinov's moral depravity when we hear him say to his interlocutors, "I also have a boss – the presidential envoy to the region," thereby implicating himself as a client of Sergei Kirienko.

On the face of it, this documentary film, as it was called, broadcast during an evening news program, had many of the trappings of a muckraking news story. It originated as a leak from anonymous sources, it was presented as breaking news, and it contained evidence both of criminal conspiracy and moral depravity of a high-ranking public official. It was judged by journalists as a cause for grave concern and as an occasion for moral outrage, warranting a press conference. By shielding their sources, the journalists at *The New Sentinel* (where the press conference was held) and at the Volga TV station (where the film was shown) signaled that they were assuming the risks associated with speaking truth about people in power. The grainy image, the jerky camera movements, and the poor sound quality of the recording all worked to underscore the presumed authenticity of the surveillance tape at the core of the film.

There were, however, other features of this film and its presentation to viewers that had little to do with conventions of investigative reporting. First, about a minute into the film, there was a small caption that briefly flashed on the screen and read, "Paid for from the [election] fund of [mayoral] candidate V. V. Barinov."

Victor Barinov was the editor of *LS Plus*, the political tabloid launched to partake in wars of *kompromat* on the eve of the election in Nizhny Novgorod. Barinov and two other journalists were among several red herring candidates who entered the 2002 mayoral race to deflect votes from frontrunners like Bulavinov and Klimentiev. Another reason why people like Barinov registered as mayoral candidates – without the intention of winning the election – had to do with a provision in the 2002 election law discussed in Chapter 2. The law required that every piece of electoral advertising, including negative campaign ads, be labeled as paid for by a particular candidate. But few candidates – in Russia and elsewhere – usually want their names directly associated with a negative advertising campaign. In their stead, groups formally or informally affiliated with candidates, similar to political action committees (PACs) in the United States, end up doing the "dirty work" of authoring negative attack ads against other candidates. In Nizhny Novgorod, the red herring candidates such as Victor Barinov were functionally equivalent to PACs in that they could legally run (primarily negative) advertising campaigns against other candidates.

Importantly, though, the appearance of the caption "Paid for by candidate X" did not necessarily mean a hard-and-fast separation of political advertising from editorial content, as discussed in Chapter 2. The 2002 election law defined *political advertising* extremely broadly as "activity aiding to create a positive or a negative impression of a candidate among voters," effectively erasing any distinction between advertising and publicity. Media outlets were required to mark as advertisement many segments of election-time coverage that in other circumstances would appear as regular news. For instance, on the same evening news program a week later, following yet another discussion of the grainy video, the anchor introduced a brief interview with Andrei Klimentiev (the candidate whose assassination was discussed in the video) as the next news item. Klimentiev's measured reaction to the news of an assassination plot against him was accompanied by none other than the caption "Paid for from the [electoral] fund of candidate A. A. Klimentiev."

Still, there were other features of this "documentary film" that clearly pointed away from the standards of documentary truth-telling and toward the standards of fictional storytelling. In the opening sequence of the film, for instance, the camera pans across the main square of Nizhny Novgorod to the tune of ominous-sounding music as passers-by cross the square in slow motion. As this picture of the city fades out, the title of the film – *The Bandits of Nizhny* – slowly appears on the screen in large red letters, conveying a sense of foreboding. An off-screen voice professionally trained to communicate intrigue and suspense narrates the story of secret meetings between Bulavinov and the leaders of the criminal underworld. The off-screen narrator speaks in short, telegraphic sentences as viewers watch shadowy figures of men in suits get out of cars, talk on the phone, sit at restaurant tables, and shake hands. "July 2002. Café Gardenia. Two o'clock in the afternoon. Here is the leader of the most daring organized crime group in our city … Here is Bulavinov's car. Here he is himself. The criminal leaders stand up to greet him." After rolling for another half a minute, the film is then abruptly cut to a still frame that says, "To be continued during the screening of a feature film around ten o'clock in the evening." As promised, at ten in the evening, Volga TV aired another short segment of the film. Three days later a longer segment of *The Bandits of Nizhny* was aired in the same evening news program where it first appeared.[24]

What is going on here? What are the cloak-and-dagger aesthetic and other conventions of fictional storytelling doing in an evening news broadcast? Could the journalists be somehow inviting their audiences not to take what they are seeing at face value? Could they be subtly mocking the genre of political news itself, similar to what comedians Jon Stewart and Stephen Colbert have done in the United States? While tempting, this interpretation is not likely because journalists' other actions clearly contradict it. A week after the initial airing of *The Bandits of Nizhny*, the head of the news division at Volga TV, Alexander Rezontov, appeared before viewers.[25] Rezontov told viewers that the station received two defamation lawsuits and an official warning from the regional telecommunication authorities after airing the film. By Russian law, an official warning is an especially serious threat to a television station because after two such warnings received over a twelve-month period, the station's broadcasting license is automatically revoked. Even though neither the lawsuits nor the warning were actually in connection with *The Bandits of Nizhny*,[26] Rezontov conjectured that those moves were none other than Bulavinov's retaliation for the airing of *The Bandits of Nizhny*. Rezontov went on to indirectly implicate Sergei Kirienko, the presidential envoy to the region and the patron of Vadim Bulavinov, as being behind the issuing of the warning.

Rezontov then went on to defend the truthfulness of *The Bandits of Nizhny* and the television station's right to air it. He drew his viewers'

---

[24] A segment of that broadcast is available at http://youtu.be/uHGZpWKP8gU (accessed April 3, 2014).

[25] A segment of that broadcast is available at http://youtu.be/jtJvP34ztJs (accessed April 2, 2014).

[26] The official warning was issued for a broadcast that was similarly directed against Bulavinov: several weeks earlier, Volga TV journalists had reported rumors that, if elected, Bulavinov would build public housing in Nizhny Novgorod for thousands of refugees from Chechnya. The regional telecommunication authorities judged that report to contain incitement of ethnic hatred, a punishable offence by Russian law.

attention to the fact that Bulavinov made no public statements denying that his image or voice appeared in the film. Rezontov also noted that Bulavinov did not file a libel suit against the television station after airing of the film, choosing instead to seek help from his patrons (*pokroviteli*) in the office of the presidential envoy. It is striking how, in defending the authenticity of the grainy videotape, Rezontov and his colleagues at Volga TV did not seem to be bothered by the fact that what was shown to audiences was not the videotape itself but a *film* about it – a film that was brought into the editorial offices of *The New Sentinel* by "unidentified individuals." Who were those individuals? Who might have made the film (rather than the tape)? Who named it *The Bandits of Nizhny?* Who supplied the subtitles? Who wrote the music? These questions remain unanswered.

Accuracy in the conventional journalistic sense of getting the facts straight or in the sense suggested by Bernard Williams (2002) – as the persistence in trying to get to the bottom of things – does not seem to be a prominent concern for Rezontov and his colleagues at Volga TV. They do establish several "hard" facts about the film: that someone was handing it out to passers-by at train stations, that some of the copies were mailed from Moscow via DHL, that the off-screen narrator speaks with a Moscow accent, and that "influential businessmen" in Nizhny Novgorod received their own copies of the film. We are also told that a subtitled video identical to the grainy footage featured in *The Bandits of Nizhny* simultaneously appeared on a website that "experts say" is patronized by the security services. This exhausts the list of hard facts Volga TV journalists establish about the film. Based on those facts, Volga TV conjectures that the film was "probably" made in Moscow, and "by all appearances," the security services had something to do with it.

Viewers are then offered some evidence of journalists' efforts to verify the authenticity of the videotape, but that evidence is hardly convincing. We learn, for instance, that Volga TV ordered an expert examination of the tape by "an organization specially certified for those purposes." "Experts painstakingly studied the voice on the tape," Alexander Rezontov tells his evening news audience, "and based on a combination of acoustic and linguistic factors, they concluded with a high degree of certainty that the voice on the tape belongs to V. Bulavinov." "What was obvious to many," Rezontov sums up, "has now been officially confirmed by specialists." In another instance that could be interpreted as journalists signaling to viewers that they are trying to get at the bottom of the story, viewers are told that Volga TV sent official inquiries to the Department of Internal Affairs, the Federal Security Service, and the prosecutor's office asking for more information about Bulavinov's potential connections with the criminal world. Those inquiries were left unanswered, but instead of seeking other sources of information, Volga TV journalists left it at that.

In the absence of what professional journalists call *hard facts*, and in the absence of demonstrated efforts to obtain those facts, Volga TV journalists are left without reliable ways to offer performative assurances that they stand by what they say. Instead, Volga TV journalists invite viewers to trust them by invoking the authority of unidentified experts, of guesswork, and of common sense. "Specialists agree," "lawyers are wondering," "in all likelihood," "obvious to many," and "not far from the truth" are stock phrases used throughout the report in *The Bandits of Nizhny*. Signals of sincerity and reflexivity – other important characteristics of speech aiming at truth, as identified in the Introduction – are sorely missing, leaving audiences without crucial cues to form moral judgments about journalists' integrity and trustworthiness. Without those signals, the chances for media producers to connect with audiences on the level of intersubjective experience dwindle, increasing the opportunities of instrumental and manipulative uses of communication instead.

Unable to assure viewers of the accuracy of their texts or of their own sincerity and reflexivity, Volga TV journalists end up heavily relying on pathos – yet another criterion of truthful speech, as discussed earlier – to convey that they mean what they say. In ancient Greek, *pathos* meant "feeling" or "suffering" in everyday usage, but Aristotle turned it into an analytical term, understanding it as an essential component of tragedy and as a constitutive element of both poetry and rhetoric. Simultaneously, an artistic and a rhetorical device available to writers of both fact and fiction, pathos is what helps to make narratives "work" (Ettema 2005). In an important way, the cloak-and-dagger aesthetic of *The Bandits of Nizhny* could be seen as an example of the use of pathos to aim at truth, where truth is what resonates with universals of human experience, what plugs into viewers' desires and disappointments, and what viewers can understand and accept (Ettema 2005).

Pathos is also generally at work when speakers wish to raise the stakes in a conversation, to emphasize the gravity of the situation, and to invoke ideals and values. Volga TV journalists upped the ante when, in response to the defamation lawsuits and to the official warning issued to them after airing the film, they portrayed themselves as targets of a hostile attack against freedom of the press. "There was basically a declaration of war against our television station this week," Alexander Rezontov spoke gravely into the camera on August 31, 2002. "In the past, there were other attempts to put pressure our station, but after the airing of *The Bandits of Nizhny*, we are being openly terrorized." "Someone is clearly very dissatisfied with our honest and principled journalistic positions." "The goal is clear: to make us go silent before the upcoming elections. Someone is in horror of another screening of *The Bandits of Nizhny* film." With the raised pathos of statements like these, Volga TV journalists presented themselves as courageous truth-tellers speaking boldly into the face of power, as people with ideals and values who stand by what they say. "Yes, our judgments are often harsh and unflattering for public officials, but such is our creed and our journalistic position ... We are stopping the further screening of *The Bandits of Nizhny* until the courts examine our appeal. But nothing can force us to stop doing our professional journalistic work."

It is, of course, an open empirical question whether and how these invocations of honesty, courage, and integrity were taken up by the actual audiences of Volga TV. The raised pathos of *The Bandits of Nizhny* may have rung true with viewers, resonating with their gut reactions about how politics is conducted in the region. At the same time, the film and the reporting on it employed some openly manipulative smear techniques (multiple repetitions of key phrases damaging to Bulavinov, not letting him speak for himself, building cognitive associations between him and visual images of corruption, exploiting the audience's fear of organized crime, and so on). To be sure, one needs to have a good amount of media literacy to detect those techniques at work. Still, (1) the near absence of the signals of accuracy, sincerity, and reflexivity, (2) the overuse of pathos to the point that it might have fallen "flat," (3) the fact that *The Bandits of Nizhny* appeared during a period of intense electioneering and was accompanied by brief but noticeable "paid for" reminders, and (4) given the overall breakdown of the social relations between journalists and audiences – given all of these factors – it is likely that the credibility of *The Bandits of Nizhny* and of Volga TV reporting on it remained rather low. After all, despite a coordinated media attack against him, Bulavinov did end up winning the mayoral election in Nizhny Novgorod in September 2002.

I have no way of knowing, at this point, what Volga TV journalists thought they were doing as they presented and defended *The Bandits of Nizhny* to their audience. But judging by the reactions of those I knew at *The Observer*, it was probably some combination of a mercenary attitude toward the profession and some form of rationalization described earlier in this chapter, where journalists try to convince themselves that they are in the right even as they engage in professionally dubious actions. Without such forms of professional accommodation, it would have been very difficult to stay active in the production of *kompromat*.

As always, it is important to pay attention to the unintended consequences of these attitudes and practices for the profession as a whole. During my time in Nizhny Novgorod in 2001–2002, I met only a few journalists who undertook any kind of investigations, so I invariably asked almost everyone with whom I interacted why they were not pursuing investigative work. Some of the answers confirmed what I was already observing in the newsrooms: compared with the Soviet and especially to the perestroika period, the incentive structure for undertaking journalistic investigations was missing. As Western editors and publishers also know too well, investigative reporting is expensive, so it is first to be sacrificed when the budget is tight. For many journalists in post-Soviet Russia, the tightening of newsroom budgets meant a drastic shift from salaries to piecemeal payments. "Why would I spend several weeks working on a single investigative story," a journalist told me, "if I am going to be paid the same amount as I would for a report I could write in half a day?"

This explanation only works in conjunction with the decreased cultural standing of investigative work. After all, even under piecemeal pay arrangements, media managers could pay more per line for investigative text than for news or commentary. What was bringing down the cultural worth of investigative work? One explanation was rather straightforward and had to do with the unwillingness of media managers to enter into conflicts with advertisers over journalists' investigations. Such was the case at the *Birzha* ("Stock Exchange") publishing house, for instance, where I spent my first several months in 2001–2002. Another reason journalists gave me for *not* pursuing investigative work had to do with how unprotected they felt. Russia's Center for Journalism in Extreme Situations (CJES) and Glasnost Defense Foundation (GDF) documented over 200 murders and countless beatings and intimidations of journalists in Russia between 1991 and 2006. I have not met or heard of anyone in Nizhny Novgorod who had been harassed for their investigative work, perhaps because there were so few journalists in the city interested in conducting investigations. Journalists in Nizhny Novgorod did tell me, though, that if they were to become interested in investigative work, their editors would probably not support them and would likely refuse to stand in court with them against accusations of libel. Only the national papers with large circulations and lawyers on staff could offer journalists that kind of protection.

Still another explanation for the decreased worth of investigative work lay in the domain of perceptions. "Someone is always behind it" and "It is always in someone else's interests" were by far the most common responses to my question about the lack of interest in investigative reporting. And there *is* some truth to it: as discussed in the Introduction, by definition, most investigative reports originate with leaks from interested sources (Waisbord 2000). At least in theory, professional journalists then conduct independent investigations seeking additional sources to corroborate or refute the information contained in the leak. The problem in post-Soviet Russia has been that this last step – journalists' seeking additional sources and evidence – has been both dangerous and actively discouraged by editors, whereas the first step in the process – leaks to media outlets – has been institutionalized into *kompromat*. Given journalism's deprofessionalization, there has been no shortage of journalists willing to take the first step but not the second (i.e., to publicize the leak without verifying the assertions contained in it). Some journalists, according to Olessia Koltsova (2006: 138), went a step and a half: they collected *kompromat* provided by multiple warring parties and then drew their own conclusions, which, Koltsova argues, "was [already] much closer to a journalistic definition of genuine news than to a leak of *kompromat*."

The problem, of course, is that such nuances are lost to outsiders, including other journalists who are not directly involved in the production of *kompromat*. As I demonstrated with *The Bandits of Nizhny*, *kompromat* uses many of the same rhetorical devices as an investigative report. Even if *kompromat* only masquerades as a form of truth-telling, its overwhelming presence in Russian public space both crowds out and erodes what counts as qualitative investigative work. In public discourse about journalism in the early and mid-2000s, for instance, it became commonplace to invoke how the professions of the investigative reporter and that of a "media assassin" (*media killer*) have effectively merged. It was less surprising to see this admixing invoked by political analysts and other outsiders to the profession (e.g., CPI 2001) but more disconcerting when it was coming from respectable journalists or from journalism educators (e.g., Kashin 2016; Paniushkin 2004; Simonov 2000).

The worrisome consequence of this confusion between *kompromat* and investigative reporting is that it brings down the society-wide value of truth-seeking and truth-telling. In other words, it opens doors to widespread cynicism. Here the study of post-Soviet journalism necessarily connects with the study of broader cultural changes after the fall of the Soviet Union. What has been the relationship between journalism and cynicism in post-Soviet Russia, and what has been the dynamic of that relationship? Did post-Soviet society really lose all taste for public truth-seeking and truth-telling, and if so, how do we know, and what did it look like? Chapter 4 addresses these questions.

4 | *The Spiral of Cynicism in the 2000s*

Much changed in the media-political scene in Nizhny Novgorod throughout the 2000s. As discussed in Chapter 3, in the late 1990s and early 2000s, several cross-institutional groups (CIGs) consisting of prominent local officials, industrialists, bankers, and high-ranked representatives of the security services were vying for formal and informal control of the region. Those elite power struggles were precipitated by the abrupt departure to Moscow of the young and charismatic governor of the Nizhny Novgorod region, Boris Nemtsov, whom President Yeltsin appointed Russia's Deputy Prime Minister in 1997. The vying for power among Nizhny Novgorod elites intensified in 2001–2002 after Sergei Kirienko, another native of Nizhny Novgorod, returned to the region after his brief and unsuccessful tenure as Russia's Prime Minister. In their struggle for control of the region, CIGs, including the one led by Kirienko, began to actively buy up regional media outlets, turning them into weapons for smear attacks on political enemies.

Chapter 3 documented one such power struggle among CIGs involving the media – the mayoral campaign in the summer of 2002. That particular battle ended up being the last one of its kind in the region's recent history. The mayoral victory "won" by Sergei Kirienko's CIG allowed that CIG to consolidate political control over the region, including control over the region's media. The rival CIG, led by former oil baron turned Member of the Duma Dmitry Saveliev, disintegrated after "losing" the mayoral election in 2002 to Kirienko's CIG. A crucial sign of Saveliev's capitulation to Kirienko was Saveliev's sale of the controlling stake in Volga TV to Kirienko's son Vladimir soon after the new mayor took office.

The consolidation of political control of the region around Sergei Kirienko in the early 2000s paralleled the consolidation of power by Vladimir Putin on the national scale occurring at the same time. The accumulation of power in Nizhny Novgorod by Kirienko was also part of the process through which Putin was building his "vertical power structure" (*vertikal vlasti*) – a top-down governing mechanism meant to replace what was construed as the chaos and ungovernability of the 1990s. The key to building *vertikal vlasti* was installing regional leaders loyal to Putin but powerful enough to maintain a hold on their regions on their own. Intraelite struggles of the sort described in Chapter 3 were clearly a major impediment to building *vertikal vlasti* throughout Russia. Those struggles made regional politics unpredictable and could result in independent regional leaders capable of challenging the federal center. With Sergei Kirienko's ties to the Kremlin, his CIG's victory in the mayoral election of 2002 thus was an important component of extending *vertikal vlasti* into Nizhny Novgorod. The realigning of political vectors between Moscow and Nizhny Novgorod was complete by 2005 when the communist governor of the region, popularly elected in 2001, was replaced by Putin's appointee from Moscow. This became possible because the Russian Duma did away with direct gubernatorial elections in 2004. Many regions have followed the lead and begun canceling mayoral elections in their cities as well. In Nizhny Novgorod, the last direct election for mayor took place in 2005.

With these changes in place, public politics gradually left Nizhny Novgorod. With a single set of political players in charge, there were no more information wars to rock the region compared with the late 1990s and early 2000s. *Kompromat* and electoral advertising lost their prominence as a news genre. News outlets that relied on political advertising as their main source of income shifted to so-called government contracts (*goszakazy*) or formal public relations agreements with government organizations to stay afloat. Many private newspapers in Nizhny Novgorod closed down: such was the fate of *The Observer* and *LS Plus*. The few media organizations that had been relatively independent, such as the business publishing house (*Birzha*) where I conducted initial fieldwork, were eventually sold to entrepreneurs loyal to the Kremlin. By the end of the 2000s, most journalists I knew from fieldwork had left the profession. Some left Nizhny Novgorod for Moscow, and some took jobs in public and government relations.[1]

---

[1] A telling sign of the devolution of journalism in Nizhny Novgorod was the fact that after the sale of *Birzha*, one of its former editors became a public relations manager for Russia's Atomic Energy Agency *while* continuing with her duties as the head of the regional chapter of the Russian Union of Journalists.

This chapter investigates what was going on in Russian public culture, of which journalism was part, during that long decade starting in the early 2000s and ending in the early 2010s. This was the decade that witnessed a thorough and seemingly effortless consolidation of authoritarianism in Russia. We still know very little about the cultural factors that allowed for and helped with the consolidation of authoritarianism during that decade and specifically about the role journalism played in that process. Discussions of authoritarianism usually center on sham elections, extralegal violence, and the curtailment of freedoms as defining institutional features of authoritarian regimes. State patronage of the military, the bureaucracy, and the elderly is sometimes mentioned among the social and economic factors that can sustain authoritarianism.

Much less, though, has been written about the cultural practices – those that involve public work with meaning – that helped to consolidate authoritarianism, aside from an important general point that authoritarian governments encourage citizens' depoliticization. There is a key cultural difference, political scientists tell us, between authoritarian and totalitarian regimes: totalitarian governments work to mobilize their populations for national, social, military, and other goals, whereas authoritarian governments try to demobilize and depoliticize their citizenry. This is done through a variety of means, including, centrally, via the mass media. The main focus of media offerings under authoritarianism is on diversion and entertainment rather than on political agitation and propaganda (Linz 2000).

This chapter builds on these insights but argues that depoliticization can mean different things in different historical periods and places and that those meanings need to be empirically investigated rather than assumed. This chapter asks what kind of depoliticization was occurring in Russia in the 2000s, how it was culturally produced, and what role journalism and the mass media played in that process. Chapters 2 and 3 already began answering these questions. I traced how the perception of investigative journalists as public truth-seekers went into sharp decline during the 1990s and early 2000s and how that has helped to devalue the very idea of press freedom. This chapter examines the consequences of this devaluation. What does public discourse look like in a society that seems to have lost interest in seeking truth and speaking it to power? Did the kernel of truth-seeking disappear entirely from public space, or was it channeled somewhere else, and if so, where? Answers to these questions will help us to understand what kind of depoliticization was produced in Russia in the 2000s and how it was different from its Soviet counterpart. To answer these questions, this chapter shifts gears – away from fieldwork and toward the analysis of public discourse, away from Nizhny Novgorod and toward Moscow, and away from localized news production and toward the circulation of themes and ideas in Russia's public space.

Depoliticization is commonly discussed through the concept of cynicism. Both are seen as negative categories – that is, defined by the absence or withdrawal of political engagement, ideals, hope, and trust. Indeed, anthropologists working in post-Soviet Eastern Europe have documented unprecedented levels of cynicism in the region (Greenberg 2014; Oushakine 2009; Ries 2002; Shevchenko 2009). These levels have been widely interpreted as evidence of democratic failure (Greenberg 2010). This chapter brings more nuance to these claims, suggesting that cynicism need not be defined only negatively (through absences and failure) but as a structure of feeling that may still contain some traces of truth-seeking in it.

Because I am interested in the circulation of the cynical zeitgeist, I draw on a variety of sources of data for this chapter. Among them are public statements by Russia's officials and other public figures that could be construed as especially cynical and that have widely resonated across traditional and new media. Other sources include scholarly work by Russian sociologists, including their interviews with Russia's top media managers conducted on conditions of anonymity, discussions about cynicism in journalists' blogs, analyses of entertainment trends by Russia's television critics, and changes in patterns of language use as noted by anthropologists, sociolinguists, and literary scholars.

What Is Cynicism?

Cultural anthropologists and other scholars have been increasingly interested in studying cynicism as a structure of feeling that feeds political action and inaction, especially in contexts with high levels of violence, prolonged economic crises, political impasses, and a history of authoritarian rule. Despite the growing number of ethnographic works invoking the concept, studying cynicism remains difficult. As one commentator aptly put it, "[T]ools of social theory were not designed with investigation of cynicism in mind" (Chaloupka 1999: 47).

The difficulty with studying cynicism lies in the protean and fluid nature of the concept. As noted earlier, *cynicism* is commonly defined as disenchantment with ideals, resulting in citizens' apathy, passivity, and disengagement. Another, older view of cynicism sees it as synonymous with open immorality or nihilism. Under that definition, one is called a cynic when one openly declares to be unashamed by anything, unconstrained by any ethical criteria, living in the world of "anything goes."

Still another way to define cynicism is through its association with skepticism or realism. This involves what the ancient Greeks called an *exercise in deflationary rhetoric* (Williams 2002: 9), where one first postulates a distinction between higher and lower dimensions of the same phenomenon – such as between argumentation and force, between truthfulness and manipulation, between altruism and self-interest, and so on. Then the cynical move is to deny the higher element of the pair while affirming the lower. So a show of conviction becomes mere performance, romantic love is reduced to sexual instincts, and sincerity is taken as a sign of inexperience and naiveté. Politics, at bottom, comes down to manipulation of desires and fears, strategy and tactics, deception and force.

Finally, there is a view of cynicism that connects it with irony rather than with apathy, skepticism, or nihilism (although there is a close relationship among all of these concepts). An ironist is not looking to discover the naked truth behind appearances. Rather, he or she "steps above the events and flows of time ... to posit some ultimate point of view beyond difference" (Colebrook 2004: 135–138; Deleuze 1990). Irony draws its power from ambiguities and paradoxes, from what is unresolvable about the human condition. An ironic stance relieves speakers of the necessity to commit to a particular moral position; instead, one can "hover" above viewpoints and perspectives (Hutcheon 1995). Philosopher Peter Sloterdijk (1987) has argued that cynicism of this detached, ironic variety has been prevalent among Western intellectuals from the 1970s onward. He calls this sensibility "enlightened false consciousness" or "cynical reason" (see also Žižek 1989). Sloterdijk is here playing with the classic Marxist definition of false consciousness, whose formula was "they do not know it, but they are doing it." With enlightened false consciousness, the formula becomes "they know what they are doing, but they are doing it anyway." This is a form of modern cynicism, Sloterdijk (1987) suggests, that incorporates moral comfort, ironic detachment, and borderline melancholia, none of which prevents people from keeping on working.

Regardless of their preferred definition, philosophers and cultural critics studying cynicism note that the kind of cynicism one will practice depends crucially on where one is positioned in relation to power. There is what Sloterdijk (1987) has called "master cynicism," or the "cynicism of domination." It manifests as a particular kind of disinhibition where those in power violate their own proclaimed ideals or simply admit that they are in the business of manipulating aspirations and hopes. Then there is what Žižek (2012) and Sloterdijk (1987) have called the "bitter cynicism of the oppressed," the "truth of servants," or the "intelligence of the disadvantaged." This is a different kind of cynicism, and it manifests in a variety of ways – from low-lying suspicion of the ideological pronouncements of those in power to active hostility toward the masters. This variety of cynicism informs a wide repertoire of social critique. It also serves as fertile ground for conspiracy theories (Marcus 1999; West and Sanders 2003).

Finally, there is what I would like to call the *cynicism of the friends of power*. These are people on the inside of politics and in cultural production who for one reason or another identify with the powerful and mimic them by acting "as if universal laws existed only for the stupid, while that fatally clever smile plays on the lips of those in the know" (Sloterdijk 1987: 3). Crucially, friends of power can tap into the intelligence of the disadvantaged by displaying straight-talk jadedness, openly declared weariness, or tough-minded distrust of ideological proclamations. Through such actions, friends of power nudge their disadvantaged interlocutors "to likewise draw their identities from the master's needs" (Chaloupka 1999: 22).

Where one is located in relation to power is thus very important to the kind of cynicism one might practice. This is one of the key insights of Peter Sloterdijk's (1987) influential magnum opus on modern cynicism. Another core contribution of the *Critique of Cynical Reason* is the observation that at the heart of modern cynicism there is a tension between wanting to distance oneself from a set of ideals and beliefs and wanting to cross that distance, reasserting another set of truths instead. Sloterdijk (1987) does not put it in those terms, but we could call the former component *ideological disengagement* and the latter *ideological disinhibition*. Even as an act of closing oneself off to politics, then, cynicism bears traces of a revelation, thus carrying a shadow of truth-seeking in it.

Finally, there is Sloterdijk's original idea that the old link between cynicism and evil has finally come undone, at least in twentieth-century Europe.[2] "The person with the clear, 'evil gaze' has disappeared into the crowd . . . Modern cynics are integrated, asocial characters who . . . are a match for any hippie . . . Instinctively, they no longer understand their way of existing as something that has to do with being evil, but as participation in a collective, realistically attuned way of seeing things" (Sloterdijk 1987: 33). The untying of cynicism and evil in this way might not seem like a serious problem at first sight and may even seem like a good thing. After all, in many corners of the contemporary West, the late modern moment has been celebrated as the age of healthy ironic distancing. While Sloterdijk acknowledges (ancient) *kynicism*'s provocative and liberating potential, he sees modern mass cynicism that has taken hold in the West from the 1970s onward as a discouraging trend that undercuts critical thinking, knowledge-seeking, and other ideals of the Enlightenment. Sloterdijk (1987) worries about modern mass cynicism because he sees it as a distant relative of mass demoralization that had set in during the Weimar period in Germany and that eventually led to fascism. Weimar cynicism's "first descendant was fascism and [its] second descendant is us" (Sloterdijk 1987: 7).

So while the connection between cynicism and disinhibited evildoing may have come undone in late modernity, there is likely still a connection between cynicism and what Hannah Arendt (1963) called the "banality of evil."[3] Sloterdijk (1987) does not make a direct connection between cynicism and thoughtlessness (which Arendt famously placed at the center of her thesis about the banality of evil). But the material from Russia during the 2000s begs for that comparison. Modern mass cynicism and Arendt's thoughtlessness share a crucial indifference toward politics – an indifference to genuine communication, as Arendt understood it. Next, both mass cynics and the likes of

---

[2] In the Russian language, the words *cynical* and *cynicism* still carry the overtones of evildoing. Those connotations come to the fore when one is described as acting "in an especially cynical way" (*s osobym tsinizmom*).

[3] Sloterdijk (1987: 299, n.16) recalls that watching a rebroadcast of an interview with Hannah Arendt on German public television became a major inspiration for his book on modern cynicism. After hearing Arendt discuss her work on *Eichmann in Jerusalem*, Sloterdijk says, the book "began to write itself."

Adolph Eichmann live with a vague sense of moral dissonance, but they do not feel compelled to deal with that dissonance.[4] As a result, both cynicism and thoughtlessness become mechanisms through which people can shield themselves from the risk and discomfort of examination – of self and others – and from the pain of making up one's mind (Arendt 2003). Instead, like Eichmann, mass cynics end up relying on clichés and stock phrases as banisters to guide their thinking ("There is nothing anyone can do about it," "I was only doing my job"). Because of this lack of interest in critical examination of self and others, both mass cynicism and banal thoughtlessness lead to inertia that prevents people from taking principled moral action. As a result, both encourage non-contestation of power. More tragically, as I will argue toward the end of this chapter, they contribute to a loss of the world known in common, where "the very concept of truth [loses] its meaning" (Arendt 2000).

The Cynical Zeitgeist

In his influential examination of the origins of modern cynicism, Sloterdijk (1987) argues that some historical epochs are more prone to cynicism than others. Postwar and interwar periods – especially for countries that were defeated in war – stand out as particularly good candidates for the emergence of a cynical zeitgeist. For modern Europe, Sloterdijk (1987) locates the first full-scale crystallization of mass cynicism in the political culture of the Weimar period. After the signing of the Versailles treaty, "everywhere the bitter feeling of having been deceived hung in the air" (Sloterdijk 1987: 410). Resentment of the victors of the war (who "did not have in mind any chivalrous gestures of honor toward the conquered") and disappointment in the ideals over which the war had been fought were shared by the German elites and the powerless alike (Sloterdijk 1987: 411).

While there are obviously many important historical differences between Weimar Germany and post–Cold War Russia, there are also many striking similarities. As defeated empires, both Germany and Russia ended up plunging into a set of interlinked crises co-occurring

---

[4] "Unaccustomed to any optimism about the future ... we live from day to day, from vacation to vacation, from news show to news show, from problem to problem, from orgasm to orgasm, in private turbulences and medium-term affairs, tense, relaxed. With some things we feel dismay but with most things we can't really give a damn" (Sloterdijk 1987: 98–99).

in multiple areas of social life.[5] In addition to the military defeat and collapse of ideology, both countries experienced a profound crisis of parliamentarianism and an economic collapse, resulting in spiraling hyperinflation and unemployment, accompanied by a cultural crisis of masculinity. To cope with all of it, Sloterdijk (1987: 470) says, residents of the Weimar Republic developed a particular optic – that of the "observer of catastrophes, of the war voyeur." For many, this meant acquiring "nausea about politics" and training oneself in having a "productive lack of conviction" (pp. 470, 472).

At the level of everyday experience, living in the Weimar Republic meant living with a diffuse sense of anxiety and restlessness. "A dull feeling of instability of things penetrated into souls, a feeling of lack of substance, of relativity, of accelerated change, and of involuntary floating from transition to transition" (Sloterdijk 1987: 483). The Weimar experience also trained people in mistrust. "Cases of fraud, deception, misleading, breach of promise, charlatanism, and so forth multiplied ... The impostor grew into a character type of the times par excellence" (p. 484). Deceivers became ubiquitous *and* socially indispensable, Sloterdijk (1987) argues. They helped to reinforce one of the few convictions Weimar residents did have: that no one was to be trusted, that anyone could be deceived at any moment.

Most profoundly, a sudden collapse of ideology after World War I left many Germans with an uneasy sense of meaninglessness of it all at the end of the day. It was particularly difficult, Sloterdijk (1987) says, for the soldiers who fought in World War I to come to terms with the seeming meaninglessness of the pain of the war. "To admit that 'everything had been for nothing' and that the untold torments had no political meaning at all – for many contemporaries that was unbearable" (p. 461).

To deal with their uneasiness and confusion, Weimar residents embraced cynicism as a way to anesthetize themselves against the perceived meaninglessness and amoralism of the world. Cynicism for them became a defensive strategy, "an armoring of the ego against its suffering ... a No to inner wounds, to weakness and neediness" (Sloterdijk 1987: 467–468). It is at this historical juncture that the cynicism of the powerless articulated especially well with the cynicism

---

[5] Alexander Yanov (1995) was the first to raise the possibility of a "Weimar scenario" in post-Soviet Russia. See also Medvedev (2014); Oleinik (2015); Revzin (2012).

of domination. Mistrustful, resentful, and restless, those without any real power began to "train themselves to play master of the situation" precisely in circumstances "where things have gotten out of control" (p. 386). World-weary realpolitik ways of thinking readily availed themselves to "the small ego[s]" tempted "to think in parallel with the trains of thought of a great strategic brain" (p. 470). Friends of power (people such as Oswald Spengler, Sloterdijk suggests) encouraged realignment of the two cynicisms and gave them wide cultural circulation.[6]

Despite all the "armament, wall-building ... and self-hardening" in which Weimar residents engaged to protect themselves from the unnerving experience of a permanent crisis, political fermentation within their psyches continued (Sloterdijk 1987: 468). Even though everyone's masks were now "half lowered" and everyone's motives presumably exposed, both the powerful and the powerless remained existentially dissatisfied (Sloterdijk 1987: 384). The key to understanding cynicism of the Weimar period, says Sloterdijk (1987: 468), is to recognize that those who build up psychological armoring to protect themselves from politics "will one day 'build down' and let lose." A psyche nauseated by politics eventually demands a movement of disinhibition and simplification.

Fascism became such a movement. Out of the existential anxiety of the Wemiar period was born "a readiness ... to turn away from this incommodious state of the world and to remold the hate against it into a Yes to sociopolitical and ideological movements that promise ... the most energetic return to 'substantial' and reliable states of affairs" (Sloterdijk 1987: 483). The success of fascism "was based not least of all on the seductive trick of enticing the bulk of the refusers, the unhappy, and the no men with the prospect that they themselves are the true realists, and summoned coshapers of a new, grandiose, and simplified world" (p. 501). Fascism's allegiance to a politics of pure violence was similarly enabled by the cynicism of the Weimar period, Sloterdijk (1987) argues. Amida general fatigue with politics after World War I, violence became the only true, "valid and ineluctable" political reality toward which there was no nausea (p. 467).

[6] Spengler's *Decline of the West* was an enormously popular book in post-Soviet Russia in the early 1990s.

It is striking how many parallels one can find between the political culture of Weimar Germany and that of post-Soviet Russia. In the first two decades after the fall of the Soviet Union, Russian sociologists documented tremendous levels of generalized disappointment, frustration, anxiety, and hopelessness among ordinary Russians going through the post-Soviet transition.[7] Results of one national poll conducted in 2006, for instance, revealed that over two-thirds of Russians were living with a sense of loss, three-quarters with a sense of an external threat to their lives, and over four-fifths with a sense of vulnerability and danger. Two-thirds of respondents said that they did not have any certainty about the future, and over three-fifths said that they were experiencing less joy and more fear compared with several years earlier (Dubin 2006a). Other national polls conducted between 1991 and 2005 showed consistently low levels of trust in public institutions (in the single digits), a chronic sense of helplessness in the face of instability, and a growing sense of aggression and resentment (Gudkov 2005).

Ethnographic accounts of everyday life in post-Soviet Russia have bolstered and enriched these general findings. Ethnographers have been offering poignant accounts of how, at least in the first two decades after the fall of the Soviet Union, everyday life in post-Soviet Russia was experienced as a permanent, never-ending crisis (Kruglova 2014; Ries 2002; Shevchenko 2009), similar to the way it was experienced in Weimar Germany. Cynicism – as mistrust of people and institutions, as the sense of being manipulated and deceived, as bracing oneself for the worst – became an adaptive mechanism for living under the conditions of that permanent crisis. As sociologist Olga Shevchenko (2009) has argued, creating emotional distance between oneself and the substance of politics became an important way for ordinary Russians to assert their moral agency and to maintain a semblance of control over their lives. Shevchenko (2009: 144–171) describes how ordinary Muscovites trained themselves in developing an explicitly dismissive view of any kind of political engagement. Prepared to be deceived at any moment, they reinforced their cynical armoring and that of others as they exhibited their jadedness and political detachment to one another. Interestingly, Shevchenko (2009) notes, while this rhetorical

---

[7] See Dubin 2005, 2006b; Gudkov 1999, 2005, 2009; Levinson 2011; Shevchenko 2009.

practice did give people a chance to assert their moral worth and to develop some solidarity with one another, this solidarity was immediately undercut by people's collective refusal to believe in the possibility of any meaningful collective action.

Cynicism before and after 1991

It is tempting to see the cynicism toward politics and public institutions in post-Soviet Russia as a phenomenon of path dependency – that is, as a leftover from the Soviet period when citizens kept some emotional distance from official institutions and practices, as described, for instance, by Alexei Yurchak (1997, 2006). As discussed in the Introduction, the majority of Soviet citizens, according to Yurchak, had a very particular relationship with official Soviet politics and public culture. They practiced what Mikhail Bakhtin called being *vnye* (*vnyenakhodimost'*) – a position of being very aware of official rhetoric yet remaining uninvolved in it.

It is tempting to draw parallels between people's attitudes toward politics in Soviet and post-Soviet Russia, particularly during Putin's presidency (e.g., Yurchak 2016). It is beyond doubt that some historical memory of distrusting high-minded political pronouncements was reactivated in the post-Soviet context, after the failure of democratic reforms became apparent in the 1990s. Nevertheless, I believe that there are crucial differences between how cynicism was practiced in the late-Soviet and post-Soviet periods.

To begin with, one simply could not admit publicly to being a cynic in the Soviet Union, particularly if one was a cultural producer, party or state official, or any other kind of public figure (Gudkov 2005). That is, one could not openly engage in ideological disinhibition, which I identified earlier as one of the two components of cynicism as a cultural practice (the other being ideological distancing or disengagement). In the 1990s and 2000s, however, openly calling oneself a cynic became a badge of honor, especially among journalists. Veteran Soviet journalist Inna Rudenko (2005), discussed in Chapter 1, lamented this state of affairs in an interview in the mid-2000s:

Here, a colleague writes that journalists are cynics by definition. What is that supposed to mean?! Back in our days it was simply shameful to admit to being a cynic. Impossible. There were different kinds of journalists, but to publicly admit to something like that ... Why was not Yury Shchekhochikhin a cynic? And Sima Soloveichik was not one, and neither was my late husband Kim Kostenko. Nor was Yura Rost, or my teacher Boris Pankin [all well-known Soviet journalists]. I grew up among those people. And how is today's cynicism better than yesterday's hypocrisy?

One devil's advocate response to Inna Rudenko's lament would be to say that it is probably not the individual journalists who became more cynical (and, Rudenko implies, less moral) but rather the profession itself. As I have discussed throughout this book, journalists in the Soviet Union saw themselves primarily as coparticipants in the governing of society – as educators, community organizers, and spokespeople for citizens unjustly wronged by Soviet bureaucracies. This kind of hands-on journalism was arguably less conducive to breeding cynicism than reporting on crime, disasters, accidents, and trumped-up dramas in the Anglo-American reportorial tradition (Chalaby 1996). It is precisely this kind of fast-paced conflict- and scandal-driven reporting that entered Russia's public space with the removal of press censorship in the late 1980s. If Sloterdijk (1987: 307–315) is right in thinking that modern journalism and cynicism are phenomenologically related, then the arrival of the journalism of information in Russia might have meant the arrival of a particular kind of media cynicism as well.[8]

Another devil's advocate response to Inna Rudenko's lament might go like this: even if Soviet officials and cultural producers did not engage in open ideological disinhibition, surely many Soviets, both powerful and ordinary, engaged in ideological distancing – the other component of cynicism I identified earlier in this chapter. Alexei Yurchak's (2006) ethnography is often cited to illustrate precisely this point: that Soviet citizens routinely placed some emotional distance between themselves and official-sounding words and phrases as they

---

[8] Sloterdijk (1987: 307–315) views media cynicism as one of the most fundamental varieties of modern cynicism and devotes substantial attention to exploring its origins. He speculates that media cynicism stems from journalists' full awareness that they feed on people's unspoken "hunger for misadventure" and demand for sensations (p. 307). The media also bring a deluge of information to their audiences, and in that deluge the important and the unimportant are mixed together in pseudoequivalences. "Here, some are eating; there, some are dying. Here, the second car is discussed; there, a nationwide, catastrophic draught" (p. 309). Repeated exposure to pseudoequivalences, argues Sloterdijk, dulls our senses and helps to build our cynical muscle.

practiced living *vnye* (staying uninvolved in official politics but being acutely aware of it).

True, Yurchak (2006) would probably respond to all of this, but with one crucial exception. Soviet citizens' seemingly mindless participation in official events and other ideological formalities did not occur on its own but rather side-by-side with the more positive and meaningful experiences of state socialism. Despite their dissatisfaction with having to take part in ideological formalities, Soviet citizens generally considered state socialism a legitimate form of government and endorsed many of its tenets. Those included an orientation to the future, a belief that life can be continuously improved, a value placed on the pursuit of knowledge, collectivist ethics, an emphasis on sincerity, an ambivalence toward money, and so on. Dull ideological formalities and meaningful experiences of state socialism coexisted in the same cultural and cognitive space. Yurchak's (2006) ethnographic interlocutors refer to these meaningful aspects of life under socialism as opportunities to pursue "deep truths" (as opposed to the surface truths of ideological formalities) and as "work with meaning" (as opposed to pro forma performances of ideological tasks). It is crucial, Yurchak (2006: 141) emphasizes, that these positive meanings were not antithetical to the coercive experiences of Soviet officialdom but were "an indivisible, if somewhat paradoxical, element" of those experiences.

The same could be said about Soviet journalism. There were many aspects of working in Soviet newspapers that journalists found dull, frustrating, and outright oppressive. But there were many other aspects of being a Soviet journalist that one found meaningful and rewarding. Those, as detailed in Chapter 1, had to do with developing strong bonds with readers, having opportunities to be creative, acting on one's sense of fairness and justice, and knowing that the journalist could make a difference in ordinary people's lives (see also Wolfe 2006). Again, it is very important that the development of these social identities and bonds was occurring within the very same institutional structures of the party press where official Soviet ideological discourse was also produced.

So, on many occasions, ordinary Soviets disengaged from official politics *in order to* pursue values and ideals that were nevertheless congruent with the main tenets of state socialism. Nothing of this sort can be said for post-Soviet Russia. As Lev Gudkov (2005: 51) has argued and as ethnographers of postsocialism have shown, the roots of post-Soviet cynicism are in the passive-aggressive *ressentiment* of the people who for a brief moment believed in the redemptive possibility of a new political order and who were then bitterly disappointed. As Gudkov's colleagues at the Levada Center put it, after the fall of the Soviet Union, the majority of Russians "found themselves in a historical nowhere" (Levinson 2011; see also Levada 2006). The ideals and value orientations of state socialism receded, while the new positive meanings of liberalism, democracy, and the market failed to materialize. As in Weimar Germany, cynicism in post-Soviet Russia became the adaptive mechanism for coping with the meaninglessness of it all.

The Disinhibition of Domination

Let us now take a look at some examples of post-Soviet cynicism in Russian public culture throughout the long 2000s and consider their cultural implications. As discussed earlier in this chapter, the kind of cynicism one practices depends on where one is located in relation to power. Among those whom Sloterdijk (1987) called the "master cynics," the two constitutive components of cynicism – distancing and disinhibition – often go hand in hand. When the powerful display their emotional distance from the political issues at hand, they signal to the rest of us that they presumably have no personal investment in the content of political life and their role in it. In so doing, they admit to having power but not wanting the responsibility that comes with being a political actor – the sort of responsibility that Weber (1946) spoke about in *Politics as a Vocation*. Admitting to power without responsibility is how master cynics "bare all" through a combination of disinhibition and disengagement. Sloterdijk (1987: 111) put it best: "Modern cynicism ... is the masters' [response] to their own idealism as ideology and as masquerade ... In its cynicisms, hegemonic power airs its secrets a little, indulges in semi-self-enlightenment, and tells all" (Sloterdijk 1987: 111).

As Russian sociologist Boris Dubin (2005) pointed out, Russian President Vladimir Putin has been among the most adept performers of cynical disinhibition disguised as lack of interest in the issues at hand. When it suits him, Putin enjoys portraying himself as being *vnye* – aware of but emotionally distanced from the issues and problems brought to his attention, whether by journalists during press conferences or by bureaucrats or "regular people" during his televised encounters with them. As Dubin (2005) rightly notes, it is difficult to imagine Putin heading a mass demonstration or speaking spontaneously and passionately to a large crowd. One of the earliest and ill-famed examples of Putin's projected noninvolvement was his response to a question posed by Larry King on CNN in August 2000. Earlier that month, a Russian nuclear submarine exploded in the Barents Sea, killing the entire crew. Putin did not interrupt his vacation in Sochi to attend to the tragedy. When Larry King asked him later what had happened to the submarine, Putin famously responded, with a smirk on his face, "It sank." Putin then clarified that he considered the sinking of the submarine to be "a technical issue" and that politicians should leave technical issues to experts. On another tragic occasion, when one of Russia's leading investigative journalists, Anna Politkovskaya, was assassinated in her apartment building in October 2006, Putin famously remarked that Politkovskaya's death brought the Kremlin more problems than her publications ever did. This remark once again was an attempt to feign noninvolvement: it implied that neither Putin himself nor people under his command had been particularly worried about, interested in, or bothered by Politkovskaya's muckraking work.

On less infamous occasions, Putin similarly portrayed himself as uninterested in whatever he was being asked about, especially if the topic made him uncomfortable. Responding to a journalist's inquiry about the second trial of Mikhail Khodorkovsky (a former oil tycoon who spent ten years behind bars on false allegations), Putin shrugged his shoulders and said that he was not following Khodorkovsky's fate and did not even know there was a second trial going on (Pavlovsky and Gelman 2010). When legendary rock musician and civic activist Yuri Shevchuk unexpectedly confronted Putin at a televised charitable event, making critical remarks about corruption becoming rampant under Putin's presidency, Putin pretended not to know who Shevchuk was and evaded the question.[9] When asked by another journalist, also in 2010, why riot police routinely and violently break up the small demonstrations organized by opposition groups in Moscow, Putin claimed he knew nothing about it and was not particularly interested in finding out.[10] And during a televised phone-in with the nation at the end of 2011, when asked about the emergency meetings in the Kremlin

[9]   www.novayagazeta.ru/politics/3315.html (accessed July 3, 2014).
[10] www.kommersant.ru/doc/1495411 (accessed July 3, 2014).

after the first mass political protests in Moscow, Putin responded that he had not heard of any emergency meetings, nor was he particularly concerned about protests. "I have not noticed any panic in the Kremlin, although I have not really been there in a long time," Putin said nonchalantly. "I have actually been trying to learn to play hockey ... so I have not really been paying attention to what has been going on."[11] Gleb Pavlovsky, a long-time political consultant for the Kremlin who has since fallen out of favor, made an apt remark about this pattern of behavior by Putin. "[He thinks he] created a stable Russia, and you [journalists] are pestering him with these details, with these names [of Khodorkovsky, Shevchuk, and opposition leaders]. He is not interested in any of this, believe me!" (Pavlovsky and Gelman 2010).[12]

To be sure, when it suits him, Putin is also adept at showing disinhibition *without* the accompanying need to disengage. Historian Michael Gorham (2013) has usefully written about the images of the "strongman" (*silovik*) and of the "good ol' boy" (*muzhik*) Putin has cultivated throughout his tenure. Indeed, Putin has been fond of using prison and gang jargon to connote toughness toward his adversaries. Commonly, he hints at his desire to destroy his political opponents but stops short of openly threatening them. Gorham (2013: 88) suggests that in such cases Putin's speech is "equivalent to what in boxing is known as pulling a punch." This is a kind of disinhibition that "acknowledges existing codes of proper behavior ... while at the same time violating them" (Gorham 2013: 88).

In the early 2010s, instances of Putin's disinhibition began to be more frequent and more pronounced. In November 2011, for instance, in a televised meeting with the leadership of his party, United Russia, Putin revealed that during the financial crisis of 2008, he considered dissolving the Russian Duma and transferring its decision-making powers to the cabinet of ministers (which he headed at the time). Putin then further revealed that he was assured by the head of the United Russia party that the party "would act quickly" and would pass anything Putin wanted through the Duma (where the party held

---

[11] www.rg.ru/2011/12/15/stenogramma.html (accessed July 17, 2014).

[12] Of course, Putin could also simply be lying about his disinterest in topics that put him on the spot. For an indication of that, see Trudolyubov (2011). Or he could be trying to convince himself (as well as his audiences) that he is still coolly living *vnye* (aware of but not too concerned or worried about whatever is brought to his attention).

absolute majority), so there was no need to dissolve the Duma.[13] One of the few journalists in Moscow who noticed that piece of official news was Oleg Kashin. "If I understand right," Kashin (2011b) wrote, "[Putin is telling us that] there had been a serious discussion of something like a coup [in 2008], and the only reason it did not occur was because the Duma was already controlled by the executive branch anyway. Had the Duma been headed by different people, the executive branch would have dissolved the Duma and would not have made a big deal out of it."

In 2012, first at a summer camp for pro-government youth and then at an annual press conference, Putin further disclosed that he "could have easily changed the Constitution" back in 2008 in order to "stay on" as president for the third term in a row, but in the end, he resisted the temptation.[14] At least two things were remarkable about this statement. First, Putin once again signaled that he did not need the Duma or the courts to initiate major constitutional changes: he spoke as if he could do it alone. Second, in talking about the possibility of "staying on" for a third presidential term, Putin effectively implied that he did not need elections either. The way he framed it, the decision of who becomes the next president was his alone, not that of the voters.

Over time, Putin's repertoire of cynical disinhibition began to expand beyond feigning disinterest toward political opponents or hinting at his desire to destroy them. Starting in the early 2010s, Putin began to try his hand at mocking his adversaries, bordering on bullying and insults. During the wave of political protests in the winter of 2011–2012, for instance, Putin famously made fun of the protesters by comparing the look of their protest symbol – a white ribbon – to a used condom. In the same televised phone-in with the nation in December 2011, he likened the protesters to a tribe of monkeys (the Bandar-logs) from Rudyard Kipling's *Jungle Book*. On another occasion in 2012, he called the protesters "chaff" (*shelukha*) that would need to be sifted through in order for anyone worth paying attention to to emerge.[15] On still another occasion, he publicly called a professor at the Moscow Higher School of Economics a "moron"

---

[13] www.vz.ru/news/2011/11/24/541328.print.html (accessed July 8, 2014).

[14] http://vz.ru/politics/2012/7/31/591175.html and http://kremlin.ru/transcripts/17173 (accessed July 7, 2014).

[15] www.kommersant.ru/doc/2039603 (accessed July 8, 2014).

(*pridurok*) when the latter suggested that the Arctic region needs to be managed internationally and not by Russia alone.[16]

Even Putin's image of the "good ol' boy" began to be transformed under the influence of cynical disinhibition. In the national phone-in episode in April 2014, for instance, a working-class man from the Far East region of Khabarovsk turned to Putin with a plea to help build a road into his village. "I own a car and I pay a road tax of 4,000 rubles a year," the man said into the camera during the phone-in, "but we have no road! There is fifty kilometers from our village to the nearest federal highway, and there is no road!" On the split screens of their TV sets, the viewers could see Putin beginning to laugh hysterically as the man spoke. "If you don't have a road, why do you need a car?!" Putin sneered at the man. "Where do you drive your car, anyway?! Is this some kind of joke (*provokatsija*)?" Stunned, the caller was at a loss for words for a few of seconds. Eventually, he mumbled, "It's not a joke. It's an urgent problem here." The camera then cut to another caller.[17]

If Gorham (2013: 88) is right that Putin's main rhetorical strategy in the 2000s was one of pulling punches, then in the early 2010s Putin appeared to no longer be interested in being bound by existing conventions. Instead, he seemed to be more interested in creating a reality to which others would have to adjust.[18] Putin confirmed this indirectly in October 2012, when he gave an extended interview on a television program devoted to his sixtieth birthday. "I do whatever I like anyway," he said contentedly into the camera. "People have different opinions about it, but I do not deny myself anything."[19]

As the Russian saying goes, "the fish rots from the head down." Other powerful bureaucrats have been taking cues from Putin, and in recent years there has been no shortage of cynical disinhibition coming from high-ranking officials, members of the Duma, and other powerful political players. Several particularly egregious cases of official disinhibition have caught the attention of journalists and bloggers. But

[16] http://tvrain.ru/articles/putin_nazval_professora_vshe_pridurkom-353637/ (accessed July 8, 2014).

[17] http://youtu.be/MIcpQgwtMhY (accessed July 8, 2014).

[18] Compare this to the attitude widely attributed to Karl Rove of the George W. Bush administration: "We're an empire now, and when we act, we create our own reality. And while you're studying that reality ... we'll act again, creating other new realities, which you can study too, and that's how things will sort out" (Suskind 2004).

[19] www.ntv.ru/peredacha/CT/m23400/o113999/ (accessed July 8, 2014).

instead of becoming major public scandals, they generated little public commotion and no official reaction. One well-publicized case involved Alexander Tkachev, the governor of the Krasnodar region in the south of Russia until 2015. In the summer of 2012, massive flooding occurred in a mountainous area of that region. Almost 200 people died, and 30,000 people lost their homes. Thanks to the investigative work of citizen journalists, it quickly became clear that the region's authorities knew about the upcoming flood hours in advance. Not only did the authorities fail to evacuate people from the zone of the fast-approaching flood, but they also failed to sound any emergency warnings whatsoever. As tens of thousands of people went to sleep suspecting nothing, the governor, the mayor, and other regional and local officials busied themselves airlifting their families from the zone of the impending tragedy. When Governor Tkachev was confronted by outraged citizens demanding to know why no one had been warned about the flood, Tkachev famously declared, with a straight face and with cameras rolling, "Yes, we knew about the possibility of the flood about three hours in advance ... And what was I supposed to do? To knock on every door? With what resources? And then – even if we did knock on every door – do you really think you all would have gotten up and left?"[20] As the Russian blogosphere reeled at this galling admission of official negligence, Governor Tkachev flew to Moscow where his patron, President Putin, commended him for the handling of the tragedy. Only the mayor of the town most affected by the flood lost his job.

Another regional leader who became known for his openly dismissive attitude toward citizens is Georgy Poltavchenko, governor of the St. Petersburg region. During a visit to St. Petersburg of Russia's Prime Minister, Dmitry Medvedev, in October 2012, some residents demonstrated what they thought of their Prime Minister by disapprovingly honking their horns and making offensive gestures at Medvedev's motorcade. When asked to publicly comment on the incident, Governor Poltavchenko, disparagingly, called those who honked and made gestures at Medvedev "scumbags" (*zhloby*).[21] Since that day, Poltavchenko is apparently known in St. Petersburg as "the scumbag governor."[22]

[20] http://echo.msk.ru/blog/echomsk/907179-echo/ (accessed July 10, 2014).
[21] www.gazeta.spb.ru/885650-1/ (accessed July 14, 2014).
[22] http://navalny.com/p/3675/ (accessed July 14, 2014).

Cynical disinhibition among Russian officials has become especially pronounced in their encounters with journalists. This is probably because officials come into contact with journalists more frequently than with ordinary citizens. Journalists working for independent and semi-independent media organizations, as well as their inexperienced colleagues elsewhere (as opposed to experienced "court" reporters), became an especially good target of official mocking and bullying throughout the 2000s and early 2010s. Several factors worked together to make this happen. First, officials at all levels have been taking cues from the top that they can increasingly mock, ridicule, and insult anyone with less power, including journalists, with impunity. Second, there continues to be widespread contemptuous perception of all journalists as members of the "second oldest profession" – a perception that did not wane throughout the 2000s. Lastly, Russian journalism continues to be plagued by an abysmal lack of professional solidarity. Journalists I knew in Nizhny Novgorod and their colleagues in Moscow I was following online complained tirelessly about being treated as "servants" (*obsluga*) by officials at all levels (Mostovshchikov 2011; Svetova 2012). The journalists also complained that ordinary people turned away from them or hurled insults at them when they learned they were talking to journalists (Dikov 2011b; Turkova 2011).[23]

Some high-ranking officials seem to be deriving special pleasure from insulting, mocking, or threatening nonconforming journalists. For instance, Alexander Bastrykin, Putin's classmate and head of the Investigative Committee of Russia,[24] entered into an open conflict with *Novaya Gazeta*, one of the few remaining independent publications with national distribution, in July 2012. Bastrykin was displeased with the way *Novaya Gazeta* correspondent Sergei Sokolov had portrayed Bastrykin in one of his earlier stories. In retaliation, Bastrykin ordered his security staff to forcibly take Sokolov into a wooded area outside of Moscow, where Bastrykin personally threatened Sokolov's life and safety. "If I wanted to," Bastrykin told Sokolov, "I could order to kill you and then head the investigation into your murder."[25] Sokolov and his editor

---

[23] See also www.facebook.com/sergey.mayorov.7/posts/511756545534466 (accessed July 10, 2014).

[24] Formally an independent government agency, formerly under the office of the Prosecutor General of the Russian Federation.

[25] www.gazeta.ru/politics/2012/06/13_a_4624173.shtml (accessed July 10, 2014).

made the incident public,[26] yet no official reaction followed. Bastrykin was not held accountable in any way for openly threatening the life of a journalist.

Russian officials' contemptuous attitude toward journalists culminated in a public speech given by Deputy Minister of Mass Communication Alexei Volin at the Department of Journalism at Moscow State University (MSU) in the fall of 2012. Pulling no punches, Volin told journalism educators at MSU that their most important job was to teach students how to take orders from whoever is paying them (*slushat'sia diadiu*).[27] The exquisite irony of the situation was that Volin was speaking at a conference held at MSU and titled, "Journalism and Its Public Mission." "Journalism has no mission," Volin declared. "Journalism is a business. Young journalists should know that they will be writing whatever their owner tells them. If you are not teaching them about that part of their job, you are committing a crime." During the question and answer session, one journalism professor, still in shock from Volin's remarks, asked Volin if he had considered the reaction his words would elicit among the MSU professoriate. "I don't give a damn about your reaction," Volin shot back, unperturbed. Another shocked audience member asked how Volin's remarks squared with the freedom-of-speech provision in Russia's law on the press. "You should first figure out what you want," Volin retorted. "Do you want to talk abstract generalities or do you want to talk business?"[28]

While mistrustful attitude toward journalists has been around since the mid-1990s, as Chapters 2 and 3 demonstrated, the open slighting of the profession – of the kind demonstrated by Volin – became more of a phenomenon during the long 2000s. In the 1990s, most officials did not yet feel that they could snub or insult journalists to the extent that became possible by the late 2000s. Back in the 1990s, it was only the owners and sponsors of media outlets who allowed themselves to act as if they owned not only the media outlets but also the people working for them. Bureaucrats and officials who did not own or sponsor media organizations but who interacted with journalists on a daily basis did not yet feel like they could treat journalists in an openly dismissive or

---

[26] *Novaya Gazeta* had four staff journalists, including Anna Politkovskaya, assassinated since 2000. Fear for Sokolov's life likely made the editor of *Novaya Gazeta* decide to publicize the incident.

[27] www.msunews.ru/news/3061/ (accessed July 10, 2014).   [28] *Ibid.*

insulting manner. This changed by the late 2000s, when, regardless of their status, many officials began to openly treat journalists as if they were indeed their servants.

With the proliferation of Twitter in the late 2000s and early 2010s, the mocking and bullying by officials – of journalists and disagreeable others – became even more widespread. Members of the Duma elected in 2011 were particularly fond of using Twitter to mock and insult those with less power who stood in their way. In March 2013, for instance, a Member of the Duma named Andrei Isayev tweeted: "A snide little put-down against three women-MPs in a vile little tabloid paper today. The slimeballs who did this had better know: we will not forgive, we will not forget!"[29] Isayev was referring to an article published in *Moskovsky Komsomolets* (*MK*), a semi-independent private newspaper in Moscow, about recent political scandals around three female members of the Duma. The article was titled, "Political Prostitution Has Changed Gender." As if his first tweet was not enough, Isayev followed up with a more direct threat against the newspaper: "Little scum, relax [*melkie tvari, rasslabtes'*], we do not care about you. But our retaliation against the author [of the article] and the editor [of *MK*] will be harsh and tough."[30] Perhaps because this threat was so direct and so public, or perhaps because the tide finally began to shift, this incident led to a small show of solidarity among professional journalists in Moscow. Isayev was publicly shamed in several news outlets across the city. He let the criticism pass, and the incident was over.[31]

So what is going on here? Why this compulsion among the powerful to openly threaten, mock, and insult one's political adversaries, journalists, and even ordinary citizens? One explanation would be to say that the powerful in Russia are doing it simply because they can, especially when they feel they are being provoked by those with less power. This is precisely what Sloterdijk (1987: 218) calls "master

---

[29] https://twitter.com/AK_Isaev/status/312618265098727425 (accessed July 11, 2014).

[30] https://twitter.com/AK_Isaev/status/312636557792256000 (accessed July 10, 2014).

[31] For additional examples of Russian MPs insulting and mocking citizens, see https://twitter.com/A_Sidyakin/status/202328538500710400, https://twitter.com/NickValuev/statuses/223835315297722368, https://twitter.com/Rogozi n/status/233229407853096961, and https://twitter.com/ildrozdov/status/2812 90763957063680 (all accessed July 10, 2014).

cynicism" or the "cynicism of domination." As he reminds us, power only likes to laugh at its own jokes. When the joke comes "from below" and is at the master's expense, "the master lifts the mask, smiles at his weak adversary, and suppresses him" (Sloterdijk 1987: 111).

A related way to make sense of the bullying and mocking of citizens by officials is to see it simply as villainy. This sends us back to the old Christian definition of cynics as clear-headed ill-willed characters who effectively embody evil.[32] This interpretation works for the preceding examples where the powerful attack the powerless without any apparent provocation from the latter. Vladimir Putin ridiculing the man from a faraway village for owning a car he does not drive or the Deputy Minister of Mass Communication humiliating a group of journalism professors without any apparent reason could certainly be understood as examples of plain, old evildoing.

When the powerful who attack the powerless (with or without provocation) can give an account of what they are doing, we are dealing with finite evildoing (Arendt 1971). Real villains – that is, evildoers who acknowledge themselves as such – are relatively rare, according to Arendt. They are usually driven by – and in that sense limited by – their motives (jealousy, envy, resentment, and the like). Most of the evil in the world is *not* done by villains, Hannah Arendt (1971) argued, but by "the non-wicked everybody who has no special motives and for this reason is capable of infinite evil" (p. 445). Sloterdijk (1987) makes a similar observation, noting that cynical disinhibition by the powerful is a rare occurrence. There are many people in power who might never "lift their mask" so as to publicly humiliate their weaker adversaries. Disinhibition among the powerful is rare, argues Sloterdijk (1987), because on some level it is still about irreverence and cheekiness and, in that sense, about nonconformity. Only it is "a cheekiness that has changed sides" (p. 111).

So plain, old villainy can account for some of the official disinhibition I described earlier, but it is not enough to explain why cynicism among the powerful in Russia continues to be seen as a growing trend.[33] That the powerful are more willing than ever to lift their

---

[32] The Christian connotations of cynicism as an embodiment of evil carried over into the Soviet era. See, for instance, the *Soviet Dictionary of Ethics*, published in 1975 (quoted in Lipovetsky 2014).

[33] See Gerasimov 2014; Guriev 2013; Kamyshev 2012; Lipovetsky 2014; Sorokina et al. 2012.

masks and not give it a second thought must be connected to the deepening of mass cynicism in Russia that took place during the long 2000s (Gudkov 2005; Shevchenko 2009). The disinhibition of the powerful and the cynicism of the powerless likely developed in lockstep throughout this period, resonating with and reinforcing each other.

A key role in aligning the two cynicisms during this period was played by the people I have called *friends of power*. These were cultural producers, including TV and radio personalities, who drew their identities from their proximity to power. Despite identifying with the powerful, these journalists, producers, and hosts remained popular with their nonelite audiences – in part due to the particular variety of cynicism they practiced. What was their cynicism about? How did it articulate with the cynicism of the powerful and the powerless? What were the long-term consequences of those articulations? The next section addresses those questions.

Friends of Power and the New *Stiob*

To examine the dynamics of cynicism among the friends of power, let us turn to the cultural products made by them. Entertainment programs (talk shows, cabaret sketches, standup comedy, and so on) were among the most popular genres of TV cultural production in the 2000s and early 2010s (Borodina 2014). That the ratings for entertainment programs would stay exceptionally high throughout this period is indeed what one would expect in the increasingly authoritarian climate of Putin's Russia.[34] One would not necessarily expect, however, the pervasive cynicism that became the signature aesthetic of those programs. A cynical aesthetic became especially prominent in what became known as the "new humor" with such shows as *ProzhektorPerisHilton, Vecherny Urgant, Multlichnosti,* and *Kamedi Klab* distinguishing themselves from their late-Soviet and early post-Soviet predecessors (Aleksandrov 2009; Sheremet 2009; Prorokov 2014).

There was both continuity and break between the new humor of the long 2000s and the forms of irony that preceded it in the 1980s and

---

[34] Political communication scholars have long recognized that authoritarian governments work hard to maintain robust entertainment industries (e.g., Porto 2012).

early 1990s. In late socialism, the most common form of irony in nonofficial public culture was known as *stiob* (Boyer and Yurchak 2010; Yurchak 2006, 2011). *Stiob*'s humorous effect was achieved through speakers' overidentification with official Soviet rhetoric. Such overidentification created an all-important ambiguity to the point that it was sometimes difficult to tell whether the speaker was serious or joking – that is, whether he or she genuinely endorsed communist rhetoric or was subtly mocking it.[35] As an aesthetic practice, *stiob* also worked as a class and education marker among Soviet artists and intellectuals. Instantly recognizing *stiob* for what it was, Soviet intellectuals could mark their distance from the presumably naive others who might be confused by the ambiguity of *stiob*.

Needless to say, irony through overidentification was one of the most effective and safe ways to distance oneself from Soviet officialdom without openly challenging it. Through *stiob*, one could signal to others that one was not fooled by Soviet ideological pronouncements, that one could tell the difference between ideological formalities and the more meaningful aspects of socialism, and that one could do it safely, without showing up on the official radar.[36] But, Yurchak (2006: 250) insists, *stiob* was a complex phenomenon and should not be reduced to anti-Soviet resistance through humor. Through the ambiguity contained in *stiob*, the speaker could also show some "affinity and warmth" toward socialist ideals and goals.[37]

For a generation of educated Soviets born between the 1950s and 1970s, then, *stiob* and living *vnye* (aware of what is going on but not involved in it) became key modes of relating to power. This ironic, semi-detached relation to power became part of the habitus – a set of

---

[35] In some respects, *stiob* was not unlike what Stephen Colbert practiced on his show on Comedy Central in the United States, where he overidentified with his ideologically conservative rivals in order to mock them (Boyer and Yurchak 2010). In other important ways, though, *stiob* was very different from Colbert's satirical work. Colbert's audiences were rarely in doubt about where Colbert stood politically and morally: he has made his political stances clear off the show. This cannot be said about the late-Soviet practitioners of *stiob*.
As Yurchak (2006: 251; 2011) demonstrates, when asked directly, the late-Soviet *stiob* artists were either unable to or uninterested in clarifying their political and moral stances for their audiences.

[36] There are important similarities here between the social workings of *stiob* and of "knowing smiles" analyzed by Alena Ledeneva (2011).

[37] For a similar argument on the working of sympathetic irony in special period Cuba, see Tanuma (2007).

transportable dispositions – that many educated Soviets took with them into the post-Soviet period. In the 1990s, it was no longer only communist rhetoric but a much greater range of political discourses, including liberalism, feminism, capitalism, and democracy promotion, that began to be treated with ironic detachment (Yurchak 1999; 2006).

Somewhere during the 1990s, though, *stiob* lost the ambiguity through which its ironic effect was achieved. Post-Soviet *stiob* increasingly became simply about mocking or ridiculing something (Lipovetsky 2014; Nesterenko 2008; Sorokin 2013; Yurchak 1999). Without that ambiguity, the new *stiob* began to move out of the space of irony and into the space of satire, where open mocking is the norm.[38] At the same time – and this is the key difference – the new *stiob* retained some elements of irony, namely, the ironist's emotional detachment from the topic at hand.[39] Unlike the satirist, the *stiob* artist is not passionate about what he or she satirizes. The new *stiob* mocks from no place of conviction; it is passionless mockery.[40]

With its nondiscriminating attitude about what to mock, the new *stiob* has been working particularly well for Putin's Russia. Whenever something is off limits, there is always something else that could be made fun of, since for the new *stiob* any topic is as good as any other. If one cannot mock Russian political elites, one can always take jibes at Western leaders, ridiculing their hypocrisy, double standards, and liberal values. Western frills such as toleration of otherness and respect for the law have become very popular objects of mockery on Russian

[38] Several nightly entertainment programs on Russian TV have tried to model themselves on popular satirical shows in the United States, including "The Late Night Show" and "The Daily Show." Unlike their US counterparts, though, the Russian shows are prerecorded and undergo strict censorship (Bazarova 2009; Dikov 2011b; Grymov 2012; Gubin and Loshak 2011). Needless to say, this has severely undercut their satirical potential (Benyumov 2012; Petrovskaya 2010; Sheremet 2009; Trudolyubov 2013a).

[39] In Sloterdijk's terms, the satirist is a *kynic* (not a cynic): an irreverent truth-seeker whose mocking challenges the status quo from within a particular system of ideals and values. The *stiob* man, on the other hand, is a bona fide cynic – someone who feels occasional dismay but "with most things . . . can't really give a damn" (Sloterdijk 1987: 99).

[40] One could argue that *stiob* died with the collapse of the Soviet Union, and what I am calling the *new stiob* is no *stiob* at all but simply mockery. The problem is, Russians still use the word *stiob*, now more so than ever. I believe we are witnessing a transformation of a phenomenon rather than its disappearance. Literary critic Mark Lipovetsky (2014) makes a similar argument.

radio and television. Other humanist values – such as compassion for the weak, honoring the dead, standing by one's words, and the like – have also been suitable objects of *stiob* (Dubin 2005; Nesterenko 2008; Sorokina et al. 2012).

Let me illustrate this trend with a couple of examples from the early 2010s. Consider a segment from a popular cooking show that aired on nationwide Channel 1 in prime time in 2013. The show was hosted by Ivan Urgant, arguably Russia's top comedian and television entertainer today. An episode of the show was devoted to making borscht, a traditional Ukrainian beat soup. The episode aired months before Russia's military standoff with Ukraine, so there was no direct relation to the conflict that ensued. Still, the episode aired against the backdrop of a long and complicated history of interethnic relations between Russians and Ukrainians.

Ivan Urgant was cohosting the borscht episode with another screen-writer and director, Alexander Adabashian. Cutting fresh herbs in front of the camera, Urgant made a crack, "And here I am cutting up the greens like a Red Army commissar would cut up some Ukrainian villagers [during World War II]." Urgant's cohost, Adabashian, did not miss a beat. Vigorously shaking his hatchet to get rid of the bits of greens stuck to it, Adabashian chimed in, "And here I am shaking off the remains of the villagers [into the borscht]" (Petrovskaya 2013). When liberal television critics and bloggers attempted to shame Urgant for having crossed a moral line, Urgant tried to laugh it off at first. Eventually and under some pressure from colleagues, Urgant did apologize for the joke in a subsequent episode of the program.

Not so with the hosts of another talk show that aired on Mayak, a state-owned national radio network, in 2012. Since its inception, the show (*Bolyachki* ["Sore Spots"]) was in the habit of entertaining listeners by discussing symptoms of different diseases. Over the years, it morphed into what one television critic called "The Program Otherwise Known as 'Let's Laugh at the Sick'" (Petrovskaya and Larina 2012). A memorable broadcast in October 2012 was devoted to a discussion of cystic fibrosis in children. As usual, the producers invited a medical doctor into the studio to speak at length about the symptoms of the disease. The hosts then spent almost an hour inter-rupting the doctor, taunting him, mocking his descriptions, cracking jokes, and laughing at the debilitating symptoms of the disease (Tankova 2012).

This was not the first time the hosts of *Bolyachki* made fun of a disease in their program. But it was the first time an online discussion about it ensued, in part in response to the outrage of parents with children with cystic fibrosis.[41] Ruslan Orekhov, a host at *Komsomolskaya Pravda-TV*, tried to explain why the genre of laughing at the sick has been in demand in Russia. "I am trying to understand the hosts at the Mayak station," Orekhov wrote. "Yes, it has become difficult to make jokes these days. So many topics are off limits – politicians, sponsors, VIPs who can offend and take offence. But the morning show must go on. And it is important that it is not heavy, because everyone is tired of heavy topics. It is imperative to demonstrate a carefree attitude to things, to anything. The easiest way to do that is not to think about the details of what is being discussed ... Then 'professionalism' becomes about keeping the conversation smooth-going, chuckling in a well-trained voice, and cracking jokes about whatever comes your way, *without giving it any thought*" (Orekhov and Pomidorov 2012, emphasis added).

Sociologist and philosopher Boris Dubin (2005) offered further insight into why laughing at the sick or joking about war crimes became acceptable on Russian radio and television. The people who ended up in charge of broadcasting in post-Soviet Russia, says Dubin, belong to the generation who came of age amid the culture of late-Soviet *stiob*. The power of *stiob*, we may recall, lay in the presumed uncertainty of the naive listener as to the sincerity and seriousness of the speaker. Dubin (2005) sees the same dynamic reemerging in what I am calling the *new stiob*. The new *stiob*, as we saw, is no longer about over-identification with official rhetoric – it is now about indiscriminate mockery. Still, the new *stiob* can leave audiences confused or uncertain as to the intentions of the speaker. Could Ivan Urgant really be making light of murders of civilians during World War II? Did the Mayak radio hosts really mean to laugh their heads off at the debilitating symptoms of cystic fibrosis? The image of the naive listener who is either confused by what he or she is hearing or takes it at face value reemerges in the new *stiob*.[42] Once again, *stiob* becomes a marker of class distinction

---

[41] The program was eventually closed in the aftermath of the scandal.

[42] This disparaging attitude of many media producers toward their audiences is encapsulated in a popular meme, *pipl havayet* ("the masses are eating it up," a creative neologism drawing on English words "people" and "to have" and referring to the belief that mass audiences unthinkingly absorb whatever they

among "those in the know" (*svoi* in Dubin's phrase). Practiced by media producers and hosts as a condescending "smile of augurs," *stiob* is now also a vehicle through which TV and radio personalities can align their identities with those of the powerful.

If all this is going on, we may ask, why haven't viewers and listeners figured this out yet – that they are being treated like idiots? Well, many of them have, says Dubin (2005: 28), and they have turned away from *stiob* entertainment altogether or consume it without enthusiasm, especially when no alternatives are within easy reach. But another problem with the new *stiob* that contributes to its resilience is that it actively disavows itself as an intelligent and intelligible practice. It is not a coincidence, Dubin (2005: 27) says, that starting in the late 1990s, many entertainment programs explicitly featured "all kinds of dummies and nitwits" (*durni i pridurki*) as hosts and protagonists. "Their communicative formula can be summarized this way: by demonstrating total idiocy,[43] the mass communicator offers a position that is neither in on the action nor fully removed from it – a point of being *vnye* that is actually very addictive. It can be compared with looking through a peephole – into the world of power, politics, history, sex, and so on" (Dubin 2005: 27). While looking through a collective peephole may be mesmerizing, it discourages relating to, reflecting on, and forming opinions about what one is witnessing and doing. In such acts of mass communication, Dubin argues, the main message that ends up being transmitted is the idea of being *vnye* itself – the idea of "indeterminacy, transiency, and evaluative uncertainty of the entire social whole" (Dubin 2005: 27).

To see a particularly good example of what Dubin means, consider a news story that ran on October 16, 2012, on major Russian TV networks.[44] Journalists reported on a unique scientific experiment that had apparently just been conducted on humans. For a month, six volunteers were locked in an improvised gas chamber inhaling

---

are fed). The remarkable fact about *pipl havayet* is that media executives and on-the-air personalities feel they can invoke this meme publicly, in classic acts of cynical disinhibition, in front of the very masses they deride (Dubin 2005; Petrovskaya 2011; Shestopal and Kachkaeva 2006). See also Loshak (2011b).

[43] Dubin is probably aware that the modern word *idiot* descends directly from the Greek word for "private." For the Greeks, the private was a dehumanized realm where we live our biological lives as animals. It is only in the public realm that our actions acquire intelligibility and meaning (Arendt 1958).

[44] http://www.1tv.ru/news/techno/217775, accessed December 8, 2014.

excessive amounts of carbon monoxide at 38°C. The experiment was led by Yevgeny Chazov, a well-known cardiologist and member of the Russian Academy of Sciences. Speaking to REN-TV journalists about the purported success of the experiment, Chazov did not hide his excitement: "Your crew is the first in the world to see this. You are lucky ... These conditions [of overexposure to carbon monoxide] usually cause severe injuries in people. The death toll is high. What can help people in such circumstances?" (Taroshchina 2012). Chazov and his team now have a chance to find out. And what about the volunteers who spent a month in the gas chamber? They could not be interviewed because they were in a rehabilitation program recovering from the experiment.

What can viewers take away from a news report like that? Well, they will likely pick up on the fact that carbon monoxide is toxic and therefore dangerous for humans – that message and its moral valence are clear. But what about the morality of conducting a toxic experiment on humans in the first place? That question is raised neither by the scientists nor by the journalists. Lest viewers begin to wonder about that on their own, academician Chazov reassures them that the experiment is of great value to humanity. At the same time, Chazov *is* clearly worried about the high death toll from overexposure to carbon monoxide. That once again might suggest to viewers that such an experiment cannot possibly be a good thing. But then again, Chazov and his team are already excited about the next phase of the trial: in addition to injections of carbon monoxide and high temperatures, sudden changes in atmospheric pressure will be introduced into the gas chamber as a new variable (Taroshchina 2012).

Communicatively speaking, Dubin (2005, 2011) would say, a report such as this is an empty vessel: it prevents the transmittable content from being comprehended and available for reflection, let alone moving past it. The back and forth between the worry and the excitement about carbon monoxide overexposure clears the very idea of "a toxic experiment on humans" of negative moral valence. When concepts are unhinged from their moral valences like this, the process of communication loses intelligibility. Communication begins to occur "outside [*vnye*] the structures of subjectivity formation – outside our ability to hold onto values, outside our ability to experience embarrassment and shock, outside the production of new meanings, outside the inescapability of making choices and being held responsible for them" (Dubin 2005: 29).

Losing the World in Common

Hannah Arendt (1951, 1958, 1968) likely would have recognized in this state of affairs symptoms of the loss of the world known in common. Arendt understood the world in common to be the world of shared meanings and human relations on which people rely to orient themselves in the ever-changing flow of events. Such a world emerges when we speak in public, stand by our words, and mean what we say. This world allows us to hold steady amid uncertainty, to temporarily hold some things constant so that we can act. The world in common is thus both an achievement and a need: without it, we are disoriented and do not know what we are doing.

The condition of worldlessness – of people losing the world in common – is central to Arendt's theorizing of totalitarianism (1951). Totalitarian movements, Arendt argued, destroy the webs of human relations and shared meanings from which the world in common springs, replacing them with brand-new alternative realities. In those realities, things start to be called the opposite of what they are, and evil loses "the quality by which most people recognize it – the quality of temptation" (Arendt 1963: 150). Compared with the reality of the world in common, though, the alternative realities of totalitarian movements are impermanent and "wobbly" and cannot serve as the foundation from which people can meaningfully think and act. Yet these realities do have an effect: they invite "a peculiar kind of cynicism – an absolute refusal to believe in the truth of anything" (Arendt 2000: 567). "The result of a consistent and total substitution of lies for factual truth is not that the lies will now be accepted as truth, and the truth be defamed as lies, but that the sense by which we take our bearings in the real world – and the category of truth vs. falsehood is among the mental means to this end – is being destroyed. And for this trouble there is no remedy" (Arendt 2000: 567–568).

During the long 2000s, Russia was obviously far from classic totalitarianism as theorized by Arendt, but there were many signs that the world in common from which people would normally take their bearings slowly began to erode. By the early 2010s, for instance, a growing number of journalists, bloggers, and other public figures began to remark on the disorientation they felt in their professional and personal lives – disorientation from not recognizing the reality in which they increasingly found themselves. One frequent complaint has been about the disorienting speed with which the boundaries around what is acceptable – politically, professionally, and morally – began to be removed.[45] Those working in television, for instance, began to note that for some of their colleagues, coercing someone to speak on camera has become a regular occurrence. This could be achieved through a combination of physical violence against the interviewee, verbal provocations by the journalist, and plain, old trickery.[46] The video footage obtained in this way can then be used as TV producers see fit: an off-screen voice can finish the sentences for the people caught on camera, the recording can be cut up and spliced back together to mean the opposite of what the interviewee said, and so on (Gazeta.RU 2012; Oss 2012). In the classic manner of cynical disinhibition, some of those practicing reportorial coercion are openly unapologetic about what they are doing (Bykhovskaya 2011, 2012; Shmelev 2013). NTV reporters, for instance, have admitted that they misrepresent themselves to citizens, falsify interview questions, and likely hack into people's phones to get the information they want (Gazeta.RU 2012; Semin 2014). Hacking into e-mail accounts of nonconformist public figures has also been publicly celebrated rather than condemned (Izvestia.RU 2012; Malgin 2012a). As Daniil Dondurei (2011), magazine editor and cultural critic, woefully summed it up, "It is as if we all found ourselves inside a Zimbardo experiment. We suddenly realized we are allowed to use violence with impunity."

Another indicator of people losing the world in common has been cases of literal breakdown in communication between journalists I was following online and those of their colleagues who appear to treat beliefs as if they were opinions.[47] "I run into more and more people who do not understand that changing their beliefs for money, or to please somebody, [or for fun] is not a good idea in principle," writes publisher, blogger, and radio host Sergei Parkhomenko (2011). "When you point it out to them and reproach them for it, they honestly do not understand what they are being accused of." Distressed by one such encounter, blogger Alexei Novikov (2012) decided to publicize it. Novikov published his e-mail exchange with a reporter for Russia One, the government's official TV channel. The reporter asked Novikov

---

[45] See Guriev (2013); Sonin (2012); Sorokina et al. (2012); Troitsky (2011).
[46] See Dikov (2011a); Kichanova (2012); Malgin (2012b); Turovsky (2011).
[47] See Glaeser (2000), particularly chap. 5 ("Challenging Sincerity"), on the anxiety about changing beliefs "as often as shirts" in postunification Berlin.

(who lives in Kiev) to go on the record as someone who lives abroad and who is paid to subvert the Russian government through social media. "It really doesn't matter if it's true or not," the reporter assured Novikov. "We just need someone gregarious, cynical, technically proficient, and with an excellent Kievan accent." In disbelief, Novikov refused, saying that he found such an offer "massively insulting." The reporter seemed unperturbed. "Hmm," he wrote back to Novikov. "I did not want to offend you. It's just business. Too bad we did not find any common points here."[48]

Why are Parkhomenko, Novikov, and other writers disturbed when their interlocutors treat their (and their own) beliefs as opinions? Because assertions of belief, unlike expressions of opinion, are fundamental to how we acquire knowledge about the world (Williams 2002). Assertions of belief are invitations to rely on, to trust the speaker and his or her message. And trusting, as much as doubt, is central to the production of all knowledge: We can only doubt something if we can check it against the sources we trust (Shapin 1994). Expectations of constancy and consistency of beliefs are precisely what separates belief from opinion. Those expectations are akin to promises: we rely on them as we struggle to judge, act, and think (Arendt 1958; Williams 2002). When those promises are invalidated, we feel disoriented because we suddenly lose a crucial navigational tool for taking our bearings in the world of perpetual change.[49]

One final source of discomfort coming from concerned journalists, columnists, and bloggers worth mentioning is their sense that the rules of logical reasoning no longer apply in much of public discourse in Russia, particularly when it comes to establishing cause-and-effect relations. Moscow journalist Kyrill Rogov (2005) captured this sense of logical disorientation particularly well:

If you say that Putin is destroying democracy in Russia, you will hear, in response, that there was never any democracy in Russia to destroy. If you say that Putin is robbing capitalists of their property only to hand it to his own

---

[48] See also Shenderovich (2011); Romanova (2012); Shmelev (2013).

[49] Keeping one's beliefs consistent does not mean one can never revise them. Sometimes one has to reevaluate what one holds dearly, perhaps even to a point of entering into a moral conflict. One might have to reconcile ideas and principles that have become incommensurable or decide which principle is more operative in a particular situation. Publicly acknowledging this process is an important part of maintaining one's integrity (Halfon 1989).

kind, you will hear that there was never any private property in Russia to begin with – there was only robbery. If you say that the Kremlin has turned the legal system into a cover-up for its dubious machinations, you will hear that the laws were never obeyed in Russia anyway. So what are we supposed to do?! We do not need democracy *because* there is none and has never been any. Private property will not be protected *because* we tend to steal from one another anyway ... *Because* the owner of NTV, media mogul Vladimir Gusinsky used his television for mercenary ends [in the 1990s], that is why all of our television channels can now be filled with propaganda ... The logic of these responses is very telling and important for understanding the current historical moment in Russia [emphasis added].[50]

Psychologist and columnist Anna Fenko (2012) offers a useful explanation why such twists of logic are indicators of a serious problem in contemporary Russia. Fenko (2012) draws on Jean Piaget (1950), who argued that logical reasoning is not something we are born with or something we can take in from authority figures but rather something we must discover on our own through social and intellectual cooperation with others. It is in the presence of others, argued Piaget, that a child starts to follow the rules of logic for the first time, which are fundamentally the rules of social behavior as well. What happens, asks Fenko (2012), when those rules come undone? When we find no logic in the actions of a single person, says Fenko (2012), we call such actions stupid. When we find no logic in the behaviors of many people, we call such behaviors absurd. But when we start seeing distortions of logic everywhere, we start to lose the ground under our feet.

This sense of disorientation from the absurdity of Russian political life as a whole was summarized particularly well by Yulia Muchnik, a prize-winning journalist from the city of Tomsk. Muchnik wrote her blogpost after one of the activists in the Russian opposition, Leonid Razvozzhayev, was kidnapped in Kiev in October 2012. Razvozzhayev later turned up in a Russian jail, where human rights activists saw him and claimed he had been tortured. The Russian officials denied he had been tortured, claiming instead that he had willfully surrendered. Reflecting on those events and claims, Muchnik wrote:

I think the comparisons people are making right now with [Stalin's Great Terror] are emotionally understandable, but they are not very helpful in

---

[50] See also Fenko (2012); Gerasimov (2014); Kamyshev (2012); Muchnik (2012); Panyushkin (2005); Rubtsov (2012); Yampolsky (2014).

comprehending the reality we are in right now. This reality is hideous, disgusting, absurd. But most importantly – it is different. In this new reality, human rights activists have no problem getting access to a prisoner; one can watch YouTube clips of the prisoner who says 'I was tortured'; and all of this can be discussed on Facebook and on [remaining independent] radio and television stations. All the while, no one believes anybody, anything can turn out to be true or not true. Everything is relative, no one's authority is respected, all words are worthless, all slogans disgusting . . . This is a very different reality where none of us had been before.[51]

This loss of the world in common I have been describing here and the moral disorientation that accompanies it are mentally and emotionally taxing. Based on her ethnographic research in the city of Perm in the late 2000s and early 2010s, anthropologist Anna Kruglova (2014) documents how ordinary Russians, overtaxed in their ability to deal with the world around them, aimed for a certain kind of "emptiness of mind" in interactions with others. "Everyone [felt] so vitally, mentally, and psychologically fatigued" that they wanted "the topics, registers and sounds of conversations [to] be very sensitively kept 'clean' or 'empty'" (Kruglova 2014). The desire for mental cleanliness or emptiness was the result of anxiety around communication as a polluting process, argues Kruglova (2014). Speech was polluting when it was high in pathos, contained declarative assertions and logical appeals, and made frequent use of concepts and abstract terms. Polluting speech unnecessarily "loaded" people "down" with excessive information (*gruzit'*), overtaxing their capacity to feel, think, and act. It is no surprise that the mass media, particularly those covering politics, were seen as an especially rich source of communicative pollution. It is also no coincidence that during the long 2000s, the television set was appropriately nicknamed "the zombie box" (*zomboyashchik*).[52]

Cultivating nonthinking became a communicative goal, albeit a difficult one, for many Russians (Kruglova 2014). Commenting on the difficulty of achieving a "clean and empty" mind, Kruglova's interlocutors spoke of being "burdened by education" or even of having been "indoctrinated into the values of critical thinking" (Kruglova 2014). "Keeping one's interiority empty [and] clean of any specific, especially gripping and tenacious thoughts, while maintaining a generally positive

---

[51] www.facebook.com/mucnik.ulia/posts/390615357674471 (accessed December 11, 2014).

[52] www.emory.edu/INTELNET/dar294.htm (accessed January 24, 2015).

attitude" was seen as an achievement (Kruglova 2014). To help one another achieve that goal, people would remind one another "not to load" one another with unnecessary information. If someone appeared worried, concerned, or undecided about something, a frequent response would be "not to sweat it" (*ne par'sya*), "not to think too much about it" (*ne zamorachivaisya*), or simply to "give it up" (*zabei na eto*). If conversations veered excessively toward anything conceptual or political, people would remind one another to bring it back to the "here and now," to "you and I," to personal concerns (Kruglova 2014).

Everyday language quickly picked up on those communicative struggles. Linguists, writers, and literary critics have all commented on the ambiguity and inarticulacy of everyday speech as a key feature of language practices throughout the 2000s.[53] According to sociolinguist Alexander Asinovsky (2011), for instance, frequent pauses, other markers of hesitation, and the overuse of demonstrative pronouns (in place of nouns and entire sentences) have been largely responsible for that sense of ambiguity and inarticulacy in everyday speech. Instead of naming things and states of mind, people seem to take refuge in the safety and vagueness of pointing to them instead. The most common pointers that replace entire sentences, according to Asinovsky, are *there* (*vot*), *it* (*eto*), *here* (*tut*), *kinda* (*kak by*), *gotta* (*nado*), and *so* (*tak*). Anna Kruglova (2014) documents the same phenomenon: "Nouns could be substituted by pronouns, their effects – by motions, impressions ... vectors of movement: 'it,' 'they,' 'stuff,' 'out there,' 'exudes,' 'heap,' 'load,' 'on top' [and so on]."

Russian writer Vladimir Sorokin equally laments the language of the 2000s, calling it "flat," "empty," "powerless," "mute" (Arkhangelsky 2013; Sorokin 2012). For cultural critic Andrei Arkhangelsky (2013), the language of the 2000s becomes a distant other:

It does not have any thickness, any volume. There is nothing to play with – because words simply refuse to be. They do not carry any messages. They do not belong to anyone ... Interjections, silences, omissions, and false-starts are the only place where one can find any truth in the language today. It is not a coincidence that in contemporary art-house film, protagonists' inability to communicate is seen as a rare moment of authenticity. Any literariness,

---

[53] See Arkhangelsky 2013; Asinovsky 2011; Epstein 2012; Gerasimov 2014; Rubinshtein 2015; Shargunov 2011; Sorokin 2012; Yampolsky 2014.

versatility, or even clarity and certainty of speech comes across as a sign of untruth. (Arkhangelsky 2013)

Taking developments in public culture as evidence, this chapter set out to track what kind of depoliticization was produced in Russia in the long 2000s. I examined the upsurge in cynical disinhibition among the powerful over that period and the emergence of a new aesthetic form – the new *stiob* – among cultural producers who identify as (or can be identified as) friends of power. This chapter drew on research, journalism, and commentary by scholars, cultural critics, and other public intellectuals who had been thinking about these topics – for judgments about how cynicism of the powerful and the friends of power resonated with ordinary Russians.

Documenting the growing sense of social and moral disorientation and the emerging desire to withdraw into thoughtlessness, this chapter argued for the presence of strong Arendtian links between cynicism, worldlessness, and thoughtlessness. These links notwithstanding, however, it is not likely that people in Russia in the 2000s lost *all* interest in seeking truth and telling it to others. After all, as Sloterdijk (1987) reminds us, cynicism is an unsettled and dynamic state of mind. To a large extent, it is driven by dissatisfaction and anxiety, and insofar as it exhibits those qualities, it retains a shadow of truth-seeking in it. Emotional distancing bordering on thoughtlessness is only one component of cynicism, as this chapter established; the other component is disinhibition. "A psyche nauseated from politics" eventually demands a revelation (Sloterdijk 1987: 467). One form such revelation can take, Sloterdijk says, is *kynicism* – the cheeky, irreverent, joyful, and often risky modality of speaking truth to power as exemplified and developed by Diogenes of Sinope in Ancient Greece. Another form such revelation can take, we may add with Foucault, is *parrhesia* – taking the risk to shame or criticize power from a position of moral duty.

This is precisely what happened in Russia in late 2011 and early 2012. On September 24, 2011, in the lead-up to Russia's parliamentary and presidential elections, Putin (then Prime Minister) announced that he and Dmitry Medvedev (then President) "had long ago agreed" that they would simply "swap jobs" come the May 2012 presidential elections. Such cynical disinhibition on the part of Putin and Medvedev was widely perceived to have been the cultural catalyst for the wave of mass political protests that took place across Russia between December 2011 and May 2012 (Gabowitsch 2013; Greene 2014; Lipovetsky 2014). As Mark Lipovetsky (2014) put it, up to that point, many Russians had likely simply lived with, and put up with, the political and cultural cynicism that had become the norm in Putin's Russia. However, Putin's cynical admission of the plan to swap jobs with Medvedev may have just been one disinhibition too many (Barry 2011; Fishman 2011; Gorokhova 2011). As Sloterdijk (1987: 244) explains, in their disrespect for the powerless, master cynics sometimes lose track of the fact that they still have to occasionally differentiate themselves "from mere criminality." When they fail to do that – as was the case with Putin's "job swap" revelation – master disinhibition can backfire and provoke outrage rather than indifference among the powerless. "Too much" disinhibition forces the powerless to suspend *their* cynicism and to demand that the powerful be held to account. This, in turn, can provoke the powerful toward even more *repression*, as they take revenge on those who dared to openly defy them. Sloterdijk (1987: 103) calls this chain reaction "the dialectic of disinhibition."

Such a complex dynamic at the core of cynicism helps to explain why the most cynical period of Russian history – the period many called the *null years*, time without heroes, without symbols, nauseating, dark time[54] – could be followed in the early 2010s by a most earnest attempt to return to a politics of truth-seeking that animated the political protests in 2011–2012. Sloterdijk's dialectic of disinhibition also helps to explain why those protests, invigorated by *kynicism* and par-rhesia, were, in turn, followed by an even "darker time" – the period following the annexation of Crimea – that has been characterized by the most brutal and ugly variety of political repression post-Soviet Russia has known to date. How that process unfolded is the subject of Chapter 5.

---

[54] See Auzan (2011); Dubin (2011); Ganapolsky (2011); Garros (2012); Nikitin (2011); Vostrov (2012).

5 | Trying a Life without Irony in the Early 2010s

In the six months between December 2011 and May 2012, to the surprise of many, a wave of political protests swept through not only Moscow and St. Petersburg but also smaller Russian cities as well (Gabowitsch 2013; Greene 2014). Specifically, the protesters disputed the results of Russia's parliamentary and presidential elections; more generally, they agitated for more dignity and honesty in public life. Even though the protest movement did not take off in the way its participants had hoped, it was extremely significant for Russia's public culture. More than anything else, I believe, the protests became the platform from which the value – the meaningfulness – of seeking truth and speaking it to power could once again be reasserted in Russian public space, after a long decade of widespread cynical disengagement from politics. The protests brought back the spirit of parrhesia – of courageous speech directed at the powerful – that seemed to have left Russian public space in the 2000s.

For journalists and other cultural producers who had worked throughout the deeply cynical 2000s, the protests were a jolting wake-up call, forcing many of them to face their own moments of truth (Krichevskaya 2012). A number of entertainment and consumer-oriented magazines in Moscow and St. Petersburg that used to be explicitly apolitical throughout the 2000s began to offer detailed coverage of the protests, to many people's surprise.[1] There were several unexpected high-profile resignations of editors in Moscow and beyond over pressure from owners to misrepresent the protest movement to audiences. Groups of journalists wrote open letters addressing fellow journalists, owners, publishers, and officials at the Central Election Commission, demanding dignity and honest elections. There emerged an "Occupy Media" movement in Moscow (Loshak 2012). In the summer of 2012, competition for

---

[1] These included *Afisha, Bolshoi Gorod*, and *Citizen K* (loosely equivalents of "Time Out Moscow"). They also include *Moi Rayon* ("My District") – a free, consumer-oriented weekly funded primarily by real estate, supermarket, and local business advertisements.

university slots in journalism programs was higher than usual. At the same time, the protests also sparked intense conflicts within the journalistic community itself, including professional and ethical disagreements about the extent of political compromises one can enter with the authorities and about one's right to publicly shame colleagues who do enter into such compromises.

This chapter documents the cultural and ethical struggles that accompanied the return of parrhesia into Russia's public space. As an ethical process, the return of parrhesia was intertwined with the task of reestablishing trust between public speakers and their audiences. As with any process of building something anew, it is taking much longer than it took for the practice and the value of parrhesia to collapse in the mid-1990s. Also, as in interpersonal relations, regaining trust is a delicate matter: it is difficult to know how much virtue needs to be demonstrated before trust is reestablished, and the process may never fully succeed (Asen 2013).

This chapter draws on my ethnographic observations of protest activities and discourse around them during the three months I spent in Russia in the winter of 2011–2012. I also draw on my daily monitoring of the coverage of protest events and attitudes in traditional and new media, including different blog platforms and social networking sites, for over a year after the waning of the protests. This chapter asks the following questions: What were some of the new, creative ways public speakers began to signal in 2011–2012 that they meant what they said? What did journalists' and other public speakers' attempts to regain trust with audiences look like? How were those efforts taken up? I will once again draw on the several criteria referred to throughout this book for evaluating speech and action that aims at truth, including accuracy, sincerity, seriousness (pathos), reflexivity, courage, and willingness to assert one's beliefs and to stand by them. Chapter 4 traced how those criteria were muddled in Russia throughout the 2000s as the crisis of truth-telling entered its most acute phase. This chapter evaluates the extent to which those criteria might have reemerged.

A Renewed Concern with Accuracy

When it comes to journalists' concern with accuracy as a value, there has been little change from the professional standards that have now been in place for over twenty-five years in Russia. As examined in Chapter 1, some accuracy-related practices that Western journalists would scoff at were tolerated and even encouraged in Soviet journalism. Those included guesswork (*domysel*), fabrication of detail (*vymysel*), quotes reconstructed from memory, use of journalist's internal dialogue, and other techniques of narrative enhancement. After Russian journalists were exposed to Western reportorial practices in the late 1980s and early 1990s, *domysel* and *vymysel* gave way to professional norms emphasizing properly sourcing a story, taking care in quotations and paraphrasing, not taking statements out of context, and so on. Of course, not all Russian journalists accepted these new norms as binding – in fact, as I demonstrated in Chapter 3, the opposite was often true. Disregard for accuracy survived in the production of *kompromat* (reputation-damaging falsehoods) in many media outlets in the late 1990s and early 2000s – as part of information wars between oligarchs and powerful media moguls.

Beginning in 2012, there was a new spike in *kompromat* – this time on state television, as journalists loyal to the Kremlin began to openly mock and grossly misrepresent the protest movement. Yet, for the first time in almost two decades, journalists began to openly shame their colleagues for the production of *kompromat*. Public denunciation of misbehaving colleagues is part and parcel of any occupational field that has been sufficiently professionalized. As I demonstrated in Chapter 3 in particular, occupational solidarity and peer criticism virtually disappeared from Russian journalism after the fall of the Soviet Union due to journalism's profound deprofessionalization during that period. The 2011–2012 wave of political protests, however, seemed to have begun reversing that trend. The protests compelled many journalists to reengage in peer criticism (Allenova 2011; Kucher 2011; Larina 2012). The open shaming of colleagues involved in the production of government-mandated *kompromat* has survived the 2011–2012 protests and has become relatively common, particularly among journalists in Moscow and St. Petersburg (Gubin 2013; Parfenov 2013).

The protests sparked yet another development around the practices of accuracy worth noting. In 2012, a genre of political theater emerged that deliberately erased the border between theater and journalism. Three different theaters in Moscow (*Teatr Praktika, Teatr Dok*, and *Politeatr*) rose to prominence for their productions based on ongoing news events (Boyakov 2012; Kaluzhsky et al. 2013; Nekrasov 2013; Ugarov 2012;). In some respects, these theaters began doing what

Aaron Sorkin did in his HBO series "Newsroom": sending a political message *to* journalists, modeling how news events *should* be covered. Dialogues for plays performed at these theaters were carefully researched and were based on actual quotes from police reports, court hearings, interviews with newsmakers and victims of crime, and street conversations overheard by scriptwriters.

When journalism enters a profound crisis and systematically fails to aim at truth, morphing into *kompromat* and propaganda, other social actors may feel the need to take on journalism's roles instead. This is precisely what Moscow political theater was inspired to do (and audiences were ready to receive) at the cusp of the protest movement in 2012. A related development was the notable increase in investigative reporting pursued by citizens from different walks of life instead of journalists. At the height of the protests, outraged by the abuses of power they had witnessed, many election observers, volunteers, and civic activists investigated those abuses and published the results, while many journalists watched from the sidelines.[2] Again, an upsurge in investigative reporting such as this, professional or not, was impossible to imagine during the cynical and apathetic 2000s. Since then, investigations conducted by nonjournalists have become the norm: the majority of investigative reporting in Russia today is done by the Anti-Corruption Foundation (FBK) – a nonprofit organization led by lawyer and opposition leader Alexei Navalny.[3]

The Importance of Being Earnest

It is perhaps inevitable that a large wave of public protests would be accompanied by an increase in the public significance of sincerity. And yet the spike in signals of sincerity during the winter of 2011–2012 took many observers of Russian public culture by surprise. The yearning for sincerity was particularly noticeable in the new media, but also in speeches delivered at rallies and other public gatherings and even in rock, punk, and rap music.[4] There was much commentary on how

---

[2] See, for instance, Cherkasov et al. 2012; Kalashnikov 2012; Lindele 2012b; Navalnyi 2012; Shultz 2012; Zheleznova 2013.

[3] See https://fbk.info/english/about/ (accessed June 7, 2016).

[4] Political performances by rappers Noize-MC and Dino MC-47, by rock musician Yuri Shevchuk, by punk groups Rabfak, Barto, and, of course, by Pussy Riot are emblematic of this trend.

readers and viewers missed sincere speech (*istoskovalis' po iskrennosti*) after the profoundly cynical "null years." Several months prior to the protests, a well-known business weekly, *Kommersant-Vlast*, had run a popular column in which that yearning was palpably expressed. In the column, journalists wrote would-be memoirs of several members of Putin's inner circle (former "ideology chief" Vladislav Surkov, head of a state-controlled television channel Konstantin Ernst, former head of the youth wing of the ruling United Russia party Vasily Yakemenko, and Putin's "puppet oligarch" and Chelsea soccer club owner Roman Abramovich).[5] Those imaginary memoirs, written by journalists, were wonderfully full of "naked truths"– would-be confessions of what those powerful men must "really" feel about their role in politics and in Russia's history – whether it is remorse or regret, shame or fear, contentedness or gleeful delight.[6]

The 2011–2012 parliamentary and presidential elections that sparked the protests were as usual preceded by official election campaigns that were full of official speeches and slogans. But somehow this time around there was a greater public demand, verbalized in new and social media, for first-person narratives – a particular form of "telling it like it is" – from politicians running for reelection. Even journalists and commentators relatively loyal to the political establishment complained that the campaigns that were run were devoid of passion and personal touch and were therefore unconvincing. *Let mi spik from mai hart* became a popular meme that opposition leader Alexey Navalny successfully used with his audiences (Navalny would say the phrase in English with a heavy, stereotypical Russian accent, thereby reducing the pathos of the phrase through humor, which is another important tactic aiming at trust-building and truthfulness [more on this below]).

Among the active (and not so active) participants in the protest movement, first-person narratives (in blogs, online media, and different social media platforms) proliferated during 2011–2012. There was a striking, although understandable, similarity in the structure of many of those narratives. One common story was some variation on "I was completely uninterested in politics, but one thing led to another, and after having witnessed a particularly egregious case of injustice, I realized I can no longer stay by the wayside." As these people (popular

---

[5] See Prilepin (2011); Kashin (2011a); Smirnova (2011); Belkovsky (2011).
[6] See also Saprykin 2012.

bloggers, journalists, musicians, TV entertainers, and others) signed up to be election observers, attended rallies, spoke at rallies, covered the rallies as reporters, volunteered for a cause, and so on. They kept a public record of what they were doing, thinking, and feeling, including their hopes and anxieties, their fear and shame, their indignation and despair. Many willingly admitted their naiveté and idealism and engaged in various forms of self-criticism and self-irony, consciously or unconsciously drawing on the power of those modes of speaking to aim at truth. Admitting mistakes and making public apologies were also common and were especially valued when they came from journalists and TV producers (who were perceived to have been in the wrong for many years). Not surprisingly, discussions of those first-person narratives (both online and off) focused on whether one could believe the sincerity of those confessions and apologies and whether one was experiencing a similar range of sentiments.

That something important was going on around sincerity could also be illustrated by the frequency with which confessional first-person narratives began to appear on pro-Putin, Kremlin-backed blogs as well. According to Anton Nossik (2012), a prominent figure in the Russian blogosphere, a new online technique emerged in the winter of 2011–2012 on pro-Kremlin blogs that had been almost nonexistent before. Nossik (2012) called it "simulation of intimacy" (*imitatsia zadushevnosti*). According to Nossik, pro-Kremlin bloggers would first assure their audiences that they were speaking frankly and were drawing on personal experience. Then, having made those assurances, the bloggers would launch into ad hominem attacks against their ideological opponents (usually Putin's critics).[7] Nossik found that seemingly unconnected bloggers would post messages almost identical in structure that would begin with the confession that the blogger personally knows the individuals he is about to discuss, having been involved with those individuals "in a direct, personal, partisan way" (Nossik 2012). Then, in the next paragraph, those individuals (usually Putin's critics) "would end up being unmasked, exposed, cauterized, and made to show their true colors" (Nossik 2012). Nossik concludes that this "moldering weapon of new sincerity" (*trukhlyavoe oruzhie novoi iskrennosti*)

---

[7] Journalist Oleg Kashin (2012) talks about the same "simulation of intimacy" technique, usually "too crude" to be believable (*slishkom topornaya imitatsia zadushevnosti*), common in commercial, paid-for blogs.

must have been pulled out of the Kremlin's ideological arsenal to once again be taught "at special agitation schools for the young crop of propagandists" (Nossik 2012).

Even more interestingly, the new demand for sincerity was manifesting in the moral ambivalence around a genre of irony in Russia known as *stiob*. As discussed in Chapter 4, *stiob* was a particular form of parody that originated in the late-Soviet period, when Soviet ideological form – official-sounding turns of phrases, expressions full of pathos, whole paragraphs of "correctly" worded texts – became immutable, fixed, instantly recognizable as such and increasingly irrelevant in their literal meaning for the majority of Soviet citizens. One of the most effective (and safe) ways to mock this style of speaking in the late Soviet period was to overidentify with it, to the point that it was sometimes unclear whether one was serious or not (Yurchak 2006).

As described in Chapter 4, throughout the 2000s, the meaning of *stiob* experienced its own internal displacement, to borrow once again from Yurchak's (2006) helpful poststructuralist toolkit. The *new stiob*, as I call it, fuses elements of irony and satire. It is open mockery but from a position of emotional and intellectual noninvolvement. As writer Yuri Nesterenko (2008) put it, the (new) *stiob* is "the mockery ... of the serious, the sincere." As such, the new *stiob* has worked well for Putin's Russia, directly contributing to citizens' depoliticization. "*Stiob* works most destructively against [a certain group of young] intellectuals," Nesterenko (2008) laments. It sends the message that being sincere or serious "is not fashionable, is laughable, and anyone who thinks differently simply lacks a sense of humor and is overall 'slow' or lagging behind [*otstal ot zhizni*]. [It sends the message] that one should be ashamed of high thoughts and of civic idealism" (Nesterenko 2008).

Nesterenko may well be right that Kremlin ideology chiefs worked hard to tap into the ambiguity of the new *stiob* throughout the 2000s to turn it to their advantage (cf. Dondurei 2012, 2016). It may well be that *stiob* became "glamorous" in Russia in the 2000s; all the more interesting, then, were the changes it began to undergo during 2011–2012. In the run-up to the disputed parliamentary and presidential elections and during their aftermath, activists, bloggers, and journalists involved in the protest movement began to draw attention to the moral ambiguity of the new *stiob*. When someone would make a *stiob*-like remark in public, supporters of the movement would point out that such remark was misplaced (*ne k mestu*), badly timed (*ne ko vremeni*), was a sign of one's arrogance or disrespect toward the position or a set of ideas being discussed. In other words, people began to comment on how the moral energy of the new *stiob* fell flat in circumstances that demanded moral clarity.[8]

Reduction in Pathos

As musician Varvara Turova, active in the protest movement, pointed out in her microblog, one of the key ideas of the movement was not to devalue humor as such but "to find a way for humor to signal that one is being serious, that one means it." Seriousness indeed began to reemerge in 2011–2012 as an important marker of speech that aims at truth. Compared with other criteria of truthful speech, however, seriousness presented an added challenge: it is easy to overuse to the point that it will fall flat. In J. L. Austin's (1962) terms, if the pathos of seriousness is abused, its performance becomes infelicitous or unsuccessful – which is what I argued happened to the majority of official Soviet discourse. In important ways, the late Soviet practice of *stiob* had been a healthy antidote to the "dreary pathos" (*unylyi pafos*) of Soviet official speech (Genis 2012).

Another challenge with seriousness is that its abuse can come across as true-believer zeal, and this can be similarly off-putting to audiences. Yet, despite these challenges, seriousness as a public value *had* to reappear in Russia if trust between speakers and audiences was to be rebuilt. Protesters, bloggers, opposition politicians, and journalists who were active in the protest movement seemed to be acutely aware of this predicament. As journalist and media educator Vasily Gatov summed up this challenge in his microblog post in early 2012, "[Y]ou have to use irony, but you also have to be serious" (*bez ironii nel'zia, no i neseriozno nelzia*). One very important tactic the protesters and their sympathizers drew on is what I will call a *reduction in pathos* (*snizhenie pafosa*). This is a common turn of phrase in Russian, which means bringing down the unnecessary drama of one's speech, not overdoing it on seriousness or true-believer zeal yet still somehow signaling that one means what one says.

---

[8] See, for instance, Bershidsky 2012b; Gessen 2011; Loshak 2011a; Sorokin 2013; Troitsky 2012; Trudolyubov 2013b.

One way to reduce the pathos, or excessive seriousness, of a political statement is, of course, through humor. A striking, much-commented-on feature of the early protests in December 2011 was their festive, light-hearted atmosphere, aided greatly by the humorous signs people carried.[9] As journalist Masha Gessen (2012) noted in an afterword to her biography of Putin, many protesters were pulled into the movement precisely because it avoided being dead serious. "'There are so many people there!,'" a very young man shout[ed] into his cell phone [at a Moscow rally in December 2011], 'and they are all normal! I've heard like a million jokes, and they were all funny!'" (Gessen 2012: 288).

One important reason why humor worked so pragmatically well in those spaces is because it helped to lower the anxiety and fear many people felt as they came out into the streets with explicitly political slogans – many for the first time in their lives.[10] But there was, of course, another important task humor accomplished in those political spaces, the task identified by Gatov and Turova earlier: humor was used to signal that one was actually being serious, that one meant it. To many people who still remembered the overinflated pathos of Soviet demonstrations and parades that nobody took literally or seriously, humor this time around helped to signal that rally participants were not mocking politics or playing some political game but that they actually "meant it."

I find Gilles Deleuze's (1990) theory of humor particularly useful in explaining how humor can play a complex political and ethical role in a postironic context.[11] Deleuze (1990) explains that unlike irony, humor descends, or moves downward, helping to take meaning and subjectivity "back or 'down' to its corporeal origins" (Colebrook 2004: 137; see also Bakhtin 1984; Sloterdijk 1987). Even though Deleuze (1990) does not put it this way, we could say that humor, through this downward movement, helps to reconnect with the corporeal foundation of pathos *as*

---

[9] One hand-written sign, voted best in an online poll in December 2011, was addressed to Putin and read: "We know you want it the third time. But we have a headache!"

[10] In Nizhny Novgorod and Kazan where I attended the rallies in December 2011, as in many other cities across Russia, those rallies were "unsanctioned," which meant that the police had full discretion to arrest the participants (which, for the most part, they did not do).

[11] For a compelling perspective on this topic in the field of rhetorical studies, see Innocenti and Miller 2016.

suffering (in its original Greek meaning). An appeal to pathos (and passion) in speech is meant to invoke *compassion* in listeners, by having them connect to their own experiences of (bodily) suffering. But when pathos is overused in speech, it loses that connection to the body and, as Deleuze (1990) would say, to the depth of human experience and to a particular set of truths associated with it. Instead, pathos ends up trying to claim the space of *logos* – of lofty words, ideas, and ideals floating above everyday experience.

For Deleuze (1990), from Plato onward, this world of ideas is the world of heights rather than depths. It is from those heights that humor helps us to descend into a "vaster, stranger, richer world" of "passions-bodies" that better captures the fullness and profundity of the human experience (Deleuze 1990: 129, 131; see also Bakhtin 1984). It is interesting to note how this metaphor of the world of ideas as the world of heights finds its way into our everyday language. We speak of lofty ideals and moral high ground, of occasions being "high serious," and of people getting on their high horse, upping the ante, using highfalutin language, and being condescending. However, we intuitively understand that humor – often as *understatement* – takes it down a notch and deflates tensions.

It is important for our case that Deleuze (1990) makes a sharp distinction between humor and irony. If humor brings things down, irony is "the adoption of a point of view 'above' a context, allowing us to view the context from 'on high'" (Colebrook 2004: 135). "Instead of locating ourselves within the flows and durations of life," an ironic point of view is one of "life as a whole, the point of view of conceptuality in general" (Colebrook 2004: 135). From this perspective, the world of irony and the Platonic world of ideas have one and the same purpose – to claim final authority over "the whole reality" (Deleuze 1990: 138). And that is precisely irony's problem, according to Deleuze: irony is unable to see or "to admit what is beyond its point of view" (Colebrook 2004: 135).[12] Ultimately, Deleuze (1990) says, irony fixes us in the symbolic order of language, from which – irony tells us – we cannot escape. Humor, by contrast, discloses "the forces or

---

[12] For ambivalence about the use of irony in Western journalism, see Ettema and Glasser (1994); Harbers and Broersma (2014); Song and Lee (2015).

powers that can never be exhausted by [linguistic] representation" (Colebrook 2004: 138).

Seen in this way, it makes sense why the new *stiob* – as a form of irony rather than humor – was met with moral ambivalence by those sympathetic to the protest movement, whereas humor was widely embraced. Russia's main business newspaper, *Vedomosti*, named Alexei Navalny (blogger and anticorruption activist, who emerged as a leader of the opposition during the rallies) the "politician of the year." The newspaper explained that this was in recognition of his unique contribution to Russian politics: "Navalny is the first person who has offered young people a politics without animal-like seriousness" (Vedomosti 2011). Other commentators have called him the "first politician to avoid excessive pathos" (*nepafosnyi politik*). Navalny's sharp sense of humor no doubt helped to establish and maintain his popularity. Yet, when Navalny was given the microphone to address a rally of 100,000 people for the first time, he began yelling in dramatic, declamatory slogans: "Who is the power here? We are the power! Yes or No? Yes or No?" People in the crowd reacted negatively: they were reluctant to chant the slogans after him and began to turn to one another and ask, "Why is he yelling so much?" (*zachem on tak krichit?*). In subsequent interviews with him, journalists made Navalny explain his exalted style of speaking at the rally. He responded that he had never seen 100,000 people in his life before, and his emotions had gotten the better of him.

These kinds of public admissions, too, helped to lower one's pathos just enough to begin to build trust. The pragmatic success or failure of a speaker (or sign holder) during the 2011–2012 events seemed to crucially depend on whether one was able to contain the "unnecessary drama" (*lishnii pafos*) one did not want to be identified with in a postcynical context. During the rally on December 10, 2011, in Yekaterinburg, a group of students, with smiles on their faces, held a sign that said, "Nothing Special, Just Honest Elections."[13] During a rally in Moscow on December 24, 2011, several protesters, again, with smiles on their faces, wore identical signs that said, "I don't usually go to these rallies-shmallies. But even I have had it!" Another common refrain among rally participants and supporters was their insistence that

---

[13] See http://veved.ru/press/13610-v-ekaterinburge-sazhali-medvedya-na-kol-tancevali-rugali-izbirkomy-i-blagodarili-policiyu.html (accessed June 8, 2016).

"this is not a revolution" and that "nobody wants a revolution" (e.g., Bunin 2012). Television anchor and journalist Leonid Parfenov captured this sentiment and the historical tension around it in his own address to one of the rallies. We all understand, said Parfenov, that "Russia has exhausted its limit on revolutions. But it has exhausted its limit on stagnation, too!"

Interestingly, and importantly, humor was not the only tactic to counter the perception of excessive seriousness of public speech. Another tactic that seemed to work toward the same goal of building solidarity and trust was the appearance – again, in spaces of politics – of generalized, often understated tokens of goodwill. We could see this as an attempt to repair the sense (and the space) of "the public" as something where "we are all in this together," as discussed in the Introduction, a sense that was damaged in the early post-Soviet moment. During the December 24, 2011, rally, for instance, one group of protesters in Moscow carried a long horizontal spread with a colorful drawing of a shining sun and the words "Good Morning!" on it (there was probably a second meaning there of Russia "waking up" as well). Another sign, taped to the back of a car during another political event in Moscow, said in hand-written letters, "Everything Will Be All Right." Still another of my favorite images from a rally in Moscow is a picture of a young man carrying some kind of placard. The front of the placard could not be seen in the photograph, but the back of the placard says in large handwritten letters: "Looking for a Girlfriend."

Another pathos-reducing tactic, which Alexei Navalny used successfully with apathetic citizens, was to argue that becoming politically or civically involved can be "easy and fun." Navalny managed to get large numbers of people involved in his team's various political and civic projects, including working as an observer during elections, anticorruption monitoring, and partaking in the operations of his "well-meaning machine of propaganda."[14] The choice of "well meaning"

---

[14] This is a project Navalny's team launched to counteract the pro-Kremlin messages on state television and in government-controlled newspapers, and supporters of the protest cause were invited to participate. Participation could range from face-to-face agitation, to printing and distributing leaflets, to renaming your wi-fi connection "Putin is a crook." Interestingly, at first, Navalny called this project "a well-meaning machine of propaganda" but has since been referring to it as "a well-meaning machine of truth" (*dobraya mashina pravdy*). When called on it, Navalny explained, "We tell the truth. Distributing a leaflet about [the criminal past of an important public official] – you can call it propaganda; you can call it telling the

(*dobraya*) is crucial here because it signals having no intention to deceive that is usually associated with propaganda and manipulation, as discussed in the Introduction. Importantly, Navalny was also the first in Russia to have successfully carried out a crowd-funding campaign to help set up a foundation for fighting corruption in the Russian government. In urging people to donate to his cause, Navalny argued that it would be "fun" to fight corruption together. The organizers of the 2011–2012 rallies also succeeded in crowd funding the logistical provisions for the rallies. Throughout the process, they publicized where every ruble went, including how much it cost to set up the stage, to provide the bathrooms, and to ensure strong free wi-fi signal throughout the territory of the rallies. As one protest supporter observed, "[I]t is much more fun to donate to a cause when you know where your money is going."

It is equally telling that invitations to get politically involved because it would be fun appeared in the most serious of contexts, which once again underscored that references to fun were not gratuitous but were part of a careful balance between "underdoing" and "overdoing" it on seriousness and gravity. On the eve of the second mass rally that took place in Moscow in December 2011, over 200 artists, writers, musicians, and other cultural producers appealed to their fellow citizens from the pages of an entertainment magazine. "Dear spectators, listeners, readers!," the address said. "Time has come to openly state your civic position. We call on you to join us in attending the rally that will take place on December 24th on Sakharov Prospect ... [Those of us attending the rally] will be shamed, threatened, provoked. [We] will be called victims of political technologies. Don't give in. Let us fight for our rights in a fun (*veselo*) and well-meaning (*dobrozhelatelno*) way. This is just the beginning."[15]

In online discussions during the winter of 2011–2012 and afterwards, a reduction in pathos was also manifesting in speakers offering an upfront "apology for the pathos" (*izvinite za pafos*) of their statements, especially if one was about to post a political remark to one's

truth; you can call it informing people. In any case, it just needs to be done. Because you will wait in vain for this information to come from [state television channels]" (Navalny 2012).

[15] http://bg.ru/society/obrashhenie_deyateley_kultury_i_media-9839/ (accessed February 3, 2015).

blog or to one's "wall" on a social networking site, especially if one had not previously written on political topics. With social networking sites, it became almost a matter of good taste to apologize for the upcoming pathos before filling up friends' news feeds with political statements and references. Another interesting feature was the heavy use of emoticons (usually, a massive number of smiley faces) that supporters of the protest movement left in commentary sections on blogs, in new media, and on social networking sites. People did that even when talking about the most serious of issues – again, presumably to undercut a possible perception of themselves as "overdoing it" on pathos. Additionally, people often ended their passionate status updates or their equally passionate comments on a note of understatement – finishing off with expressions like "my two cents" (*moi dve kopeiki*), "in my humble opinion" (IMHO), "or something along these lines" (*vot kak-to tak*). These all worked as important markers that the speaker did not presume to know the whole truth, may be mistaken, and was leaving room open for dialogue.

Finally, there was also a tendency among protest supporters toward the generous use of terms of endearment, particularly in reference to the online spaces themselves. Such uses included endearing names for one's own blog hosted on Live Journal, Russia's most popular blog platform (*zh-zh-shechka*), for one's space on Facebook (*feisbuchen'ka*), its Russian equivalent *VKontakte*, as well as an endearing reference to one's blog in general (*blozhik, uyutnyi blozhik*). Both men and women seemed to use these markers of endearment equally. One explanation for this might be political: public displays of endearment are probably seen as harder to fake, compared, say, with seriousness or assertiveness in expressions of belief. For this reason, endearment in these online contexts might have worked as an additional felicity criterion for signaling truthful speech.[16]

The Return of Parrhesia

Chapter 4 discussed how the 2000s were experienced as an epoch without ideals. Russian linguists, writers, and journalists were noting that something difficult to pin down was occurring in the 2000s on the

---

[16] For philosophical perspectives on how trust is built specifically in online environments, see Ess and Thorseth (2011).

level of language use itself: people seemed unwilling to commit to positions, tended to "talk round corners" (*nedogovarivat'*), choosing vague wordings to express their thoughts. As Chapter 4 argued, this phenomenon had everything to do with the erosion of truth-telling as a value. The wave of public protests in 2011–2012 likely began to reverse that trend, demonstrating that there might be a limit to how far one can blur the content of one's speech before the demand to mean what one says reappears. In the winter of 2011–2012, when the wave of protests was strong, there was an upsurge in statements from both well-known public figures and regular bloggers who seemed most interested in going on record, so to speak, to clarify where one stood in relation to politics.[17] Asserting one's beliefs and being willing to stand by them are the most basic ways of aiming at truth, as discussed throughout this book. Moreover, there is also an expectation that one will maintain consistency of one's beliefs across contexts and across time, that one will not change one's beliefs too often, and, ideally, that one will give a public account of one's inner moral processes that led one to change one's position. This, as Halfon (1989) explained, is what we generally understand as possessing integrity of character.

These were exactly the expectations that seem to have resurfaced in Russia's public spaces in the winter of 2011–2012. As mentioned earlier, many public figures, especially those who were known to be especially apolitical in the 2000s, came forward to say that they could no longer be silent and felt the need to explain what brought them to this point (a narrative genre that is sometimes humorously referred to in Russian as *kak ya doshel do zhizni takoi*).[18] Those who failed to come forth with such statements (as in the case of Russian musicians who remained silent and showed no interest in expressing solidarity with the jailed performers from the punk-group Pussy Riot, for instance) were publicly shamed (e.g., Troitsky 2012). In the face of such revelations, many professional journalists engaged in another round of soul-searching. A most interesting case of it, to

---

[17] For some examples, see Baronova (2012); Lindele (2012a); Parushina (2012); Varfolomeyev (2012); Yashin (2012).

[18] Including, perhaps most famously, entertainment talk-show host Xenia Sobchak, as well as lesser-known popular culture figures such as Tatiana Lazareva, Maxim Vitorgan, Bozhena Rynska, and many others.

my mind, was questioning whether a personal friendship between two or more journalists should suffer if the journalists find themselves on different sides of the political barricades. Should a journalist publicly call on his or her friend or colleague to point out that the colleague is doing something politically and morally wrong? Or should such matters be settled privately? Those were simultaneously professional, political, and ethical questions that reemerged in internal discussions among journalists during 2011–2012.[19]

Public assertions of one's belief and clarifications where one stands politically and morally are most closely connected with another criterion of truthful speech I have considered throughout this book – the courage of speaking truth to power or what Foucault called "parrhesia." Since about 2010, instances of parrhesiastic speech began to reappear in Russia's public space. At first they were isolated instances of whistle-blowing or of telling unpleasant truths into the faces of one's colleagues and superiors. One can think, for example, of the speech that Leonid Parfenov, the well-known TV journalist and anchor, gave at the ceremony in October 2010 when he was awarded the first (and only) Vladislav Listyev[20] memorial prize. Parfenov was extremely nervous as he spoke in front of heads of state and private television channels about the illegal practice of television censorship on Russian TV and about the unprofessional practice of self-censorship among his colleagues.[21]

Another instance of journalistic parrhesia before 2011–2012 occurred at a small but all-important rally, also in 2010, when

[19] See, for instance, Bershidsky 2012a; Faibisovich 2012; Shenderovich 2011; Sheremet 2012.

[20] Vladislav Listyev was perhaps the most popular, highly regarded talk-show host of the glasnost and perestroika era in Russia. He was assassinated in 1994 as television was becoming a big business. On the day he was murdered, all national broadcasting was interrupted in Russia in a sign of mourning. Over 100,000 people came to his funeral in Moscow. This public reaction was very different from the one that followed Anna Politkovskaya's murder a mere twelve years later, with which I started this book. Yet the fact that the Russian Academy of Television launched a Vladislav Listyev Memorial Award in 2010 is significant and could be seen as a sign that the television community is once again in need of some ideals to live by.

[21] Parfenov remains the one and only recipient of the Vladislav Listyev Memorial Award to this date. It might be the case that his parrhesiastic award speech was too much of a shocker for the Russian Academy of Television, and the Academy does not want to risk hearing something similar from another awardee.

journalists from across Moscow gathered and spoke in support of their colleague, Oleg Kashin, who was nearly beaten to death but survived. This was the first public demonstration of journalistic solidarity in over ten years, and the mere fact of it took many in the profession by surprise. One can also recall the interview given by Natalia Vasilieva, the aide to the judge who delivered the second verdict to Mikhail Khodorkovsky, Russia's most famous political prisoner. Also extremely nervous, Vasilieva came forward and testified before cameras that the judge had not written the verdict himself. Still another early case of parrhesia in the 2010s was a video recorded by a police officer named Alexei Dymovsky, in which he publicized cases of corruption among his superiors. The video went viral on YouTube, and Dymovsky was fired from his job and later arrested (Knobel and Sanders 2012).

It was really in the winter of 2011–2012, though, that publicly speaking truth to power seemed to have become more prevalent, after over a decade of abeyance. Men and women who worked as election observers spoke out, having witnessed numerous procedural irregularities or plain crimes at polling stations.[22] Several election commission members went on the record to talk about the political pressure on them to manipulate election results in United Russia's and Putin's favor. Rap, rock, and punk musicians wrote new songs to perform at rallies and elsewhere. Journalists wrote open letters protesting their superiors' decisions.[23] A few journalists refused to go on air in December unless they could cover the protests. Others quit in a very public way[24] (in one case, in the city of Yaroslavl, the whole staff of a television station nearly quit over pressures to portray United Russia, Putin's party, in a positive light). Other journalists were fired for what they said not even on air or in print but in blogs or on social networking sites. It is important *not* to give the impression that parrhesiastic speech has since become the new norm in Russian journalism – far from it. There continue to be many in the profession who

[22] Countless examples can be found; one representative text is Sivyakova (2012).
[23] The most well-known instance was the open letter journalists working for *Kommersant* (one of Russia's leading media conglomerates) wrote to *Kommersant*'s owner (Putin's ally) protesting the firing of the editor of *Kommersant-Vlast* (a magazine belonging to the media conglomerate) that published a picture of a spoiled ballot with an obscene reference to Putin scribbled across it.
[24] See, for instance, Urzhanov (2012).

practice various forms of political conformity instead, and their numbers seem to have only increased with the roll-out of full-blown government propaganda in 2014. This is precisely what makes these instances of parrhesiastic speech stand out. But these instances became more frequent compared with the 2000s, and they seem to have lost the stigma of eccentricity or naiveté – and that is an important development worth noting.

With parrhesia possibly becoming a respectable practice once again, at least in some circles, there emerged a very important, unintended, and historically contingent development around it. As instances of parrhesia became more frequent, they sometimes stood at odds with another thing protesters *also* wanted – solidarity with their fellow citizens in opposition to Vladimir Putin's rule. Protesters' "telling it like it is" sometimes came across as a harsh speech tactic that could provoke discord and undercut solidarity and trust instead of helping to build it. This was especially the case when parrhesiastic acts were a moral reaction to some public figure's loyalty or conformity to Putin's rule. In the run-up to the presidential election in March 2012, for instance, hundreds of Russia's cultural producers – theater directors, actors, musicians, and others – explicitly endorsed Vladimir Putin's bid for reelection, having become his "election agents." As such, many of them recorded political advertising videos in which they called on their compatriots to vote for Putin in the upcoming election. Among those several hundred was Chulpan Khamatova, a first-rate internationally acclaimed actress (perhaps best known to foreign audiences for her lead role in *Good Bye Lenin!*). Since the early 2000s, she has also been the head of a philanthropic organization and, overall, was publicly known in Russia for her moral probity and integrity. In early 2012, Khamatova recorded a promotion video in which she expressed her support for Putin. Yet, in the recording, she appeared to have tears in her eyes and looked dejected.[25] This led many commentators to speculate that she might have been forced to record the video in exchange for continued state support for her philanthropic organization.

The Khamatova story broke the protest community apart. Many wanted her to come forward and tell everyone if she had, indeed,

---

[25] Video available at http://piter.tv/event/Shiritsya_skandal_vokrug_r/ (accessed April 10, 2017).

been a hostage of the situation. If she spoke up and admitted that she was forced to record that video, they argued, it would deliver a very strong moral blow to Putin and would bring down his remaining popularity because Khamatova's reputation was beyond reproach. Others argued that Khamatova had a right to do whatever she wanted, that one's decisions and beliefs ought to be respected, and that the kind of public "ganging up" on Khamatova that was going on was morally reprehensible. They also argued that using Khamatova to deliver any kind of "blows" was a form of violence, even if of a verbal kind, and that violence is never effective as a form of solidarity building. Still others replied that what Khamatova did, or did not do, was not simply her personal issue, but a public one, and that it was a matter of dignity for other cultural producers to speak out on the issue and to distance themselves from her. This latter group argued that Khamatova, in fact, owed an explanation to her fans and to voters – an explanation of the inconsistency of messages she had sent with that video. Khamatova remained resolutely silent and refused to give any public comments. Many, in anger and disappointment, accused Khamatova of betrayal, conformity, duplicity, and "collaborationism." Such harsh varieties of truthtelling led to more infighting among protest supporters, causing the first major rift in the nascent movement. Many feared that the infighting over this issue would discredit the protest movement among the majority of Russians. Many, in fact, suspected that this was the authorities' goal all along: to breed discord among the protesters, to confuse, and to once again turn people away from politics.[26]

The Khamatova case showed especially well how the renewed desire to "call things by their real names" – a desire for moral clarity – was at odds with a particular history of truth-telling in Russia that includes public denunciations during the Stalinist purges and the more recent history of character assassinations in the "free" media of the 1990s. To many people, ganging up on somebody to denounce them (*shapkozakidatel'stvo, travlia*) was still too reminiscent of the purges and other notorious practices of public

---

[26] See Sanders and West (2003) and Marcus (1999) on conspiracy theories as a reservoir of social knowledge about the workings of power rather than as bizarre and irrational beliefs with no grounding.

denunciation in the Soviet Union. But not saying anything was starting to be experienced as undignifying in its own way, suggesting one's conformity with the status quo. In this intellectual climate, activists in the protest movement, which included many journalists, tried to delineate, for themselves and for others, new criteria for ethical yet honest public speech. Among these new suggestions were calls to avoid making and reacting to provocations and calls to learn to forgive and to apologize, to maintain the ability to compromise, to use public denunciation extremely sparingly, and as a last resort, to practice self-irony and self-doubt and to admit mistakes. In effect, the challenge the protesters were up against was how to gauge the right combination of passion and restraint, pressure and leniency, and seriousness and humor.

In an interesting twist, many journalists active in the movement argued that the most important thing their colleagues could do in the current situation was actually to have more face-to-face conversations about politics with "average people," whether they were the police, Putin supporters, or apolitical others (Kupriyanov 2012; Sokolov 2012; Turova 2012). Some of the coverage of the rallies in March 2012 included explicit reports on how the journalist, in fact, spent most of his or her time at the rally trying to establish a "human connection" with riot police and with various passers-by (Bikbov 2012; Chudinova 2012; Kuznetsov 2012). "Our profession has discredited itself so thoroughly that only a personal conversation can help," said one regional journalist in an online discussion after the rally on March 5, 2012. Another said, "You cannot convince people of anything if you do not know them, care about them." Still another said: "I do not like the word 'agitation,' but we have to do it to get anywhere."[27]

As Russian writer Boris Akunin (2012) summed it up, "[W]hat the opposition has been doing all of these months is fighting not for election mandates or for fair verdicts, but for people's hearts and minds" (Akunin immediately added, "I am sorry I do not know how to formulate this with less pathos"). Protesters' (re)learning how to ethically speak truth to power in 2011–2012 was thus conjoined with

---

[27] That Lenin's original precepts are, once again, relevant – particularly his distinction between agitation and propaganda and his conceptualization of "the newspaper as the collective organizer, propagandist, and agitator" – has not escaped journalists' attention. See, for instance, Bershidsky (2012b).

their learning of pluralism and toleration – key ethical practices that can be at odds with parrhesia, yet it is precisely that tension that sustains meaningful liberal politics. Protesters and protest supporters were learning to do it against the continuing tide of general suspicion and distrust; this made their predicament historically specific and particularly challenging.

Conclusion

This book has told the story of the professional unraveling of journalism in Russia over the past thirty years. At the same time, it has argued that a journalism crisis is not like any other. Since journalism is linked to the pursuit of truth by definition, when journalism devolves, the value of truth-seeking devolves with it. There is a long tradition in Western public imagination and in Western media scholarship of equating journalism with democracy; my book has argued that journalism's more fundamental connection is with truth first. Journalism *can* exist in nondemocratic settings, as I have argued in the case of the Soviet Union, if it maintains the ethos of truth-seeking at its core. But journalism is existentially threatened when truth-seeking begins to lose its appeal as a value – both for journalists and for society at large.

The political protests of 2011–2012 discussed in Chapter 5 seem like a distant history now, after Russia's headlong dive into an atmosphere of aggressive nationalism and earnest warmongering leading up to and following Russia's annexation of the Crimean Peninsula from neighboring Ukraine in February 2014. News programs and talk shows on state television have since turned into a daily ritual of identifying Russia's external and internal enemies – the "duplicitous" and "degenerate" West, the "fascist usurpers" in Ukraine, the "traitorous liberals" at home – and blaming those enemies for all of Russia's real and imagined ills (Arkhangelsky 2015; Kashin 2016; Medvedev 2014; Skorkin 2014). Feeding on people's anxieties and resentments, acid-tongued commentators and show hosts have been pumping audiences with hostility and paranoia, creating a sense of a country under siege that must aggressively defend itself. News programs on federal channels did away with the last traces of a commitment to journalism: actors dressed up as factory workers, refugees, and injured rebels have made regular appearances in the news (Bykov 2014; Pomerantsev 2014; 2015), and gruesome stories spawned by someone's twisted imagination have been presented to audiences as true events (Stopfake.Org

2014). When confronted with the evidence of their own mendacity, propaganda workers have either ignored such evidence or have skirted the issue, defending themselves as information warriors who must act accordingly (Channel One 2014; TVRain.RU 2014).

It is tempting to see in these developments a return to Soviet-style propaganda methods, especially at the height of Cold War tensions. Yet there are crucial differences between Soviet propaganda and mass manipulation as it exists in Russia today. First, Soviet propaganda coexisted with professional journalism, particularly in the late-Soviet period. Unlike the propagandists, the journalists understood themselves as particular kinds of truth- and justice-seekers. However imperfectly, they helped to maintain some degree of accountability of Soviet bureaucracies to citizens. In contemporary Russia, however, the profession of journalism – as an institution that aims to provide at least some restraint on the powerful – is near extinction (Parfenov 2015). The number of news organizations that need journalists rather than propagandists is exceedingly small, and these organizations lead a precarious existence both in Moscow and in the regions. Outside those organizations, and sometimes even within them, whoever decides to practice journalism is completely on their own – unprotected by law, misunderstood by society at large, doubted by colleagues, and thus unable to count on any professional or societal sympathy, solidarity, and support.

The second crucial difference between Soviet and contemporary propaganda has to do with its epistemological foundations. As journalist Peter Pomerantsev (2015) pointed out, Soviet propagandists took the idea of truth seriously, even as they concealed it: "Soviet propaganda went to great lengths to 'prove' that the Kremlin's theories or bits of disinformation were fact. When the U.S. government accused the Soviets of spreading disinformation – such as the story that the CIA invented AIDS as a weapon [for instance] – it would cause howls of outrage from top Russian figures, including General Secretary Mikhail Gorbachev." To contemporary propagandists, however, the notion of factual accuracy has become superfluous. As a result, made-up stories, nonexisting events, pseudodocumentaries, invented threats, and phantom realities populate news and commentary on federal television today like at no other point in the country's recent history. Such news and commentary enjoy high ratings, and that seems to matter more than anything else to media overseers in the Kremlin.

Contemporary propagandists also differ from their Soviet counterparts in the kinds of goals they pursue, according to Pomerantsev

(2015). The goal of the new propaganda is not to persuade anyone but to confuse and distract, spawning ever more grotesque interpretations of reality and spreading distrust in any and all truth claims (see also Gudkov 2015; Petranovskaya 2014; Yampolsky 2014). Any truth claim is as good as any other. All governments are corrupt, and everyone is compromised, so the only thing people can be trusted with is pursuit of their own interests. All one can do in this situation is decide where one's interests lie. Once such determination is made, the games of truth can follow. Logics like this, for instance, explain the results of a recent national poll that would otherwise make little sense to observers. According to this poll, conducted soon after the annexation of Crimea, 72 percent of Russians considered it normal that the media would hide information from viewers if it served Russia's national interests. A whopping 54 percent went further and said that they saw nothing wrong with the media distorting information if it served national interests (FOM 2014).

All in all, what we are observing in Russia today is what the world looks like when journalism is made superfluous. For Hannah Arendt (1972, 2000), this was the world of *defactualization* – the world where disregard for factual truths leads to a suspension of reality. As facts are reduced to opinions and opinions masquerade as facts, boundaries between fact, opinion, and fabrication disappear, and with them disappears the stability of a shared reality. When defactualization is rampant, as in contemporary Russia, even reports of people's deaths can be perceived as something not fully real, only seeming, imaginary. Cultural critic Mikhail Yampolsky (2014) has pointedly observed, for instance, that Russian propaganda reports on war casualties in Ukraine have left the viewer without the certainty about the absoluteness of those deaths: "Maybe those deaths happened and maybe they did not. Did those people really die or did they somehow disappear into thin air without a trace? Everything starts to be perceived as only a version of reality, an illusion."

Arendt saw journalism and the academy as bulwarks against the dangers of defactualization. Those dangers, for Arendt, were present wherever politics were present. Lying and self-deception, for Arendt, were still forms of acting in the world, and as such, they have always been part of politics. Arendt worried, though, that in the modern world, disregard of factual reality could become massive and self-perpetuating. This is why modern institutions like journalism were particularly important for Arendt. In trying to get to the bottom of things, journalists dig up facts that possess resiliency and "infuriating stubbornness" against which political fabrications ultimately cannot compete in stability. We need journalists, Arendt insisted, for "without them we should never find our bearings in an ever-changing world and, in the most literal sense, would never know where we are" (Arendt 2000: 572).

My book, then, has told the story of how a country could get to a point where the institution of journalism could become superfluous. Journalism did not disappear in Russia with the annexation of Crimea in 2014. Nor did it disappear with Putin's crackdown on the press in the early 2000s. This process began in the early 1990s and lasted over twenty years. A crucial component of that process, I argued, was journalism's headlong collision with capitalism. Journalism's devaluation began there, as journalists began to think of themselves as merchants of pathos and members of the "second oldest profession." Putin's authoritarianism landed on already well-prepared ground. By the time Putin began to consolidate his influence, manipulation of public opinion was expected; indignation about it was absent; it was no longer news.

Why did journalism not survive its encounter with capitalism in Russia? After all, the relationship between journalism, liberalism, and capitalism is old and complex, and there are many countries where journalism has managed to coexist with capitalism without having to fully subordinate itself to money and power. The reason has to do with the institution of the public sphere famously theorized by Jürgen Habermas (1989) that mediates between journalism and capitalism in liberal democracies. That institution is precisely what imploded in Russia in the 1990s. The public sphere – the "common human world," as Arendt called it – is the space where private persons come together to discuss matters of common concern. In a liberal democracy, private capital does not run the show completely because there remains the public sphere where citizens feel that they all have something in common. Journalism as a public institution feeds off that sense of shared humanity. The common, the social, the public, the sense of "we are all in this together" are precisely what suffered the most blows in Russia in the 1990s. Capitalism's logics of money and power prevailed without the emergence of a necessary counterweight of the public sphere to sustain democracy and capitalism in a productive tension.

In many ways this book has been an examination of the collapse of the public *at the expense* of the private. At the end of Chapter 2, I drew attention to the cultural significance of privatization – the hallmark of all transitions to capitalism. I noted that privatization is never simply a change in forms of ownership: it has a profound effect on the public and social realms, reconfiguring people's senses of solidarity, obligation, and commitment. Privatization pries open and sets loose the meanings and structures of public and private. Anthropologists of post-Soviet Russia documented an unprecedented explosion of the cultural significance of the private throughout the 1990s (Rivkin-Fish 2005). In the immediate post-Soviet period, private interests and logics quickly expanded into various domains of social life, primarily as a reaction against the collectivism of the Soviet period. The private realm was celebrated and elevated in significance.

This book has demonstrated that a corollary process – devaluation of the public realm – must have been going on at the same time, PARADOX parallel to the triumph of the private. This is the crucial difference between post-Soviet Russia and established capitalist democracies. In the older democracies, the categories of public and private have remained in productive tension through the concept of the public sphere, as liberal-democratic and capitalist institutions codeveloped. In post-Soviet Russia, the private triumphed over the public as part of the rejection of communism, and that process stunted the development of the Russian public sphere. The institution of journalism and its public mission were caught in the wheels of that process.

Chapters 2 and 3 offered a detailed explanation of how this happened. Rapid media privatization, compounded by Russia's economic collapse and the absence of foreign media investments, meant that former Soviet journalists had to think about money all the time. They had to quickly reinvent themselves as capitalists, engaging in none other than the primitive accumulation of capital. They had to find ways to sell what they knew how to do. In short, they had to monetize fact-gathering and truth-seeking – and they had to do it under circumstances where the only viable market was one of electoral promotion and political persuasion.

Of the various ways of aiming at truth I have identified throughout this book, pathos (unlike accuracy, sincerity, reflexivity, or courage) turned out to be the easiest to monetize. Accuracy – as persistence in getting to the bottom of things – was expensive to demonstrate, and Soviet journalists did not have a very good institutional record of it to begin with. Demonstrations of sincerity and reflexivity might have been considered too revealing of the professional turmoil journalists were experiencing in the 1990s, and courage was risky. Pathos, however, was familiar to former Soviet journalists. It was cheap to produce, and it was in demand on the new market of electoral persuasion. So of all the criteria for judging the truthfulness of someone's speech, pathos became the easiest to convert into capital. In this battle between truth, money, and power, though, truth rather quickly bowed out. As pathos became a commodity, its value was unmoored from the conditions of its production. When the source of rhetorical passion is obscured, when no one knows who is suffering the passion and why, pathos loses its opportunity to aim at truth and to be perceived as such.

Lastly, Soviet journalism might have been especially ill prepared for a standoff with capitalism because the two were built on incompatible epistemological foundations, as I discussed in Chapter 1. Like Marxism, and socialism more broadly, Soviet journalism was premised on a degree of epistemological realism. Truth was out there: it might have been concealed, it might have been feared, other things might have been masquerading for it, but its very existence was undeniable, and finding and speaking it were considered a virtue. Official propaganda laid claims to truth, but so did journalists, dissidents, and other intellectuals. Solzhenitsyn and Havel meant what they said when they called for living not by lies. Idealists were generally respected, whistle-blowers were taken seriously, and journalists and other cultural producers could not possibly admit to being cynics.

Capitalism generally operates within a very different epistemological frame. Capitalism is built on the creation of false values. It requires a toleration for, and even some indifference to, lying: advertising, marketing, and political campaigning would not survive without it. Capitalist actors are more interested in being effective rather than in being true. A large dose of epistemological relativism is thus built into capitalism, with money being the greatest relativizing force of all, as Marx noted a long time ago.

When capital boldly entered the spaces of journalistic production in Russia, where it previously did not belong, logics rooted in obfuscation of value trumped the logics of transparency associated with the idea of citizenship and concern for public good. It is important to recall that political liberalism – particularly the notion of the democratic republic – is similarly rooted in epistemological realism. So, in principle, the relativizing logics of capitalism were not destined to reign if political liberalism were to take hold in Russia at the same time. But as we know from elsewhere, capitalism's forces are stronger than those of democracy and liberalism (Brown 2015), which is probably why capitalism succeeded and liberalism failed when the two were introduced in Russia side-by-side. The public realm – to which both socialism and liberalism have a commitment – ended up being weakened, while the private realm of capitalist relations and practices rose in significance.

The weakening of the public is also a core feature of neoliberalism (Boggs 2000; Brown 2015). As a result, some of the processes examined in this book have distinct parallels in older democracies, particularly in the United States. As I worked on this book, I sometimes thought that I might be studying the future of journalism and public culture in the United States. It has become commonplace to acknowledge that as an institution, American journalism has similarly been undergoing a profound economic and cultural crisis from which it has not yet emerged (but see Zelizer 2015). Newsrooms and resources have been cut, staff positions eliminated, and legacy newspapers closed or sold off to private equity firms. Understandably, this has bread disorientation and demoralization among many journalists. Professional journalism in the United States has been further challenged by the growing presence of money in elections, by the prevalence of "oppositional research" conducted by super PACs, by the popularity of partisan punditry, and by the growing appeal of "truthiness" in the news. Some of the same developments can also be found in Western Europe, but to a lesser extent – there the fate of professional journalism is tied up with the continuing commitment to the institution of public broadcasting, with government subsidies to the press, and with limitations on the role private money can play in election campaigns.

Similar to the story I told in this book, the crisis of journalism in the United States has been accompanied by a growing spread of cynicism in American political and public culture (Capella and Jamieson 1997; Chaloupka 1999). This cynicism is the disappointment and hopelessness many Americans feel at the inability of public institutions, including journalism, to bring about much-needed political and social change (Boggs 2000; Jacoby 1999). Mounting economic dispossession, growing moral righteousness, and unending political strife have eroded many people's faith in rationality, modernity, progress, and justice. In this sense, Russia's fast-paced change in political culture described in this book can be viewed as a condensed version of what the West has been going through since the early 1970s. Seen in this light, this book can be read as a worst-case scenario of what a modern public institution may look like when it is fully overrun by the logics of money and power.

If anything, however, this book has also argued that within cynicism itself there remains a kernel of epistemological realism. In this sense, cynicism is more grounded and connected to reality than capitalism, and it is here that this book offers some hope (cf. Allen 2013; Greenberg 2014). Cynicism and capitalism are indeed similar, in that both are dynamic and restless states – states of economy and states of mind. But in a crucial way, cynicism's epistemology is more hopeful than that of capitalism. This is why, as I showed in Chapters 4 and 5, people are both drawn to and struggle with cynicism and its political ramifications. Without that kernel of truth-seeking at the core of cynicism, disillusionment with the state socialist project would never have resulted in perestroika. Similarly, without that kernel, the political protests of 2011–2012 would never have emerged out of the long 2000s with their prevailing attitude of political apathy and disengagement. Without that kernel, Dmitry Kiselyov, the self-assured face of contemporary Russian propaganda, would not feel the need to pass off his onscreen performances as moments of parrhesia.[1] As Foucault, Arendt, and Sloterdijk have all argued in their own ways, the desire to seek truth is a fundamental part of the human condition. In the midst of what Arendt called the "dark times," this desire may indeed fade or be folded into crippling cynicism. But this does not mean that the yearning to seek truth can ever fully disappear as long as people share a world in common. When and how that yearning will take center stage again in Russia's public space are a matter of historical contingency.

---

[1] Kiselyov's weekly signature show, *Vesti Nedeli* ("News of the Week"), opens with him speaking the following into the camera: "As far as I am concerned, freedom of the press is when you call things by their real names. I am Dmitry Kiselyov, and this is *Vesti Nedeli*. Enough mumbling! It's time to speak directly!" He then proceeds to "speak directly" about how long Russia has been humiliated, how long it kept quiet about it, and how it is finally rising from its knees to show to the world that it is still a superpower. Kiselyov's speech only masquerades as parrhesia because, most importantly, parrhesia is ethical speech from a position of little or no power that risks angering a more powerful interlocutor. Kiselyov's speech is not delivered from a position of lack of power – if anything, Kiselyov represents the power of the Kremlin today: he is the head of Russia's main government news agency, Russia Today.

Bibliography

Abbott, A. (1988). *The system of professions: An essay on the division of expert labor*. Chicago: University of Chicago Press.

Abercrombie, N., and Longhurst, B. (1998). *Audiences: A sociological theory of performance and imagination*. Thousand Oaks, CA: SAGE.

Abrams, P. (1982). *Historical sociology*. Somerset, UK: Open Books.

Agranovsky, A. (1968). *Sut dela: zametki pisatelia [The core of the matter: a writer's notes]*. Moscow: Izdatel'stvo politicheskoi literatury.

Agranovsky, V. ([1978] 1999). *Vtoraya drevneishaya: besedy o zhurnalistike [Second oldest profession: conversations about journalism]*. Moscow: Vagrius. Available at http://lib.ru/NEWPROZA/AGRANOWSKIJ_W/agran_01.txt (accessed February 5, 2017).

Akunin, B. (2012). F.A.Q. Available at http://borisakunin.livejournal.com/71491.html (accessed February 2, 2015).

Albuquerque, A., and Silva, M. (2009). Skilled, loyal, and disciplined: Communist journalists and the adaptation of the model of the American model of "independent journalism" in Brazil. *International Journal of Press/Politics*, 14(3), pp. 376–395.

Aleksandrov, A. (2009). Prozhektor postmoderna. Available at www.kommersant.ru/doc/1234968 (accessed February 2, 2015).

Alexander, J. (1981). Mass news media in systemic, historical, and comparative perspective. In E. Katz and T. Szecsko (eds.), *Mass media and social change* (pp. 17–51). London: SAGE.

Allan, S., and Thorsen, E. (2009). *Citizen journalism: Global perspectives*. New York: Peter Lang.

Allen, D. (2008). The trouble with transparency: The challenge of doing journalism ethics in a surveillance society. *Journalism Studies*, 9(3), pp. 323–340.

Allen, L. (2013). *The rise and fall of human rights: Cynicism and politics in occupied Palestine*. Palo Alto, CA: Stanford University Press.

Allenova, O. (2011). Otvet Ashotu Gabrelianovu. Available at www.snob.ru/profile/24751/blog/44448 (accessed December 17, 2011).

American Anthropological Association (AAA). (1986). *Principles of professional responsibility*. Available at www.americananthro.org

/ParticipateAndAdvocate/Content.aspx?ItemNumber=1656 (accessed February 5, 2017).

Andrejevic, M. (2008). Power, knowledge, and governance: Foucault's relevance to journalism studies. *Journalism Studies*, 9(4), pp. 605–614.

Arendt, H. (1951). *The origins of totalitarianism*. New York: Harcourt.

(1958). *The human condition*. Chicago: University of Chicago Press.

(1963). *Eichmann in Jerusalem: A report on the banality of evil*. New York: Viking Press.

(1968). *Men in dark times*. New York: Harcourt.

(1971). Thinking and moral considerations: A lecture. *Social Research*, 38(3), pp. 417–446.

(1972). Lying in Politics. In *Crises of the Republic* (pp. 3–32). New York: Harcourt Brace Jovanovich.

(2000). Truth and politics. In P. Baehr (ed.), *The portable Hannah Arendt* (pp. 545–575). New York: Penguin Books.

(2003). *Responsibility and judgment*. New York: Schocken Books.

(2005). *The promise of politics*. New York: Schocken Books.

Arkhangelsky, A. (2011). Kholuyovo – uzhe glagol. Available at www.novayagazeta.ru/comments/50278.html (accessed February 15, 2016).

(2013). Novyi Sorokin: Stantsiya Raspadskaya. Available at www.colta.ru/articles/literature/785 (accessed February 15, 2016).

(2015). God zloradstva. Available at https://slon.ru/posts/61551 (accessed June 8, 2016).

Asad, T. (2003). *Formations of the secular: Christianity, Islam, modernity*. Palo Alto, CA: Stanford University Press.

Asen, R. (2013). Deliberation and trust. *Argumentation and Advocacy*, 50(3), pp. 2–17.

Asinovsky, A. (2011). Nashi liudi postoyanno nedogovarivayut. Available at www.kommersant.ru/doc/1577180 (accessed February 7, 2011).

Aucoin, J. (2001). Epistemic responsibility and narrative theory: The literary journalism of Ryszard Kapuscinski. *Journalism*, 2(1), pp. 5–21.

Austin, J. L. (1962). *How to do things with words*. Oxford, UK: Clarendon Press.

Auzan, A. (2011). *Institutsionalnaya ekonomika dlia chainikov*. Moscow: Esquire.

Azhgikhina, N. (2004). Slukhi o konchine ocherka yavno preuvelicheny. *Zhurnalist*, 12, pp. 94–96.

(2005). Posle nostalgii. *Zhurnalist*, 4, pp. 58–60.

(2007). The struggle for press freedom in Russia: Reflections of a Russian journalist. *Europe-Asia Studies*, 59(8), pp. 1245–1262.

Bacon, W. (2006). Journalism as research? *Australian Journalism Review*, 28(2), pp. 147–157.

Baker, C. (2002). *Media, markets, and democracy*. New York: Cambridge University Press.

Bakhtin, M. (1984). *Rabelais and his world*. Bloomington: Indiana University Press.

Balcytiene, A. (2008). Changing journalistic discourses in the Baltic states: How to deal with cheap journalism. In K. Jakubowicz and M. Sukosd (eds.), *Finding the right place on the map: Central and East European media change in a global perspective* (pp. 213–226). Chicago: IntellectBooks.

Baronova, M. (2012). Pro politiku i obychnuyu zhizn. Available at http://ponny1.livejournal.com/705545.html (accessed February 2, 2015).

Barry, A., Osborne, T., and Rose, N. (1996). *Foucault and political reason: Liberalism, neo-liberalism, and rationalities of government*. Chicago: University of Chicago Press.

Barry, E. (2011). A changed Russia arches an eyebrow at Putin's staged antics. Available at www.nytimes.com/2011/10/06/world/europe/putins-diving-exploit-was-a-setup-aide-says.html (accessed June 8, 2016).

Bauer, R. (1952). *The new man in Soviet psychology*. Cambridge, MA: Harvard University Press.

(1956). *How the Soviet system works: Cultural, psychological, and social themes*. Cambridge, MA: Harvard University Press.

Bazarova, M. (2009). Pirozhnye dlia Sergeya Svetlakova: Reportazh so syomok "Prozhektorperishilton." Available at www.chaskor.ru/article/pirozhnye_dlya_sergeya_svetlakova_11887 (accessed October 31, 2009).

Belkovsky, S. (2011). Istoria Khodorkovskogo sidit v moyom serdtse zanozoi. Available at www.kommersant.ru/Doc/1653529 (accessed February 2, 2015).

Bennett, W. (1990). Toward a theory of press state relations in the U.S. *Journal of Communication, 40*, pp. 103–125.

Bennett, W., Lawrence, R., and Livingston, S. (2007). *When the press fails: Political power and the news media from Iraq to Katrina*. Chicago: University of Chicago Press.

Benyumov, K. (2012). Pered rasstrelom napoit' chaem: Na NTV debutirovalo parodiinoe sketch-shou pro Putina. Available at http://lenta.ru/articles/2013/03/05/teleputin/ (accessed March 5, 2012).

Bergman, J. (1989). The memoirs of Soviet defectors: Are they a reliable source about the Soviet Union? *Canadian Slavonic Papers, 31*(1), pp. 1–24.

Berman, H. (1948). The challenge of Soviet law. *Harvard Law Review, 62*(2), pp. 220–265.

Bershidsky, L. (2012a). Naivnye liudi. Available at www.snob.ru/selected/entry/52231 (accessed February 2, 2015).

(2012b). Pochemu idiotskie ogranichenia svobody i ne strashny, i ne smeshny. Available at www.snob.ru/selected/entry/50774 (accessed February 2, 2015).

Bikbov, A. (2012). Sekretnyi ingredient obshchestvennogo dvizhenia. Available at http://slon.ru/russia/sekretnyy_ingredient_obshchestvenno go_dvizheniya-762240.xhtml (accessed February 2, 2015).

Bird, E. (ed.). (2009). *The anthropology of news and journalism: Global perspectives.* Bloomington: Indiana University Press.

Bittner, S. (2008). *The many lives of Khrushchev's thaw: Experience and memory in Moscow's Arbat.* Ithaca, NY: Cornell University Press.

Bogdanov, V., and Zassoursky, Y. (1998). *Vlast, zerkalo ili sluzhanka? Entsiklopedia zhizni sovremennoi rossiiskoi zhurnalistiki.* Moscow: Russian Union of Journalists.

Bogdanova, E. (2005). Sovetskaya traditsia pravovoi zashchity, ili v ozhidanii zaboty. *Neprikosnovennyi zapas, 1*(39), pp. 76–83.

Boggs, C. (2000). *The end of politics: Corporate power and the decline of the public sphere.* New York: Guilford Press.

Boim, L. (1974). "Ombudsmanship" in the Soviet Union. *American Journal of Comparative Law, 22*(3), pp. 509–540.

Boobbyer, P. (2000). Truth-telling, conscience and dissent in late Soviet Russia: Evidence from oral histories. *European History Quarterly, 30*(4), pp. 553–585.

(2005). *Conscience, dissent and reform in Soviet Russia.* London: Routledge.

Borodina, A. (2014). Strana Putina i serialov. Available at http://lenta.ru /articles/2014/03/14/tvanthology (accessed February 15, 2016).

(2015). Chelovek iz televizora. Available at http://echo.msk.ru/programs /persontv/1479492-echo/ (accessed February 15, 2016).

Boudana, S. (2010). On the values guiding the French practice of journalism: Interviews with thirteen war correspondents. *Journalism, 11*(3), pp. 293–310.

Boyakov, E. (2012). Segodniashnii lozung – zhit' ne po lzhi. Available at http://interviewrussia.ru/life/977 (accessed June 26, 2012).

Boyer, D. (2003). Censorship as a vocation: The institutions, practices, and cultural logic of media control in the German Democratic Republic. *Comparative Studies in Society and History, 45*, pp. 511–545.

(2005). *Spirit and system: Media, intellectuals, and the dialectic in modern German culture.* Chicago: University of Chicago Press.

(2006). Gender and the solvency of professionalism: Eastern German journalism before and after 1989. *East European Politics and Societies, 20*(1), pp. 152–179.

Boyer, D., and Hannerz, U. (2006). Worlds of journalism. *Ethnography, 7*(1), pp. 5–17.

Boyer, D., and Yurchak, A. (2010). American *stiob*: Or what late socialist aesthetics of parody reveal about contemporary political culture in the West. *Cultural Anthropology, 25*(2), pp. 179–221.

Boym, S. (1994). *Common places: Mythologies of everyday life in Russia.* Cambridge, MA: Harvard University Press.

(2002). Kak sdelana sovetskaya sub'ektivnost. *Ab Imperio, 3*, pp. 285–296.

Brooks, J. (1989). Public and private values in the Soviet press, 1921–1928. *Slavic Review, 48*(1), pp. 16–35.

(2000). *Thank you, comrade Stalin! Soviet public culture from Revolution to Cold War.* Princeton, NJ: Princeton University Press.

Brown, W. (2010). We are all democrats now. *Theory and Event, 13*(2), available online at http://muse.jhu.edu/journals/theory_and_event/v013/13.2.brown01.html.

(2015). *Undoing the demos: Neoliberalism's stealth revolution.* Boston: MIT Press.

Bruns, A. (2005). *Gatewatching: Collaborative online news production.* New York: Peter Lang.

Bunin, I. (2012). Rossisky kommunitas. Available at www.vedomosti.ru/opinion/articles/2012/02/20/rossijskij_kommunitas (accessed April 10, 2017).

Burbank, J. (1995). Lenin and the law in revolutionary Russia. *Slavic Review, 54*(1), pp. 23–44.

Butler, J. (2001). What is critique? An essay on Foucault's virtue. Available at http://eipcp.net/transversal/0806/butler/en (accessed February 22, 2016).

Bykhovskaya, P. (2011). Ya – surkovskaya propaganda. Available at www.openspace.ru/media/air/details/32483/ (accessed December 6, 2011).

(2012). My delayem zhestkuyu zheltukhu. Available at www.openspace.ru/media/air/details/35212 (accessed March 19, 2012).

Bykov, D. (2014). Tak dalshe nelzya. Available at www.profile.ru/pryamayarech/item/81057-ulitsa-petkova (accessed February 15, 2016).

Capella, J., and Jamieson, K. (1997). *Spiral of cynicism: The press and the public good.* New York: Oxford University Press.

Carey, J. W. (1989). *Communication as culture: Essays on media and society.* Boston: Unwin Hyman.

Carlyle, T. (1849). *On heroes, hero-worship, and the heroic in history.* New York: Wiley.

Carr, D. (2013). War on leaks is pitting journalist vs. journalist. Available at www.nytimes.com/2013/08/26/business/media/war-on-leaks-is-pitting-journalist-vs-journalist.html (accessed August 26, 2013).

Cassin, B. (ed.). (2014). *Translation/transnation: Dictionary of untranslatables.* Princeton, NJ: Princeton University Press.

Cater, D. (1959). *The fourth branch of government*. Boston: Houghton Mifflin.

Cavell, S. (1979). *The claim of reason: Wittgenstein, skepticism, morality, and tragedy*. Oxford: Oxford University Press.

(1995). What did Derrida want of Austin? In *Philosophical passages: Wittgenstein, Emerson, Austin, Derrida* (pp. 42–65). Cambridge, MA: Blackwell.

(2005). Performative and passionate utterance. In *Philosophy the day after tomorrow* (pp. 155–191). Cambridge, MA: Harvard University Press.

Center for Political Information (CPI). (2001). Media-killers. Available at www.fsk.ru/jan/obozr/mediakiller.htm (accessed June 16, 2009).

Chalaby, J. (1996). Journalism as an Anglo-American invention. *European Journal of Communication, 11*(3), pp. 303–326.

Challenger, D. (1994). *Durkheim through the lens of Aristotle*. Lanham, MD: Rowman & Littlefield.

Chaloupka, W. (1999). *Everybody knows: Cynicism in America*. Minneapolis: University of Minnesota Press.

Channel One. (2014). Zhurnalisty Pervogo otvechayut na obvinenia vo lzhi v sviazi s syuzhetom pro ubiistvo rebenka v Slavianske. Available at www.1tv.ru/news/about/274369 (accessed July 2, 2015).

Chatterjee, C., and Petrone, K. (2008). Models of Selfhood and Subjectivity: The Soviet case in historical perspective. *Slavic Review, 67*(4), pp. 967–986.

Cherkasov, I., Kabanov, K., Bom, M., and Bychkova, O. (2012). Skandal vokrug spiska Magnitskogo. Available at www.echo.msk.ru/programs /magazine/904433-echo/ (accessed July 1, 2012).

Christians, C. G. (2009). *Normative theories of the media: Journalism in democratic societies*. Urbana-Champaign: University of Illinois Press.

Chudinova, K. (2012). Vy s nimi? Available at www.snob.ru/profile/8103 /blog/46773 (accessed February 2, 2015).

Coe, S. (1996). Struggles for authority in the NEP village: The early rural correspondents movement, 1923–1927. *Europe-Asia Studies, 48*(7), pp. 1151–1171.

Colebrook, C. (2004). *Irony*. London: Routledge.

Collier, S. (2011). *Post-Soviet social: Neoliberalism, social modernity, biopolitics*. Princeton N.J.: Princeton University Press.

Conquest, R. (1968). *The great terror: Stalin's purge of the thirties*. New York: Macmillan.

Cook, T. (1998). *Governing with the news: The news media as a political institution*. Chicago: University of Chicago Press.

Couldry, N. (2003). *Media rituals: A critical approach*. London: Routledge.

(2012). *Media, society, world: Social theory and digital media practice*. Malden, MA: Polity.

Couldry, N., Pinchevski, A., and Madianou, M. (2013). *Ethics of media.* Eastbourne, UK: Palgrave Macmillan.

Crouch, C. (2004). *Post-democracy.* Malden, MA: Polity.

Crowley, D., and Reid, S. E. (2010). *Pleasures in socialism: Leisure and luxury in the Eastern Bloc.* Evanston, IL.: Northwestern University Press.

Curran, J. (2011). *Media and democracy.* New York: Routledge.

Curry, J. (1990). *Poland's journalists: Professionalism and politics.* New York: Cambridge University Press.

Daly, C. (2012). *Covering America: A narrative history of a nation's journalism.* Amherst, MA: University of Massachusetts Press.

Dayan, D., and Katz, E. (1992). *Media events: The live broadcasting of history.* Cambridge, MA: Harvard University Press.

de Sola Pool, I. (1973). Communication in totalitarian societies. In I. de Sola Pool, W. Schramm, N. Maccoby, and E. Parker (eds.), *Handbook of communication.* Chicago: Rand McNally.

Deleuze, G. (1990). *The logic of sense.* New York: Columbia University Press.

Dikov, S. (2011a). EleVidenie-2. Availabe at http://onreal.livejournal.com /30569.html (accessed February 15, 2016).

(2011b). Kak rabotaet programma Malakhova "Pust' govoriat." Available at http://onreal.livejournal.com/30418.html (accessed February 15, 2016).

Dondurei, D. (2011). Pochemu khoroshie liudi sovershayut plokhie postupki. Available at http://echo.msk.ru/programs/exit/801642-echo/ (accessed June 9, 2016).

(2012). Proizvodstvo mirovozzrencheskogo musora. Available at www .diletant.ru/journal/327/article_24138/ (accessed June 9, 2016).

(2016). Smysloviki mogushchestvennee politikov. Available at www .vedomosti.ru/opinion/articles/2016/06/08/644510-smisloviki-mogu schestvennee-politikov (accessed June 9, 2016).

Druzenko, A., Karapetian, G., and Plutnik, A. (2007). *S zhurnalistikoi pokoncheno, zabud'te! O druzhyakh-tovarishchakh, drame Izvestii i raspade professii.* Moscow: Zebra E.

Dubin, B. (2005). Media postsovetskoi epokhi. *Vestnik obshchestvennogo mnenia,* 76(2), pp. 22–29. Available online at www.levada.ru/sites /default/files/vom_2005.276.pdf.

(2006a). Obshchestvo: Soyuz telezritelei. Available at www.vedomosti.ru /newspaper/article/2006/05/29/107219 (accessed February 15, 2016).

(2006b). Simuliativnaya vlast i zeremonial'naya politika: O politicheskoi kulture sovremennoi Rossii. *Vestnik obshchestvennogo mnenia,* 81(1), pp. 14–25. Available online at http://ecsocman.hse.ru/data/542/971/1219 /03_dubin_14–25.pdf.

(2011). Mass media, vlast, i kollektivnyi obraz sotsiuma. Available at www.svobodanews.ru/content/transcript/24183363.html (accessed February 15, 2016).

Dudkina, Y. (2014). Otez na syna. Kak rossiiskie semyi peressorilis iz-za Kryma. Available at http://medialeaks.ru/features/2512jd-kuhonnyie -voynyi (accessed February 1, 2015).

Dunn, E. C. (2004). *Privatizing Poland: Baby food, big business, and the remaking of labor*. Ithaca, NY: Cornell University Press.

Durkheim, E. (1915). *The elementary forms of religious life*. London: Allen & Unwin.

(1961). *Moral education: A study in the theory and application of the sociology of education*. New York: Free Press of Glencoe.

(1973). *On morality and society: Selected writings*. Chicago: University of Chicago Press.

Dzirkals, L., Gustafson, T., and Johnson, A.(1982). *The media and intra-elite communication in the USSR*. Santa Monica, CA: Rand Corporation.

Engelstein, L. (1993). Combined underdevelopment: Discipline and the law in Imperial and Soviet Russia. *American Historical Review, 98*(2), pp. 338–353.

Engelstein, L., and Sandler, S. (2000). *Self and story in Russian history*. Ithaca, NY: Cornell University Press.

Engerman, D. C. (2009). *Know your enemy: The rise and fall of America's Soviet experts*. New York: Oxford University Press.

Entman, R. (2003). Cascading activation: Contesting the White House's frame after 9/11. *Political Communication, 20*(4), pp. 415–432.

Epstein, M. (2012). Yazyk lukavogo raba. Available at www.russ.ru/Miro vaya-povestka/YAzyk-lukavogo-raba (accessed February 15, 2016).

Erikson, E. (1954). Wholeness and totality: A psychiatric contribution. In C. Friedrich (ed.), *Totalitarianism* (pp. 156–171). Cambridge, MA: Harvard University Press.

Erjaevic, K., and Kovacic, M. (2010). Relations with the media: Who are the main actors in an advertorial production process in Slovenia? *Journalism, 11*(1), pp. 91–109.

Ess, C., and Thorseth, M. (2011). *Trust and virtual worlds: Contemporary perspectives*. New York: Peter Lang.

Etkind, A. (2005). Soviet subjectivity: Torture for the sake of salvation? *Kritika: Explorations in Russian and Eurasian History, 6*(1), pp. 171–186.

Ettema, J. (1990). Press rites and race relations: A study of mass-mediated ritual. *Critical Studies in Media Communication, 7*(4), pp. 309–331.

(2005). Crafting cultural resonance: Imaginative power in everyday journalism. *Journalism, 6*(2), pp. 131–152.

(2009). The moment of truthiness: The right time to consider the meaning of truthfulness. In B. Zelizer (ed.), *The changing faces of journalism: Tabloidization, technology and truthiness* (pp. 114–126). London: Routledge.

Ettema, J., and Glasser, T. (1994). The irony in – and of – journalism: A case study in the moral language of liberal democracy. *Journal of Communication*, 44(2), pp. 5–28.

Ettema, J., and Glasser, T. (1998). *Custodians of conscience: Investigative journalism and public virtue*. New York: Columbia University Press.

Faibisovich, I. (2012). Ona prosto zashla pozavtrakat. Available at www .snob.ru/profile/11632/print/52227 (accessed February 2, 2015).

Fainsod, M. (1953). *How Russia is ruled*. Cambridge, MA: Harvard University Press.

Faraday, G. (2000). *Revolt of the filmmakers: The struggle for artistic autonomy and the fall of the Soviet film industry*: Philadelphia: Penn State University Press.

Fedotov, M. (2002). *Pravovye osnovy zhurnalistiki*. Moscow: Vlados.

Fenko, A. (2012). Vam na Zapad ili nalevo? Available at www.openspace .ru/article/561 (accessed February 15, 2016).

Ferguson, J. (2006). *Global shadows: Africa in the neoliberal world order*. Durham, NC: Duke University Press.

Firsov, B. (2008). *Raznomyslie v SSSR, 1940–1960-e gody: istoria, teoria i praktiki*. St. Petersburg: Izdatel'stvo Evropeiskogo universiteta.

Fishman, M. (2011). Tsena odnoi tainoi sdelki. Available at www.forbes.ru /ekonomika-column/vlast/74509-nenuzhnyi-prezident (accessed June 8, 2016).

Fitzpatrick, S. (1979). *Education and social mobility in the Soviet Union, 1921–1934*. New York: Cambridge University Press.

(1996). Signals from below: Soviet letters of denunciation of the 1930s. *Journal of Modern History*, 68(4), pp. 831–866.

(1999). *Everyday Stalinism: Ordinary life in extraordinary times. Soviet Russia in the 1930s*. New York: Oxford University Press.

(2007). The Soviet Union in the twenty-first century. *Journal of European Studies*, 37(51), pp. 51–71.

(2008). Revisionism in retrospect: A personal view. *Slavic Review*, 67(3), pp. 682–704.

FOM. (2014). O sredstvakh massovoi informatsii. Available at http://fom.ru /SMI-i-internet/11427 (accessed June 2, 2015).

Forde, K. (2007). Discovering the explanatory report in American newspapers. *Journalism Practice*, 1(2), pp. 227–244.

Foucault, M. (1997a). *Ethics: Subjectivity and truth. The essential works of Foucault 1954–1984*, ed. P. Rabinow. New York: New Press.

(1997b). The ethics of the concern of the self as a practice of freedom. In P. Rabinow (ed.). *Ethics: Subjectivity and truth* (pp. 281–302). New York: New Press.

(2001). *Fearless speech*. Los Angeles, CA: Semiotext.

(2010). *The government of self and others. Lectures at the Collège de France 1982–1983*. New York: Palgrave Macmillan.

(2011). *The courage of truth. Lectures at the Collège de France 1983–1984*. New York: Palgrave Macmillan.

Franklin, B. (ed.). (2006). *Local journalism and local media: Making the local news* (2nd edn.). New York: Routledge.

French, M. (2014). Reporting socialism: Soviet journalism and the Journalists' Union, 1955–1966. Ph.D. thesis, University of Pennsylvania. Available online at http://repository.upenn.edu/edissertations/1277/.

Friedrich, C., and Brzezinski, Z. (1956). *Totalitarian dictatorship and autocracy*. Cambridge, MA: Harvard University Press.

Gabowitsch, M. (2013). *Putin kaputt!? Russlands neue Protestkultur*. Berlin: Suhrkamp, 2013.

Gamayunov, I. (2009a). Pravo na pravdu. Doroga k glasnosti. Opyt 80x. Available at www.lgz.ru/article/8606/ (accessed February 15, 2016).

(2009b). Zigzag istorii. Iz dnevnika litgazetovtsa. Available at http://magazines.russ.ru/neva/2009/9/ga3.html (accessed February 15, 2016).

Ganapolsky, M. (2011). V budushcheye s Budanovym? Available at www.mk.ru/politics/article/2011/06/16/597939-v-buduschee-s-budanovyim.html (accessed February 15, 2016).

Gans, H. (1979). *Deciding what's news: A study of CBS Evening News, NBC Nightly News, Newsweek, and Time*. New York: Pantheon Books.

Garros, A. (2012). Blogpost. Available at www.facebook.com/alexander.garros/posts/485093881523934 (accessed January 15, 2015).

Gazeta.RU. (2012). Posol SShA McFaul zayavil o slezhke so storony NTV; v telekompanii sovetuyut ne udivlyatsia. Available at www.gazeta.ru/social/news/2012/03/29/n_2265441.shtml (accessed February 15, 2016).

Geertz, C. (1980). *Negara: The theatre state in nineteenth-century Bali*. Princeton, NJ: Princeton University Press.

Genis, A. (2012). Vtorogodniki. Available at www.novayagazeta.ru/society/54016.html (accessed February 2, 2015).

Gerasimov, I. (2014). Lirika epokhi zinicheskogo razuma. Available at http://net.abimperio.net/node/3353 (accessed May 26, 2016).

Gessen, M. (2011). Kak vazhno byt' serioznym, nah-nah. Available at www.snob.ru/selected/entry/39817 (accessed February 2, 2015).

(2012). *The man without a face: The unlikely rise of Vladimir Putin.* New York: Riverhead Books.

Getty, J. (1985). *Origins of the great purges: The Soviet Communist party reconsidered, 1933–1938.* New York: Cambridge University Press.

Geyer, M., and Fitzpatrick, S. (2009). *Beyond totalitarianism: Stalinism and Nazism compared.* New York: Cambridge University Press.

Gillmor, D. (2004). *We the media: Grassroots journalism by the people, for the people.* Sebastopol, CA: O'Reiley Media.

Glaeser, A. (2000). *Divided in unity: Identity, Germany, and the Berlin police.* Chicago: University of Chicago Press.

(2011). *Political epistemics: The secret police, the opposition, and the end of East German socialism.* Chicago: University of Chicago Press.

Glasser, T. (ed.). (1999). *The Idea of public journalism.* New York: Guilford Press.

Goldman, W. (2007). *Terror and democracy in the age of Stalin: The social dynamics of repression.* New York: Cambridge University Press.

(2011). *Inventing the enemy: Denunciation and terror in Stalin's Russia.* New York: Cambridge University Press.

Gorham, M. (1996). Tongue-tied writers: The Rabsel'kor movement and the voice of the "new intelligentsia" in early Soviet Russia. *Russian Review,* 55(3), pp. 412–429.

(2013). Putin's language. In H. Goscilo (ed.), *Putin as celebrity and cultural icon* (pp. 82–103). London: Routledge.

Gorokhova, E. (2011). From Russia with lies. Available at www.nytimes.com /2011/10/23/magazine/from-russia-with-lies.html (accessed June 8, 2016).

Gorsuch, A., and Koenker, D. (2006). *Turizm: The Russian and East European tourist under capitalism and socialism.* Ithaca, NY: Cornell University Press.

Greenberg, J. (2010). "There's nothing anyone can do about it": Participation, apathy, and "successful" democratic transition in postsocialist Serbia. *Slavic Review,* 69(1), pp. 41–64.

(2014). *After the revolution: Youth, democracy, and the politics of disappointment in Serbia.* Palo Alto, CA: Stanford University Press.

Greene, S. (2014). *Moscow in movement: Power and opposition in Putin's Russia.* Palo Alto, CA: Stanford University Press.

Gronvall, J. (2015). De-coupling of journalism and democracy: Empirical insights from discussions with leading Nordic media executives. *Journalism,* 16(8), pp. 1027–1044.

Grushin, B. (2000). Institut obshchestvennogo mnenia – otdel "Komsomolskoi pravdy." In A. Volkov, M. Pugacheva, and S. Yarmolyuk (eds.), *Pressa v obshchestve (1959–2000): Otsenki zhurnalistov i sotsiologov. Dokumenty* (pp. 46–65). Moscow: Moscow School of Political Research.

Grymov, Y. (2012). Pusto govoriat. Available at http://yuri-grymov .livejournal.com/99030.html (accessed February 15, 2016).

Gubin, D. (2013). Interview s zhenoi Adagamova kak professionalnyi zhurnalistski keis. Available at http://dimagubin.livejournal.com/124631 .html (accessed January 10, 2013).

Gubin, D., and Loshak, A. (2011). Kazhdyi vtoroi rasskazyvaet kakie-to dikie istorii. Available at www.kommersant.ru/doc/1783356 (accessed March 10, 2011).

Gudkov, L. (1999). Strakh kak ramka ponimania proiskhodiashchego. *Monitoring obshchestvennogo mnenia, 44*(6), pp. 46–53, available online at http://ecsocman.hse.ru/data/343/992/1219/09gudkov-46–53 .pdf (accessed February 29, 2016).

(2005). Zinizm 'neperehodnogo' obshchestva. *Vestnik obshchestvennogo mnenia, 76*(2), pp. 43–62, available online at www.levada.ru/sites/def ault/files/vom_2005.276.pdf (accessed February 29, 2016).

(2009). Priroda "putinizma". *Vestnik obshchestvennogo mnenia, 101*(3), pp. 6–21, available online at www.ecsocman.hse.ru/data/2010/05/26/12 12595112/vom3-fin_6–21.pdf (accessed February 29, 2016).

(2015). Kak vozvrashchayetsia totalitarism. Available at https://slon.ru /posts/57349 (accessed June 8, 2016).

Gulyas, A. (1999). Structural changes and organizations in te print media markets of post-communist East Central Europe. *Javnost/The Public, 6*(2), pp. 61–74.

(2000). The development of the tabloid press in Hungary. In C. Sparks and J. Tulloch (eds.), *Tabloid tales: Global debates over media standards* (pp. 111–127). Lanham, MD: Rowman & Littlefield.

(2003). Print media in post-Communist East Central Europe. *European Journal of Communication, 18*(1), pp. 81–106.

Gupta, A. (1995). Blurred boundaries: The discourse of corruption, the culture of politics, and the imagined state. *American Ethnologist, 22*(2), pp. 375–402.

(2005). Narratives of corruption: Anthropological and fictional accounts of the Indian state. *Ethnography, 6*(1), pp. 5–34.

(2012). *Red tape: Bureaucracy, structural violence, and poverty in India.* Durham, NC: Duke University Press.

Guriev, S. (2013). Kak dela? Dela otkryty! Available at http://slon.ru/russia /sergey_guriev_kak_dela_dela_otkryty_-949866.xhtml (accessed June 5, 2013).

Gutiontov, P. (2005). Iz zapisok vodoprovodchika. Vremia gniet i lomayet tekh, kto gotov gnutsia i lomatsia. Available at www.library.cjes.ru/on line/?b_id=686 (accessed May 26, 2010).

(2008). *Marzan pochti ne viden: Kniga o zhurnalistike i zhurnalistakh.* Moscow: Russian Union of Journalists.

Habermas, J. (1975). *Legitimation crisis.* Boston: Beacon Press.

(1984). *The theory of communicative action,* vol. 1: *Reason and the rationalization of society.* Boston: Beacon Press.

(1989). *The structural transformation of the public sphere: An inquiry into a category of bourgeois society.* Cambridge, MA: MIT Press.

(1990). *Moral consciousness and communicative action.* Cambridge, MA: MIT Press.

(2001). *On the pragmatics of social interaction: Preliminary studies in the theory of communicative action.* Cambridge, MA: MIT Press.

Halfin, I. (2000). *From darkness to light: Class, consciousness, and salvation in revolutionary Russia.* Pittsburgh: University of Pittsburgh Press.

(2003). *Terror in my soul: Communist autobiographies on trial.* Cambridge, MA: Harvard University Press.

(2009). *Stalinist confessions: Messianism and terror at the Leningrad Communist University.* Pittsburgh: University of Pittsburgh Press.

Halfon, M. (1989). *Integrity: A philosophical inquiry.* Philadelphia: Temple University Press.

Hall, S. (1986). The problem of ideology: Marxism without guarantees. *Journal of Communication Inquiry,* 10(28), pp. 28–44.

Hallin, D. (1994). *We keep America on top of the world: Television journalism and the public sphere.* New York: Routledge.

(2000). Commercialism and professionalism in the American news media. In J. Curran and M. Gurewitch (eds.), *Mass media and society* (pp. 218–237). New York: Oxford University Press.

Hallin, D., and Mancini, P. (2004). *Comparing media systems: Three models of media and politics.* Cambridge: Cambridge University Press.

Harbers, F., and Broersma, M. (2014). Between engagement and ironic ambiguity: Mediating subjectivity in narrative journalism. *Journalism,* 15(5), pp. 639–654.

Hardt, H. (1979). *Social theories of the press: Early German and American perspectives.* Beverly Hills: SAGE.

Havel, V., and Vladislav, J. (1989). *Václav Havel. Living in truth: Twenty-two essays published on the occasion of the award of the Erasmus Prize to Václav Havel.* Boston: Faber & Faber.

Hayek, F. (1944). *The road to serfdom.* London: Routledge.

Heinzen, J. (2007). Informers and the state under late Stalinism: Informant networks and crimes against "Socialist property," 1940–53. *Kritika: Explorations in Russian and Eurasian History, 8*(4), pp. 789–815.

Hellbeck, J. (2000). Speaking out: Languages of affirmation and dissent in Stalinist Russia. *Kritika: Explorations in Russian and Eurasian History, 1*(1), pp. 71–96.

Hellbeck, J. (2006). *Revolution on my mind: Writing a diary under Stalin.* Cambridge, MA: Harvard University Press.

Hibou, B. (2004). *Privatizing the state.* New York: Columbia University Press.

Hoffmann, D. L. (2011). *Cultivating the masses: Modern state practices and Soviet socialism, 1914–1939.* Ithaca, NY: Cornell University Press.

Holquist, P. (1997). 'Information is the alpha and omega of our work': Bolshevik surveillance in its pan-European context. *The Journal of Modern History, 69*(3), pp. 415–450.

Hooper, C. (2006). A darker "big deal": Concealing party crimes in peacetime. In J. Fuerst (ed.), *Late Stalinist Russia: Society between reconstruction and reinvention* (pp. 142–164). New York: Routledge.

(2008). What can and cannot be said: Between the Stalinist past and new Soviet future. *Slavonic & East European Review, 86*(2), pp. 306–327.

(2013). Bosses in captivity? On the limitations of the Gulag memoir. *Kritika: Explorations in Russian and Eurasian History, 14*(1), pp. 117–142.

Hopkins, M. (1970). *Mass media in the Soviet Union.* New York: Pegasus.

Hornsby, R. (2013). *Protest, reform and repression in Khrushchev's Soviet Union.* New York: Cambridge University Press.

Humphrey, C. (2002). *The unmaking of Soviet life: Everyday economies after socialism.* Ithaca, NY: Cornell University Press.

Huskey, E. (1992). From legal nihilism to Pravovoe Gosudarstvo: Soviet legal development, 1917–1990. In D. Barry (ed.), *Toward the "rule of law" in Russia? Political and legal reform in the transition period* (pp. 23–42). New York: M.E. Sharpe.

Hutcheon, L. (1995). *Irony's edge: The theory and politics of irony.* New York: Routledge.

Huxtable, S. (2012). A Compass in the sea of life: Soviet journalism, the public, and the limits of reform after Stalin, 1953–1968. Ph.D. thesis, University of London. Available online at http://bbktheses.da.ulcc.ac.uk/22/.

Huxtable, S. (2013). In search of the Soviet reader: The Kosygin reforms, sociology, and changing concepts of Soviet society, 1964–1970. *Cahiers du monde russe, 54*(3–4), pp. 623–642.

Huxtable, S. (2014). Shortcomings. Soviet journalists and the changing role of press criticism after the Twentieth Party Congress. In T. Bohn,

R. Eynax, and M. Abesser (eds.), *De-Stalinisation reconsidered: Persistence and change in the Soviet Union after 1953* (pp. 209–222). Frankfurt-am-Main: Campus Verlag.

Huxtable, S. (2016). The life and death of Brezhnev's thaw: Changing values in Soviet journalism after Khrushchev, 1964–1968. In D. Fainberg and A. Kalinovsky (eds.), *Reconsidering stagnation in the Brezhnev era* (pp. 21–42). Lanham, MD: Lexington Books.

Inkeles, A. (1950). *Public opinion in Soviet Russia: A study in mass persuasion.* Cambridge, MA: Harvard University Press.

Inkeles, A., and Bauer, R. A. (1959). *The Soviet citizen: Daily life in a totalitarian society.* Cambridge, MA: Harvard University Press.

Inkeles, A., and Kluckhohn, C. (1956). *How the Soviet system works: Cultural, psychological, and social themes.* New York: Vintage Books.

Innocenti, B., and Miller, E. (2016). The persuasive force of political humor. *Journal of Communication, 66,* pp. 366–385.

Izvestia.RU. (2012). Hacker hell: "This hacking job was very difficult." Available at http://izvestia.ru/news/528590 (accessed June 26, 2012).

Izyumov, Yu. (2011). Nepovtorimyi A.B.Ch. Available at http://izyumov.ru /Vospominaniy_LG/Chakovskiy.htm (accessed April 30, 2016).

Jacoby, R. (1999). *The end of utopia: Politics and culture in an age of apathy.* New York: Basic Books.

Jones, P. (2006). *The dilemmas of de-Stalinization: Negotiating cultural and social change in the Khrushchev era.* New York: Routledge.

Josephi, B. (2013). How much democracy does journalism need? *Journalism, 14*(4), pp. 474–489.

Kachkaeva, A., and Richter, A. (1999). Rossiiskie SMI, vlast i kapital. Available at www.medialaw.ru/publications/books/conc1 (accessed December 15, 2006).

Kalashnikov, M. (2012). Vybory Prezidenta Rossiiskoi Federatsii vyigrala Ksenia Sobchak. Available at www.niann.ru/?id=405690 (accessed February 1, 2015).

Kaluzhsky, M., Shakhina, O., and Zheno, G. (2013). Teatral'nyi arest: est li budushchee u politicheskogo teatra. Available at www.echo.msk.ru /programs/kulshok/1025184-echo/ (accessed September 3, 2013).

Kamyshev, D. (2012). Obyknovennyi tsinizm. Available at www.openspace .ru/article/263 (accessed August 15, 2014).

Kashin, O. (2011a). Mne kazalos ochen' vazhnym sdelat' tak, chtoby Putin byl objektom nasmeshek. Available at www.kommersant.ru/doc/1655286 (accessed February 2, 2015).

(2011b). Oni by raspustili parlament i sovershenno po etomu povodu ne kompleksovali by. Available at www.kommersant.ru/doc/1823411 (accessed November 25, 2011).

(2012). Okhota na "dzhinsu." Available at www.kommersant.ru/doc /1868031 (accessed February 1, 2015).

(2016). Rossia bez novostei. Available at https://slon.ru/posts/64915 (accessed June 8, 2016).

Katz, E. (1982). Publicity and pluralistic ignorance: Notes on the spiral of silence. In H. Baier, H. Kepplinger, and K. Reumann (eds.). *Offentliche Meinung und socialer Wandel/Public Opinion and Social Change* (pp. 28–38). Opladen, Germany: Westdeutscher Verlag.

([1950] 2012). "The happiness game": A content analysis of radio fan mail. *International Journal of Communication*, 6, pp. 1297–1445.

Keane, W. (2007). *Christian moderns: Freedom and fetish in the mission encounter*. Berkeley: University of California Press.

(2014). Affordances and reflexivity in ethical life: An ethnographic stance. *Anthropological Theory*, *14*(1), pp. 3–26.

Kenez, P. (1985a). *The birth of the propaganda state: Soviet methods of mass mobilization, 1917–1929*. New York: Cambridge University Press.

(1985b). Lenin and freedom of the press. In A. Gleason, P. Kenez, and R. Stites (eds.), *Bolshevik culture: Experiment and order in the Russian Revolution* (pp. 131–150). Bloomington: Indiana University Press.

Kennan, G. (1954). Totalitarianism in the modern world. In C. Friedrich (ed.), *Totalitarianism* (pp. 17–36). New York: University Library.

Kharkhordin, O. (1999). *The collective and the individual in Russia: A study of practices*. Berkeley: University of California Press.

(2001). *Mishel' Fuko i Rossia: sbornik statei*. St. Petersburg: Izdatel'stvo Evropeiskogo universiteta.

(2011). *Ot obshchestvennogo k publichnomu*. St. Petersburg: Izdatelstvo Evropeiskogo universiteta.

Kichanova, V. (2012). #surkovskayapropaganda atakuet. Available at http://kichanova.livejournal.com/83274.html (accessed February 15, 2016).

Klebnikov, P. (2000). *Godfather of the Kremlin: Boris Berezovsky and the looting of Russia*. New York: Harcourt.

Klumbyte, N. (2011). Political intimacy: Power, laughter, and coexistence in late Soviet Lithuania. *East European Politics and Societies*, *25*(4), pp. 658–677.

Knobel, B., and Sanders, J. (2012). Samizdat 2.0: The Dymovsky case and the use of streaming video as a political tool in contemporary Russia. *International Journal of E-Politics*, *3*(1), available online at http://www.igi-global.com/article/international-journal-politics-ijep /63033 (accessed April 10, 2017).

Koestler, A. (1941). *Darkness at noon*. New York: Macmillan.

Koltsova, O. (2006). *News media and power in Russia*. New York: Routledge.
Kon, I. (1999). Na poliakh i po povodu: Sotsiologia i pressa. Available at http://sexology.narod.ru/info033.html (accessed February 15, 2006).
(2000). Kazhdaya novaya publikatsia podnimala planku vozmozhnogo. In A. Volkov, M. Pugacheva, and S. Yarmolyuk (eds.), *Pressa v obshchestve (1959–2000): Otsenki zhurnalistov i sotsiologov. Dokumenty* (pp. 141–157). Moscow: Moscow School of Political Research.
Kotkin, S. (1995). *Magnetic mountain: Stalinism as a civilization*. Berkeley: University of California Press.
(2002). The state: Is it us? Memoirs, archives, and kremlinologists. *Russian Review, 60*(1), pp. 35–51.
Kozhevnikova, K. (2001). Na bulvar, v Litgazetu poshla. Available at www.vestnik.com/issues/2001/0424/win/kozhevnikova.htm (accessed April 29, 2017).
Kozlov, D. (2013). *The readers of Novyi Mir: Coming to terms with the Stalinist past*. Cambridge, MA: Harvard University Press.
Kozlov, D., and Gilburd, E. (2013). *The Thaw: Soviet society and culture during the 1950s and 1960s*. Toronto: University of Toronto Press.
Kozlov, V. (1996). Denunciation and its functions in Soviet governance: A study of denunciations and their bureaucratic handling from Soviet police archives, 1944–1953. *Journal of Modern History, 68*(4), pp. 867–898.
Kozlov, V., Fitzpatrick, S., Mironenko, S., Edelman, O., and Zavadskaia, E. (2011). *Sedition: Everyday resistance in the Soviet Union under Khrushchev and Brezhnev*. New Haven, CT: Yale University Press.
Krasukhin, G. (2005). *Stezhki-dorozhki: Literaturnye nravy nedalyokogo proshlogo*. Moscow: Yazyki slavianskoi kultury.
Krichevskaya, V. (2012). Nel'zya igrat' v zhurnalistiku. Available at www .snob.ru/magazine/entry/48082 (accessed February 15, 2016).
Kruglova, A. (2014). Dangers of articulation. Paper presented at the ASEEES Annual Meeting, San Antonio, TX.
Krylova, A. (2000). The tenacious liberal subject in Soviet studies. *Kritika: Explorations in Russian and Eurasian History, 1*(1), pp. 119–146.
Kucher, S. (2011). Mozhete vybrosit' vse Tefi, kotorye vy poluchili za luchshye informatsionnye programmy. Available at www.kommersant .ru/doc/1832621 (accessed February 1, 2015).
Kunelius, R. (2001). Conversation: A metaphor and a method for better journalism? *Journalism Studies, 2*(1), pp. 31–54.
Kupriyanov, B. (2012). Est odno intelligentskoe zabluzhdenie: subyektami v strane yavliaemsia tolko my i vlast. Available at www.kommersant.ru /doc/1922217 (accessed February 2, 2015).

Kuznetsov, S. (2012). Mashina dobra i problemy povsednevnoi zhizni nashykh sosedei. Available at http://skuzn.livejournal.com/734229 .html (accessed February 2, 2015).

Laidlaw, J. (2002). For an anthropology of ethics and freedom. *Journal of the Royal Anthropological Institute*, *8*(2), pp. 311–332.

(2014). *The subject of virtue: An anthropology of ethics and freedom*. Cambridge: Cambridge University Press.

Lambek, M. (2000). The anthropology of religion and the quarrel between poetry and philosophy. *Current Anthropology*, *43*(1), pp. 309–320.

(2007). On catching up with oneself: Learning to know that one means what one does. In D. Berliner and R. Sarro (eds.), *Learning religion* (pp. 65–81). Oxford: Berghahn.

(2010). Toward an ethics of the act. In M. Lambek (ed.), *Ordinary ethics: Anthropology, language, action* (pp. 39–63). New York: Fordham University Press.

Larina, K. (2012). Nika Strizhak kak simvol svobodnoi zhurnalistiki. Available at http://xlarina.livejournal.com/255111.html (accessed May 3, 2012).

Larson, J. (2013). *Critical thinking in Slovakia after socialism*. Rochester, NY: University of Rochester Press.

Larson, M. S. (1977). *The rise of professionalism: A sociological analysis*. Berkeley: University of California Press.

Lasswell, H. D. (1948). The structure and function of communication in society. In L. Bryson (ed.), *The communication of ideas* (pp. 37–51). New York: Institute for Religious and Social Studies.

Lazarsfeld, P., and Merton, R. (1948). Mass communication, popular taste and organized social action. In L. Bryson (ed.), *The communication of ideas* (pp. 95–118). New York: Institute for Religious and Social Studies.

Ledeneva, A. V. (1998). *Russia's economy of favours: Blat, networking, and informal exchange*. New York: Cambridge University Press.

(2006). *How Russia really works: The informal practices that shaped post-Soviet politics and business*. Ithaca, NY: Cornell University Press.

(2011). Open secrets and knowing smiles. *East European Politics and Societies*, *25*(4), pp. 720–736.

Lenin, V. (1909). *Materialism i empirio-kritizizm*. Moscow: Zveno.

Lenoe, M. (2004). *Closer to the masses: Stalinist culture, social revolution, and Soviet newspapers*. Cambridge, MA: Harvard University Press.

Lepsky, Y. (2014). Tochka Ru. Available at http://rg.ru/2014/04/28/lepsky .html (accessed April 22, 2016).

Levada, Yu. (2006). "Istina" i "pravda" v obshchestvennom mnenii: Problema interpretatsii poniatii. Available at http://polit.ru/article /2006/11/21/levada/ (accessed February 29, 2016).

Levinson, A. (2011). Nashe "my": Soprotivlenie naroda. Available at www .vedomosti.ru/newspaper/article/266021/soprotivlenie_naroda (accessed August 23, 2011).

Liebes, T., Curran, J., and Katz, E. (1998). *Media, ritual, and identity.* New York: Routledge.

Lindele, D. (2012a). Putinu. Vladimiru Vladimirovichu. Available at http:// d-lindele.livejournal.com/150767.html (accessed February 2, 2015).

(2012b). Razoblachayem slukhi o Krymske. Bez angazhirovannosti. Available at http://d-lindele.livejournal.com/145252.html (accessed July 13, 2012).

Linz, J. (2000). *Totalitarian and authoritarian regimes.* Boulder, CO: Lynne Rienner Publishers.

Lipovetsky, M. (2014). Skromnoe obayanie russkogo tsinika. Available at http://inosmi.ru/world/20140103/216227003.html (accessed May 26, 2016).

Lippmann, W. (1922). *Public opinion.* New York: Harcourt.

Livingstone, S. (2013). The participation paradigm in audience research. *Communication Review, 16*, pp. 21–30.

Loginova, N. (1992). Teatr ili tsirk? *Zhurnalist, 10*, pp. 21–24.

Loshak, A. (2011a). Eto trolling.Available at www.openspace.ru/society /projects/201/details/23787/ (accessed February 2, 2015).

(2011b). Televidenie razgovarivayet s publikoi kak s durakom. Available at http://piter.tv/event/Andrej_Loshak_Televiden/ (accessed February 15, 2016).

(2012). My ne ponimayem, chto proiskhodit v golovakh u sta millionov chelovek. Available at http://slon.ru/calendar/event/823029/ (accessed February 2, 2015).

Lovell, S. (2003). *Summerfolk: A history of the dacha, 1710–2000.* Ithaca, NY: Cornell University Press.

Lowrey, W. (2006). Mapping the journalism: Blogging relationship. *Journalism: Theory, Practice and Criticism, 7*, pp. 477–500.

Lucas, C. (1996). The theory and practice of denunciation in the French Revolution. *Journal of Modern History, 68*(4), pp. 768–785.

MacIntyre, A. (1981). *After virtue: A study in moral theory.* Notre Dame, IN: University of Notre Dame Press.

Malinowski, B. (1922). *Argonauts of the Western Pacific.* London: Routledge & Kegan Paul.

Malgin, A. (2012a). Boyus, delo konchitsia plokho. Available at http://avmal gin.livejournal.com/3167031.html (accessed July 5, 2012).

(2012b). Sovsem obnagleli. Available at http://avmalgin.livejournal.com /3473013.html (accessed February 15, 2016).

Mamleev, D. (ed.). (2003) *Alexei Adzhubei v koridorakh chetvertoi vlasti.* Moscow: Izdatel'stvo Izvestia.

Marcus, G. (1999). *Paranoia within reason: A casebook on conspiracy as explanation.* Chicago: University of Chicago Press.

Marx, K., and Engels, F. (1932). *The German ideology.* Moscow: Marx-Engels Institute.

Marx, K., and Engels, F. (1978). *The Marx-Engels reader* (2nd edn.), ed. Robert Tucker. New York: W.W. Norton.

Mason, B. (2014). Journalism practice and critical reflexivity. *Pacific Journalism Review*, 20(1), pp. 158–179.

Matusevich, V. (1999). Zapiski sovetskogo redaktora. Available at http://magazines.russ.ru/nlo/1999/37/matusev.html (accessed February 22, 2016).

Maximov, A. (2003). Kapitan. Available at http://ys.novayagazeta.ru/text /2003–07–07–10.shtml (accessed May 6, 2016).

McCormick, R. (1981). The discovery that business corrupts politics: A reappraisal of the origins of porgressivism. *American Historical Review*, 86(2), pp. 247–274.

McKay, R. (1991). *Letters to Gorbachev: Life in Russia through the postbag of Argumenty i Fakty.* London: Michael Joseph.

McManus, J. (1994). *Market-driven journalism: Let the citizen beware?* Thousand Oaks, CA: SAGE.

Medvedev, S. (2014). Russkiy ressentiment. Available at www.strana-oz.ru /2014/6/russkiy-resentiment (accessed May 24, 2016).

Merritt, D. (1998). *Public journalism and public life: Why telling the news is not enough.* Mahwah, NJ: Lawrence Erlbaum Associates.

Meyen, M., and Schwer, K. (2007). Credibility of media offerings in centrally controlled media systems: A qualitative study based on the example of East Germany. *Media, Culture & Society*, 29(2), pp. 284–303.

Mickiewicz, E. (1981). *Media and the Russian public.* New York: Praeger.

(1988). *Split signals: Television and politics in the Soviet Union.* New York: Oxford University Press.

(1999). *Changing channels: Television and the struggle for power in Russia.* Durham, NC: Duke University Press.

Mihelj, S., and Huxtable, S. (2016). The challenge of flow: State socialist television between revolutionary time and everyday time. *Media, Culture & Society*, 38(3), pp. 332–348.

Morley, D. (1992). *Television, audiences, and cultural studies.* London: Routledge.

Mostovshchikov, S. (2011). V Izvestiakh rabotayut liudi, privychnye k uni-zheniam. Available at http://slon.ru/articles/592873/ (accessed June 6, 2011).

Muchnik, Y. (2012). A note. Available at www.facebook.com/mucnik.ulia/posts/334870906582250 (accessed February 15, 2016).

Mueller, J. (1992). A new kind of newspaper: The origins and development of a Soviet institution, 1921–1928. Ph.D. thesis, University of California, Berkeley.

Muhlmann, G. (2010). *Journalism for democracy*. Malden, MA: Polity.

Muller, J. (2013). *Mechanisms of trust: News media in democratic and authoritarian regimes*. Berlin: Campus Verlag.

Nathans, B. (2007). The dictatorship of reason: Aleksandr Vol'pin and the idea of rights under "developed Socialism." *Slavic Review*, 66(4), pp. 630–663.

(2011). Soviet rights-talk in the post-Stalin era. In S.-L. Hoffmann (ed.), *Human rights in the twentieth century* (pp. 166–190). New York: Cambridge University Press.

Navalnyi, A. (2012). Blog-Out. Available at http://echo.msk.ru/programs/blogout1/912687-echo/ (accessed July 26, 2012).

Navaro-Yashin, Y. (2002). *Faces of the state: Secularism and public life in Turkey*. Princeton, NJ: Princeton University Press.

Nekrasov, A. (2013). Politicheskaya dokumentalistika: mezhdu pravdoi i propagandoi. Available at www.echo.msk.ru/programs/kulshok/1055424-echo/ (accessed March 20, 2013).

Nenashev, M. (1995). *An ideal betrayed: Testimonies of a prominent and loyal member of the Soviet establishment*. London: Open Gate Press.

(2004). Nastala pora platit' po dolgam. *Zhurnalist*, 2, pp. 10–12.

Nerone, J. (1995). *Last rights: Revisiting four theories of the press*. Urbana-Champaign: University of Illinois Press.

(2013). The historical roots of the normative model of journalism. *Journalism*, 14(4), pp. 446–458.

Nesterenko, Y. (2008). Ubit peresmeshnikov! O glumlenii nad dobrodete-liami. Available at www.apn.ru/publications/article20280.htm (accessed February 15, 2016).

Niblock, S. (2007). From "knowing how" to "being able": Negotiating the meanings of reflective practice and reflexive research in journalism studies. *Journalism Practice*, 1(1), pp. 20–32.

Nikitin, A. (2011). Nulyovye. Available at http://funt.livejournal.com/187399.html (accessed February 15, 2016).

Nord, D. (2001). *Communities of journalism: A history of American news-papers and their readers*. Urbana-Champaign: University of Illinois Press.

Nossik, A. (2012). Metodichka dlia Gapona. Available at http://dolboeb .livejournal.com/2266099.html (accessed January 8, 2012).

Novikov, A. (2012). Vchera mne bylo lichno pokazano, kak rabotayet rossiis-koye TV. Available at http://tinyurl.com/nteoav3 (accessed February 15, 2016).

Oates, S. (2006). *Television, democracy, and elections in Russia*. New York: Routledge.

Oleinik, A. (2015). Ugroza fashizma ili Veimarsky stsenariy v Rossii. Available at www.vedomosti.ru/opinion/articles/2015/02/13/ugrozafa shizma (accessed March 25, 2016).

Orekhov, R., and Pomidorov, M. (2012). Porzhat' i posmeyatsia–raznye vesh-chi. Available at www.kp.ru/daily/25970/2907346/ (accessed October 21, 2012).

Ornebring, H. (2012). Clientelism, elites, and the media in Central and Eastern Europe. *International Journal of Press/Politics*, *17*(4), pp. 497–515.

Orwell, G. (1949). *Nineteen eighty-four*. London: Secker & Warburg.

Oss, N. (2012). Anatomiya glumleniya. Available at www.gazeta.ru/column /oss/4094893.shtml (accessed February 15, 2016).

Oushakine, S. (2001). The terrifying mimicry of Samizdat. *Public Culture*, *13*(2), pp. 191–214.

(2009). *The patriotism of despair: Nation, war, and loss in Russia*. Ithaca, NY: Cornell University Press.

Overholser, G., and Jamieson, K. H. (2005). *The press*. New York: Oxford University Press.

Paletz, D., and R. Entman (1981). *Media, power, politics*. New York: Free Press.

Paniushkin, V. (2004). Komu ne nuzhen PR. Available at www.gazeta.ru /column/panushkin/158162.shtml (accessed April 30, 2014).

(2005). Passivnyi palach. Available at http://gazeta.ru/column/panushkin /361292.shtml (accessed February 15, 2016).

Pankin, B. (2002). *Preslovutaya epokha v litsakh i maskakh, sobytiyakh i kazusakh*. Moscow: Voskresenie.

Parfenov, L. (2013). Bore Korchevnikovu posle voskresnogo efira na NTV. Availale at http://parfenov-l.livejournal.com/46406.html (accessed January 20, 2013).

(2015). Zhurnalistika nikomu ne nuzhna. K 30-letiu glasnosti v Rossii. Available at https://meduza.io/feature/2015/03/17/zhurnalistika-nikomu-ne-nuzhna (accessed May 31, 2015).

Park, R., and Burgess, E. (1967). *The city*. Chicago: University of Chicago Press.

Parkhomenko, S. (2011). Ubezhdeniya – povod dlia uvol'neniya? Available at http://snob.ru/selected/entry/37667 (accessed February 15, 2016).

Parushina, A. (2012). Kak ja poshla v politiku. Available at http://grani.ru
/blogs/free/entries/195575.html (accessed February 2, 2015).

Pateman, C. (1988). *The sexual contract*. Palo Alto, CA: Stanford University
Press.

Pavlovsky, G., and Gelman, M. (2010). Interview Vladimira Putina.
Available at http://echo.msk.ru/programs/razvorot/706938-echo
(accessed August 30, 2010).

Perusko, Z., and Popovic, H. (2008). Media concentration trends in Central
and Eastern Europe. In K. Jakubowicz and M. Sukosd (eds.), *Finding the
right place on the map: Central and Eastern European media change in
a global perspective* (pp. 165–190). Chicago: Intellect Books.

Peters, J. D. (1989). Satan and savior: Mass communication in progressive
thought. *Critical Studies in Media Communication*, 6, pp. 247–263.

  (1995). Historical tensions in the concept of public opinion. In
T. L. Glasser and C. Salmon (eds.), *Public opinion and the communication of consent* (pp. 3–32). New York: Guilford Press.

  (2005). Media as conversation, conversation as media. In J. Curran and
D. Morley (eds.), *Media and cultural theory* (pp. 115–126). New York:
Routledge.

Petranovskaya, L. (2014). Chto eto s nimi?!! Available at http://spektr
.press/chto-eto-s-nimi (accessed June 8, 2016).

Petrovskaya, I. (2010). Novogodnee TV zamakhnulos na sviatoe. Available
at www.izvestia.ru/petrovskaya/article3137368/ (accessed January 10,
2010).

  (2011). Blizhe k polunochi pipl na TV prevrashchayetsia v izyskannuyu
publiku. Available at www.novayagazeta.ru/data/2011/062/26.html
(accessed June 14, 2011).

  (2013). Konveyernoe ostroumie v efire lishaet vkusa i chuvstva mery.
Available at www.novayagazeta.ru/columns/57773.html (accessed
April 19, 2013).

Petrovskaya, I., and Larina, K. (2012). Chelovek iz televizora. Available at
http://echo.msk.ru/programs/persontv/959110-echo/ (accessed December
1, 2012).

Piaget, J. (1950). *The psychology of intelligence*. London: Routledge and
Kegan Paul.

Plamper, J. (2002). Foucault's Gulag. *Kritika: Explorations in Russian
and Eurasian History*, 3(2), pp. 255–280.

Platt, K., and Nathans, B. (2011). Socialist in form, indeterminate in content:
The ins and outs of late Soviet culture. *Ab Imperio*, 2, pp. 301–324.

Pletsch, C. (1981). The three worlds, or the division of scientific labor, circa
1950–1975. *Comparative Studies in Society and History*, 23(4),
pp. 565–590.

Poltoranin, M. (1990). Ministerstvo chetvertoi vlasti. *Zhurnalist*, *11*, pp. 18–21.

(1994). Etot fond ya zamyshlial ne dlia sebia. *Zhurnalist*, *9*, pp. 12–15.

Pomerantsev, P. (2014). Russia and the menace of unreality: How Vladimir Putin is revolutionizing information warfare. Available at http://www.theatlantic.com/international/archive/2014/09/russia-putin -revolutionizing-information-warfare/379880/ (accessed June 2, 2015).

(2015). Mechta rossiiskoi propagandy – chtoby nikto nikomu ne doverial. Available at www.pravda.com.ua/articles/2015/03/31/7063251/ (accessed July 2, 2015).

Porto, M. P. (2012). *Media power and democratization in Brazil : TV Globo and the dilemmas of political accountability*. New York: Routledge.

Prilepin, Z. (2011). Kremlevskie stenaniya. Available at www.kommersant .ru/Doc/1642377 (accessed February 2, 2015).

Prorokov, N. (2014). "Seichas vse tupo delayetsia radi babok": kto pridumy-vayet shutki na rossiskom TV. Available at http://vozduh.afisha.ru /cinema/seychas-vse-delaetsya-tupo-radi-babok-kto-pridumyvaet-shutki -na-rossiyskom-tv/ (accessed July 23, 2014).

Pudovkina, E. (2000). Klub Derzanie. Available at www.pchela.ru/podshiv /26_27/club.htm (accessed February 20, 2016).

Radway, J. (1991). *Reading the romance: Women, patriarchy, and popular literature*. Chapel Hill: University of North Carolina Press.

Ranciere, J. (2004). *Disagreement: Politics and philosophy*. Minneapolis: University of Minnesota Press.

Rappaport, R. (1999). *Ritual and religion in the making of humanity*. Cambridge: Cambridge University Press.

(1979). *Ecology, meaning, and religion*. Richmond, CA: North Atlantic Books.

Remington, T. (1988). *The truth of authority: Ideology and communication in the Soviet Union*. Pittsburgh, PA: University of Pittsburgh Press.

Revzin, G. (2012). Grazhdanskie manifesty. Available at www.afisha.ru/arti cle/grigorij-revzin-arhitekturnij-kritik/ (accessed May 25, 2016).

Ries, N. (2002). "Honest bandits" and "warped people": Russian narratives about money, corruption, and moral decay. In C. Greenhouse, E. Mertz, and K. Warren (eds.), *Ethnography in unstable places: Everyday lives in context of dramatic political change* (pp. 276–315). Durham, NC: Duke University Press.

Rivkin-Fish, M. (2005). *Women's health in post-Soviet Russia: The politics of intervention*. Bloomington: Indiana University Press.

Rogers, D. (2009). *The old faith and the Russian land: A historical ethnography of ethics in the Urals*. Ithaca, NY: Cornell University Press.

Rogov, C. (2005). Politekonomiya: nedogonyayushcheye razvitie. Available at www.vedomosti.ru/newspaper/article/2005/07/06/94316 (accessed February 15, 2016).

Romanova, O. (2012). Vy vseryoz schitayete, chto takie ludi est? Available at www.facebook.com/Ooo.Romanova/posts/426576744043238 (accessed Feburary 15, 2016).

Rorty, R. (1992). Moral identity and private autonomy. In T. J. Armstrong (ed.), *Michel Foucault, philosopher: Essays translated from the French and German* (pp. 328–334). New York: Routledge.

Rosen, R. (1982). *The lost sisterhood: Prostitution in America, 1900–1918.* Baltimore: Johns Hopkins University Press.

Roth-Ey, K. (2011). *Moscow prime time: How the Soviet Union built the media empire that lost the cultural Cold War.* Ithaca, NY: Cornell University Press.

Rothenbuhler, E. W. (1998). *Ritual communication: From everyday conversation to mediated ceremony.* Thousand Oaks, CA: SAGE.

Roudakova, N. (2007). From the fourth estate to the second oldest profession: Russia's journalists in search of their public after socialism. Ph.D. thesis, Stanford University.

   (2008). Media-political clientelism: Lessons from anthropology. *Media, Culture & Society, 30*(1), pp. 41–59.

   (2009). Journalism as "prostitution": Understanding Russia's reactions to Anna Politkovskaya's murder. *Political Communication, 26*(4), pp. 412–429.

   (n.d.). "Here I stand, I can do no other": Paradoxes of legitimacy in Soviet journalism and law. Unpublished manuscript.

Rubinshtein, L. (2015). Pozhatye kamennoi desnitsy. Available at www.inliberty.ru/blog/2121-Pozhate-kamennoy-desnicy (accessed May 26, 2016).

Rubtsov, A. (2012). Politika styda. Available at www.novayagazeta.ru/politics/53907.html (accessed February 15, 2016).

Rudenko, I. (2005). Istiny Inny. Available at www.rg.ru/2005/05/05/rudenko.html (accessed February 15, 2016).

Ryabinina, E. (2003). Ni ot kogo, ni ot chego ne zavishu. Available at http://ys.novayagazeta.ru/text/2003–07–07–11.shtml (accessed April 30, 2016).

Saprykin, Y. (2012). Govori serdtsem. Available at http://lenta.ru/columns/2012/01/18/proh/ (accessed January 18, 2012).

Sartre, J. P. (1974). *Between existentialism and Marxism.* New York: Pantheon.

Scannell, P. (2014). *Television and the meaning of "live": An enquiry into the human situation.* Cambridge, MA: Polity.

Schattenberg, S. (2006). "Democracy" or "despotism"? How the secret speech was translated into everyday life. In P. Jones (ed.), *The dilemmas of de-Stalinization: Negotiating cultural and social change in the Khrushchev era* (pp. 64–79). New York: Routledge.

Scheppele, K. L. (1996). The history of normalcy: Rethinking legal autonomy and the relative dependence of law at the end of the Soviet Empire. *Law & Society Review, 30*(3), pp. 627–650.

Schill, D. (2009). *Stagecraft and statecraft: Advance and media events in political communication.* Lexington, MA: Lexington Books.

Schlesinger, A. (1949). *The vital center: The politics of freedom.* Boston: Houghton Mifflin.

Schramm, W. (1956). The Soviet Communist theory. In F. Siebert, T. Peterson, and W. Schramm (eds.), *Four theories of the press: The authoritarian, libertarian, social responsibility, and Soviet Communist concepts of what the press should be and do* (pp. 105–146). Urbana-Champaign: University of Illinois Press.

Schudson, M. (1978). *Discovering the news: A social history of American newspapers.* New York: Basic Books.

(1989). How culture works: Perspectives from media studies on the efficacy of symbols. *Theory and Society, 18*(2), pp. 153–180.

(1999). What public journalism knows about journalism but doesn't know about "public." In T. L. Glasser (ed.), *The idea of public journalism* (pp. 118–133). New York: Gilford Press.

(2001). The objectivity norm in American journalism. *Journalism, 2*(2), pp. 149–170.

(2007). The concept of politics in contemporary U.S. journalism. *Political Communication, 24*(2), pp. 131–142.

(2008). *Why democracies need an unlovable press.* Cambridge, MA: Polity.

(2010). Political observatories, databases, and news in the emerging ecology of public information. *Daedalus, 139*(2), pp. 100–109.

Schudson, M., and Anderson, C. (2009). Objectivity, professionalism, and truth-seeking in journalism. In K. Wahl-Jorgensen and T. Hanitzsch (eds.), *The handbook of journalism studies* (pp. 88–101). New York: Routledge.

Schultz, T. (2000). Mass media and the concept of interactivity: An exploratory study of online forums and reader email. *Media, Culture & Society, 22*, pp. 205–221.

Semin, K. (2014). O filme "Biokhimia predatel'stva." Available at www.nakanune.ru/articles/18622 (accessed February 15, 2016).

Shapin, S. (1994). *A social history of truth: Civility and science in seventeenth-century England.* Chicago: University of Chicago Press.

Shargunov, S. (2011). Poshlost. V obstanovke total'noi lzhi slova poteriali smysl. Available at www.mk.ru/politics/russia/2011/09/20/625288 -poshlost.html (accessed February 2, 2015).

Sharma, A., and Gupta, A. (2006). *The anthropology of the state: A reader.* Malden, MA: Blackwell.

Shatunovsky, I., and Rykovtseva, E. (2003). Chas pressy: Politicheskaya satira.Available at www.svoboda.org/programs/pr/2003/pr.111303 .asp (accessed November 13, 2003).

Shchekhochikhin, Y. ([1984] 2003a). V glaza svoim otritsatel'nym geroyam smotret' ne boyus. *Zhurnalist, 8*, pp. 21–23.

(2003b). Menia nauchili nikogo ne obmanyvat' i nikogo ne boyatsia. Available at http://ys.novayagazeta.ru/text/2003-08-11-03.shtml (accessed May 6, 2016).

(2004). *S liubovyu: proizvedenia Yu. Shchekhochikhina; vospominaniya i ocherki o nem.* St. Petersburg: Inapress.

(2010). *Tri epokhi sovetskoi zhurnalistiki. Collected ocherki, 1972–2003.* Moscow: Moscow State University Press.

Shenderovich, V. (2011). Kak ni v chem ne byvalo. Available at http://ej.ru/? a=note&id=11117 (accessed February 15, 2016).

Sheremet, P. (2009). Eto vam ne shutochki. Available at www.kommersant .ru/doc/1243633 (accessed February 15, 2016).

(2012). Eiforia i pravda zhizni. Available at http://echo.msk.ru/blog/sher emet/849936-echo/ (accessed February 2, 2015).

Shestopal, E., and Kachkaeva, A. (2006). Televidenie glazami uchenykh. Available at www.svobodanews.ru/articleprintview/271909.html (accessed February 15, 2016).

Shevchenko, O. (2009). *Crisis and the everyday in postsocialist Moscow.* Bloomington: Indiana University Press.

Shinkarev, L. (2005). Ne uveren – ne pishi. Zapovedi veterana-izvestintsa. Available at www.library.cjes.ru/online/?b_id=690 (accessed May 26, 2010).

Shlapentokh, V. (2000). Ya znal, chto dumayut chitateli "Izvestii." In A. Volkov, M. Pugacheva, and S. Yarmolyuk (eds.), *Pressa v obshchestve (1959–2000): Otsenki zhurnalistov i sotsiologov. Dokumenty* (pp. 108–123). Moscow: Moscow School of Political Research.

Shmelev, A. (2013). I Surkov, i ya v donosakh i posadkakh otchasti vinovaty. Available at www.colta.ru/docs/25070 (accessed February 15, 2016).

Shore, M. (1998). Engineering in the age of innocence: A genealogy of discourse inside the Czechoslovak Writers' Union, 1949–67. *East European Politics and Societies, 12*(3), pp. 397–441.

(2013). *The taste of ashes: The afterlife of totalitarianism in Eastern Europe*. New York: Crown Publishers.

(n.d.). Phenomenological encounters in East-Central Europe. Manuscript in progress.

Shultz, E. (2012). V zashchitu blogosfery. Available at http://eugenyshultz .livejournal.com/307517.html (accessed July 12, 2012).

Siebert, F., Peterson, T., and Schramm, W. (eds.). (1956). *Four theories of the press: The authoritarian, libertarian, social responsibility, and Soviet Communist concepts of what the press should be and do*. Urbana-Champaign: University of Illinois Press.

Siegelbaum, L. H. (2008). *Cars for comrades: The life of the Soviet automobile*. Ithaca, NY: Cornell University Press.

Silverstone, R. (2007). *Media and morality: On the rise of the mediapolis*. Malden, MA: Polity.

Simonov, A. (2000). My proskochili moment lichnoi otvetstvennosti. In A. Volkov, M. Pugacheva, and S. Yarmolyuk (eds.), *Pressa v obshchestve (1959–2000): Otsenki zhurnalistov i sotsiologov. Dokumenty* (pp. 418–434). Moscow: Moscow School of Political Research.

Simpson, C. (1994). *Science of coercion: Communication research and psychological warfare, 1945–1960*. New York: Oxford University Press.

Sims, N. (2008). *True stories: A century of literary journalism*. Evanston, IL: Northwestern University Press.

Sinclair, U. ([1919] 2003). *The brass check: A study of American journalism*. Urbana-Champaign: University of Illinois Press.

Sivyakova, Y. (2012). Mne strashno smotret' etoi pravde v glaza.Available at www.novayagazeta.ru/blogs/98/51480.html (accessed February 2, 2015).

Skorkin, K. (2014). Obshchi yazyk nenavisti. Available at www.strana-oz.ru /2014/6/obshchiy-yazyk-nenavisti (accessed June 8, 2016).

Sloterdijk, P. (1987). *Critique of cynical reason*. Minneapolis: University of Minnesota Press.

SMI-NN.RU. (2002). Alexander Veshnyakov vkliuchil Nizhny Novgorod v chislo samykh neblagopriyatnyh regionov s tochki zrenia provedenia izbiratel'nyh kampanii. Available at www.smi-nn.ru/?id=4561 (accessed June 5, 2006).

Smirnova, A. (2011). Do sih por yarostno sporiu, kogda Putina nazyvayut tiranom. Available at www.kommersant.ru/Doc/1646213 (accessed February 2, 2015).

Sokolov, S. (2012). Teper nado idti v shkoly.Available at www.novayagazeta .ru/columns/51475.html (accessed February 2, 2015).

Solomon, P. H. (1985). Local political power and Soviet criminal justice, 1922–1941. *Slavic Review*, *37*(3), pp. 391–413.

Solzhenitsyn, A. (1974). Live not by lies. *Washington Post*, February 18, p. A26.

Song, Y., and Lee, C. C. (2015). The strategic ritual of irony: Post-Tiananmen China as seen through the "personalized journalism" of elite US correspondents. *Media, Culture & Society*, *37*(8), pp. 1176–1192.

Sonin, K. (2012). Kolonka, kotoroi ne dolzhno byt'. Available at www .vedomosti.ru/opinion/news/2306101/podrugomu_byt_ne_mozhet (accessed February 15, 2016).

Sorokin, V. (2012). Proiskhodit obydlenie elit. Available at www .kommersant.ru/doc/1857067 (accessed February 15, 2016).

(2013). Smeshno? Available at www.snob.ru/magazine/entry/59097 (accessed April 8, 2013).

Sorokina, S., Oreshkin, D., and Pavlovsky, G. (2012). Kanikuly zakonchilis. Chego ozhidat' osen'yu. Available at www.echo.msk.ru/programs/soro kina/921945-echo/ (accessed February 15, 2016).

Sparks, C. (2000). Media theory after the fall of European communism: Why the old models from East and West won't do any more. In M.-J. Park and J. Curran (eds.), *De-westernizing media studies* (pp. 29–42). New York: Routledge.

Splichal, S. (1992). Media privatization and democratization in Central-Eastern Europe. *International Communication Gazette*, *49*(1), pp. 3–22.

(1994). *Media beyond Socialism: Theory and practice in East-Central Europe*. Boulder, CO: Westview.

(2001). Imitative revolutions: Changes in the media and journalism in East-Central Europe. *The Public/Javnost*, *8*(3), pp. 1–28.

Steinmetz, G. (1999). *State/culture: State-formation after the cultural turn*. Ithaca, NY: Cornell University Press.

StopFake.Org. (2014). Lozh': Raspiatie v efire Pervogo kanala. Available at www.stopfake.org/lozh-raspyatie-v-efire-pervogo-kanala/ (accessed July 2, 2015).

Suny, R. (1983). Toward a social history of the October Revolution. *American Historical Review*, *88*(1), pp. 31–52.

Suskind, R. (2004). Faith, certainty, and the Presidency of George W. Bush. Available at www.nytimes.com/2004/10/17/magazine/faith-certainty -and-the-presidency-of-george-w-bush.html (accessed June 8, 2016).

Suslov, I. (2011). Inakomyslie kak sotsiokulturnyi fenomen. Ph.D. thesis, Saratov State Technical University, Saratov, Russia.

Svetova, Z. (2012). Publichnoe zayavlenie zhurnalistov, osveshchayushikh protsess po delu "Pussy Riot." Available at www.facebook.com/zoias vetova/posts/378473238885407 (accessed August 5, 2012).

Syrokomsky, V. (2001). Zagadka patriarkha: vospominaniya starogo gazetchika. Available at http://magazines.russ.ru/znamia/2001/4/sirov .html (accessed February 22, 2016).

Szpunar, P. (2012). Western journalism's "Other": The legacy of the Cold War in the comparative study of journalism. *Journalism, 13*(3), pp. 3–20.

Tankova, Y. (2012). Umirayushchie deti–eto tak smeshno. Available at www .kp.ru/daily/25970/2907255/ (accessed October 21, 2012).

Tanuma, S. (2007). Post-Utopian irony: Cuban narratives during the "special period" decade. *Political and Legal Anthropology Review (PoLAR), 30*(1), pp. 46–66.

Taroshchina, S. (2012). Davai sverlit' drug drugu nogi. Available at www.novayagazeta.ru/columns/54960.html (accessed February 15, 2016).

Tocqueville, A. (1954). *Democracy in America.* New York: Vintage Books.

Tolkunova, T. (2002). *Dvazhdy glavnyi.* Moscow: Russkaya kniga.

Troitsky, A. (2011). Osoboe mnenie. Available at www.echo.msk.ru/pro grams/personalno/783722-echo/ (accessed February 15, 2016).

Troitsky, A. (2012). Okkupai ne okupaem? Available at www.colta.ru/docs /4253 (accessed February 2, 2015)

Trudolyubov, M. (2011). U nikh vse khorosho. Available at www.vedomosti .ru/opinion/news/1379453/nizhnyaya_chast_vlasti (accessed February 15, 2016).

(2013). Pochemu vse eto ne smeshno. Available at www.vedomosti.ru/op inion/news/10670871/ne_smeshno (accessed February 2, 2016).

Tsipursky, G. (2010). "As a citizen, I cannot ignore these facts": Whistleblowing in the Khrushchev era. *Jahrbucher fur Gechichte Osteuropas, 58*(1), pp. 52–69.

(2012). Having fun in the thaw: Youth initiative clubs in the post-Stalin years. *Carl Beck Papers in Russian and East European Studies,* 2163–839X(2201).

Tuchman, G. (1978). *Making news: A study in the construction of reality.* New York: Free Press.

Turkova, K. (2011). Strakh massovoi informatsii. Available at http://grani.ru /blogs/free/entries/191895.html (accessed February 15, 2016).

Turova, V. (2012). Blogpost. Available at www.facebook.com/VarvaraTur ova/posts/2893971512123 (accessed February 2, 2016).

Turovsky, D. (2011). "Vy – surkovskaya propaganda": Grigory Melkonyants o novom sposobe obshcheniya s zhurnalistami. Available at http://gorod .afisha.ru/archive/vi-surkovskaya-propaganda/ (accessed February 15, 2016).

TVRain.RU. (2014). *Zamministra sviazi Alexei Volin o raspiatom malchike*. Available at http://m.tvrain.ru/teleshow/harddaysnight/zamministra_sv jazi_aleksej_volin_o_raspjatom_malchike_nepatriotichnyh_smi_i_sa mom_vlijatelnom_cheloveke_v_rossijskih_media-372463/ (accessed July 2, 2016).

Udaltsov, A. (2005). *Delayem gazetu vmeste: Glavnyi redaktor, zhurnalisty, chitateli*. Moscow: Institut zhurnalistiki i literaturnogo tvorchestva.

Ugarov, M. (2012). Teatr.doc – chast' protestnogo soznaniya. Available at www.novayagazeta.ru/arts/51009.html (accessed February 13, 2016).

Underwood, D. (1993). *When MBAs rule the newsroom: How the marketers and managers are reshaping today's media*. New York: Columbia University Press.

(2008). *Journalism and the novel: Truth and fiction*. New York: Cambridge University Press.

Urzhanov, A. (2012). S etoi nedeli ja bolshe ne rabotayu na NTV. Available at www.novayagazeta.ru/blogs/126/53332.html (accessed February 2, 2016).

Vaksberg, A. (2011). Ocherk o sudebnom ocherke. Available at www.lgz.ru /article/16428/ (accessed February 15, 2016).

Varfolomeyev, V. (2012). *Postupok*. Available at http://varfolomeev .livejournal.com/652693.html (accessed February 2, 2016).

Vedomosti (2011). Politik goda: Alexei Navalnyi. Available at www.vedomosti .ru/newspaper/article/273807/politik_goda (accessed February 2, 2016).

Verdery, K. (1996). *What was socialism, and what comes next?* Princeton, NJ: Princeton University Press.

(2003). *The vanishing hectare: Property and value in postsocialist Transylvania*. Ithaca, NY: Cornell University Press.

Verner, A. (1995). Discursive strategies in the 1905 Revolution: Peasant petitions from Vladimir province. *Russian Review*, 54(1), pp. 65–90.

Viola, L. (1987). *The best sons of the fatherland: Workers in the vanguard of Soviet collectivization*. New York: Oxford University Press.

(2000). Popular resistance in the Stalinist 1930s: Soliloquy of a devil's advocate. *Kritika: Explorations in Russian and Eurasian History*, 1(1), pp. 45–69.

(2002). The Cold War in American Soviet historiography and the end of the Soviet Union. *Russian Review*, 61(1), pp. 25–34.

Volkov, A. (2000). Iz publitsistov-tekhnologov my prevrashchalis' v obshchestvovedov. In A. Volkov, M. Pugacheva, and S. Yarmolyuk (eds.), *Pressa v obshchestve (1959–2000): Otsenki zhurnalistov i sotsiologov. Dokumenty* (pp. 93–107). Moscow: Moscow School of Political Research.

(2010). *Opasnaya professiya: Nravy moego vremeni v zhurnalistike i obshchestve*. St. Petersburg: Gelikon-Plus.

(2002). *Violent entrepreneurs: The use of force in the making of Russian capitalism*. Ithaca, NY: Cornell University Press.

Voltmer, K. (2013). *The media in transitional democracies*. Cambridge, MA: Polity.

Voshchanov, P. (2003). On upertyi ili emu chto-to nado? Available at http://ys.novayagazeta.ru/text/2003–07-07–03.shtml (accessed April 26, 2016).

Vostrov, V. (2012). *Nulyovye (a documentary film)*. Available at www.youtube.com/watch?v=1OQGs5gpUhc (accessed February 15, 2016).

Wahl-Jorgensen, K. (2002). The construction of the public in letters to the editor: Deliberative democracy and the idiom of insanity. *Journalism*, 3(2), pp. 183–204.

Wahl-Jorgensen, K. (2013). Considering emotion in mediated public participation. In K. Gates (ed.), *Media studies futures*. Malden, MA: Blackwell.

Wahl-Jorgensen, K., and Hunt, J. (2012). Journalism, accountability and the possibilities for structural critique: A case study of coverage of whistleblowing. *Journalism*, 13(4), pp. 399–416.

Waisbord, S. (2000). *Watchdog journalism in South America: News, accountability, and democracy*. New York: Columbia University Press.

Waisbord, S. (2013). *Reinventing professionalism: Journalism and news in global perspective*. Cambridge, MA: Polity.

Watts Miller, W. (1996). *Durkheim, morals and modernity*. London: UCL Press.

Weber, M. (1946). Politics as a vocation. In H. Gerth and C. W. Mills (eds.), *From Max Weber: Essays in sociology* (pp. 77–128). New York: Oxford University Press.

Weiner, A. (2001). *Making sense of war*. Princeton, NJ: Princeton University Press.

West, H. G., and Sanders, T. (2003). *Transparency and conspiracy: Ethnographies of suspicion in the new world order*. Durham, NC: Duke University Press.

Whitt, J. (2008). *Settling the borderland: Other voices in literary journalism*. Lanham, MD: University Press of America.

Williams, B. (1985). *Ethics and the limits of philosophy*. Cambridge, MA: Harvard University Press.

(2002). *Truth and truthfulness: An essay in genealogy*. Princeton, NJ: Princeton University Press.

Wolfe, T. (2006). *Governing Soviet journalism: The press and the socialist person after Stalin*. Bloomington: Indiana University Press.

Woodruff, D. (1999). *Money unmade: Barter and the fate of Russian capitalism*. Ithaca, NY: Cornell University Press.

Yakovlev, Y. (2000). Pressa ravna obshchestvennomu sostoyaniyu. In A. Volkov, M. Pugacheva, and S. Yarmolyuk (eds.), *Pressa v obshchestve (1959–2000): Otsenki zhurnalistov i sotsiologov. Dokumenty* (pp. 258–271). Moscow: Moscow School of Political Research.

Yakovlev, Y., and Nenashev, M. (2003). Glavnyi redaktor – eto ne professiya. Available at http://2003.novayagazeta.ru/nomer/2003/38n/n38n-s20.shtml (accessed February 22, 2016).

Yampolsky, M. (2014). V strane pobedivsheko resentimenta. Available at http://m.colta.ru/articles/specials/4887 (accessed June 2, 2016).

Yanov, A. (1995). *Posle Yeltsina. Veimarskaya Rossiya*. Moscow: Kruk Publishers.

Yashin, I. (2012). Pro podlosti i oshibki. Available at http://yashin.livejournal.com/1118403.html (accessed February 2, 2016).

Yurchak, A. (1997). The cynical reason of late Socialism: Power, pretense, and the Anekdot. *Public Culture*, 9(2), pp. 161–188.

(1999). Gagarin and the Rave Kids: Transforming power, identity, and aesthetics in post-Soviet nightlife. In A. Barker (ed.), *Consuming Russia: Popular culture, sex, and society since Gorbachev* (pp. 76–109). Durham, NC: Duke University Press.

(2006). *Everything was forever, until it was no more: The last Soviet generation*. Princeton, NJ: Princeton University Press.

(2008). Post-post-Communist sincerity: Pioneers, cosmonauts, and other Soviet heroes born today. In T. Lahusen and P. H. Solomon (eds.), *What is Soviet now? Identities, legacies, memories* (pp. 257–276). Berlin: LIT Verlag.

(2011). A parasite from outer space: How Sergei Kurekhin proved that Lenin was a mushroom. *Slavic Review*, 70(2), pp. 307–333.

(2016). 86% podderzhki Putina – absolutnaya chush. Available at https://focus.ua/world/350070/ (accessed May 25, 2016).

Zakharko, V., Kondrashov, S., and Shinkarev, L. (eds.). (2006). *Vospominaniya ob Aleksandre Bovine: politik, zhurnalist, diplomat*. Moscow: Liubimaya Rossiya.

Zasursky, I. (2004). *Media and power in post-Soviet Russia*. Armonk, NY: M.E. Sharpe.

Zdovc, S. (2009). More stories, more readers? Feature writing in Slovene newspapers. *Journalism Practice*, 3(3), pp. 319–334.

Zelizer, B. (2004). *Taking journalism seriously: News and the academy*. Thousand Oaks, CA: SAGE.

(2013). On the shelf life of democracy in journalism scholarship. *Journalism*, 14(4), pp. 459–473.

(2015). Terms of choice: Uncertainty, journalism, and crisis. *Journal of Communication, 65*(5), pp. 888–908.

Zhao, Y. (2008). *Communication in China: Political economy, power, and conflict.* Lanham, MD: Rowman & Littlefield.

(2011). Sustaining and contesting revolutionary legacies in media and ideology. In S. Heilmann and E. Perry (eds.), *Mao's invisible hand: The political foundations of adaptive governance in China* (pp. 201–236). Cambridge, MA: Harvard University Press.

(2012). Understanding China's media system in a world historial context. In D. Hallin and P. Mancini (eds.), *Comparing media systems beyond the Western world* (pp. 143–176). New York: Cambridge University Press.

Zheleznova, M. (2013). Bloger-anonym rasskazal, kak otyskal informatsiyu o nedvizhimosti Pekhtina. Available at www.vedomosti.ru/politics/news /9041581/est_personazhi_po_kotorym_budet_neplohoj_vzryv_v_golove (accessed February 13, 2016).

Zhurnalist. (1990). Kak nas teper nazyvat?. *Zhurnalist, 8*, pp. 2–5.

Žižek, S. (1989). *The sublime object of ideology.* New York: Verso.

Žižek, S. (2012). Absolutnyi tsinizm – eto iznachalno nezhiznesposobnaya pozitsiya. Available at www.theoryandpractice.ru/posts/5280-filosof -slavoy-zhizhek-absolyutnyy-tsinizm–eto-iznachalno-nezhiznesposobnaya -pozitsiya (accessed April 10, 2017).

Index

abuses
    of power, 3, 24, 42, 79, 199
    performative, 46, 144
accuracy, 40, 41, 42, 151, 152, 197,
        198, 221
    and fidelity to reality, 63
    as care, 41
    disregard for, 198
    factual accuracy, 59, 60, 218
advertising, 98, 99, 100, 105, 107, 109,
    See political advertising
    meaning in Russia, 114
advertorials, 99, 100, 113, 118,
    See ambiguity, fake news
Agranovsky, Anatoly, 47, 64, 83
Agranovsky, Valery, 63, 64
ambiguity, 65, 103, 182, 183, 202
    of everyday speech, 193
    toward whistle-blowing, 32
Arendt, Hannah, 22, 27, 163, 180, 188,
        219
Aristotle, 38, 64, 143, 152
    neo-Aristotelian turn, 39
assassination, 84, 110, 147, 149, 172
audiences, 38, 51, 52, 62, 69, 96, 98,
    99, 118, 153, See Soviet audiences
    calling and coming to visit
        journalists, 71
    manufacturing reactions of, 61
Austin, J.L., 43, 46, 144
authoritarianism, 159, 181, 220
    vs. totalitarianism, 159
Azhgikhina, Nadezhda, 49, 54, 55

barter, 105, 109
belief, 1, 6, 27, 37, 38, 44, 139, 197,
        210, 211, 214, See conviction
    in progress, 35
    in socialism, 10, 11, 15, 22
    vs. opinions, 189, 190

beliefs, 190
blacklisting
    of possible news topics, 130, 133
blackmail, 135
bloggers, 201, 210
Brezhnev, Leonid, 60, 78
    journalism under, 82, 83
broadcasting, 112, 148, 150, 184, 185
Buzmakova, Valentina, 60, 133

capitalism, 26, 58, 98, 99, 100, 120,
        122, 142, 145, 183, 220, 222, 224,
    See privatization
    and professionalism, 100
care, 39, 41, 42, 67, 198, 215
censorship, 24, 43, 48, 59, 62, 65, 79,
        88, 91, 101, 130, 211
    and self-censorship, 52, 58, 130, 211
character assassination. See kompromat
Chechnya, 107
class struggle, 4
clubs, 20, 75, 77, 87, 94
    meeting at editorial offices, 75
cognitive dissonance, 16, 17
commitment. See standing by one's
        words
commodification
    of journalism, 142
    of news, 109
common good, 17
communication, 4, 6, 25, 30, 37, 38,
        141, 163, 186, 187, 189
    and propaganda, 37
    instrumental vs. discourse, 36
communism, 34, 79, 221
    desirability of, 60
communist media systems, 34
Communist party, 30, 51, 60
complaints, 69, 71, 72, 73, 79
    in the Stalinist period, 79

Printed in the USA
CPSIA information can be obtained
at www.ICGtesting.com
LVHW051021211223
766986LV00002B/103